# Charles Darwin's
## The Voyage of the Beagle
The Journals that Revealed Nature's Grand Plan

# Charles Darwin's
## The Voyage of the Beagle

The Journals that Revealed Nature's Grand Plan

Michael Kerrigan
*Photography by* Wolfgang Kaehler

*Saraband*

Published by Saraband (Scotland) Limited
The Arthouse, 752–756 Argyle Street,
Glasgow G3 8UJ, Scotland
hermes@saraband.net
www.saraband.net

ISBN: 1-887354-42-5

Printed in China

10 9 8 7 6 5 4 3 2 1

**Page 1:** *Galápagos sea lions snoozing peacefully on a Hood Island beach.*

**Page 2:** *Darwin referred to these marine iguanas as "imps of darkness."*

**Page 3:** *The male frigate bird uses his scarlet inflatable throat pouch to ensure that he's noticed.*

**Below:** *A great blue heron stands sentinel on Fernandina Island, in the Galápagos Islands..*

EDITOR: Sara Hunt
ART EDITOR: Deborah Hayes

# Contents

Introduction . . . . . . . . . . . . . . . . . . . . . . . . . . . . . . . . 6

Setting Sail . . . . . . . . . . . . . . . . . . . . . . . . . . . . 12

On to the Pampas . . . . . . . . . . . . . . . . . . . . 24

The Santa Fe Trail . . . . . . . . . . . . . . . . . . 38

In Patagonia . . . . . . . . . . . . . . . . . . . . . . . . 54

Land of Fire . . . . . . . . . . . . . . . . . . . . . . . . 68

An Englishman's Paradise . . . . . . . . . . . 84

The Broken Land . . . . . . . . . . . . . . . . . . . 98

Over the Andes . . . . . . . . . . . . . . . . . . . . 114

Enchanted Galápagos . . . . . . . . . . . . . 130

Oceania . . . . . . . . . . . . . . . . . . . . . . . . . . 150

On the Southern Continent . . . . . . . . 168

Homeward Bound . . . . . . . . . . . . . . . . . 184

Epilogue . . . . . . . . . . . . . . . . . . . . . . . . . . 200

Bibliography . . . . . . . . . . . . . . . . . . . . . . . 206

Index . . . . . . . . . . . . . . . . . . . . . . . . . . . . . 206

# Introduction

"I shall never forget what very anxious and uncomfortable days these two were. ...I could scarcely make up my mind to leave England.... Lucky indeed it was for me that the first picture of the expedition was such a highly coloured one."

The great paradox of exploration has always been that, while apparently charting and taking possession of our world, in important ways it leaves us much more lost than we were before. To explore is not to explain; we extend our horizons only to encompass more unknowns; far from filling in the blanks on the map, exploration is liable to tear it up completely. The great navigators like Vasco da Gama and Magellan made voyages of disorientation as much as of discovery; Columbus's encounter with the New World was to change the old one for ever. Scientific enquiry is the same: for every question answered, a hundred new ones arise, more baffling than before; the more we think we know, the less we comprehend. Copernicus's discoveries are a good example: in identifying that the Earth orbited the Sun rather than vice-versa, he brought about a necessary advance in our understanding. Yet he met with bewilderment—and, for a long time, rejection. He may have mapped out some cosmological real estate, but in doing so he threw men's and women's sense of the universe and their place in it into complete confusion.

The theory of evolution and Charles Darwin's suggestion that it might be brought about by a process he called "natural selection" were in time to prove as far-reaching as any of these earlier discoveries. And, con-

*Above: A hand-colored period photograph of Shrewsbury, Darwin's birthplace. Opposite: Sunset over the Atlantic Ocean. Below: Darwin as a young man.*

sequently, as unsettling: some still resist these ideas today, though for the most part they have passed into mainstream scientific thinking. One thing is for sure: evolutionary science has transformed our understanding of our place in the scheme of things; it has meant a wholesale reimagining of the universe— a blasphemous re-creation of it, many feel. An exciting story in itself, the voyage of the *Beagle* marked the beginning of a thrilling scientific journey to a new and more complex—and in many ways more threatening—world.

# A Shropshire Lad

Charles Darwin was not, on the face of it, the most likely of revolutionaries: he was born in Shrewsbury, Shropshire, in 1809. The quintessential English market town, Shrewsbury stands on the banks of the Severn River, not far from the Welsh border; lovely countryside surrounds it on every side. Darwin's boyhood was duly idyllic; he was more studious than most, perhaps, and had a livelier interest in bugs and rocks, but he was by no means unusual as a child of his time. At Shrewsbury's famous school he received a thorough grounding in the classics, history and math, but science was not yet on the curriculum. By the standards of his day he was superbly educated, but the English private school product was to be polished, articulate and self-confident: he was not expected to be a determined seeker after knowledge.

In giving their son the upbringing and education they did, Darwin's parents to some degree endorsed this conventionally English version of gentility, but they themselves had not been born into the landed gentry. They were very well-connected in their way, though: Charles's maternal grandfather was the self-made pottery magnate Josiah Wedgwood; his paternal grandfather was the scientist-poet Erasmus Darwin. Their children may have settled in leafy Shrewsbury, amid green fields and winding lanes, but their fortunes had come from the industrial towns of the West Midlands—and their energies and interests, for the more we look into Darwin's background, the less improbable his emergence as pathbreaking scientist starts to seem. His extended family can be seen as typifying the spirit of late-eighteenth-century Britain, between them allying entrepreneurial energy with scientific curiosity.

Wedgwood had built a ceramics empire up from nothing, transforming the entire industry in the process. A champion of innovative technology, he had valued scientific enquiry for its own sake as well, a point of contact with his friend Erasmus Darwin. They had met monthly with other like-minded men at Birmingham's "Lunar Society" to discuss the latest developments in every area of science and philosophy. They had been moral reformers too, leading campaigns on a number of social issues—most notably against the evils of the slave trade. Benjamin Franklin had been a corresponding member.

Viewed against such a background, Charles Darwin's scientific originality is easier to understand—and yet, as we have seen, in some ways his upbringing had been obstinately conventional. While tolerating his boyish enthusiasms for zoology, his parents had sent him to be educated in the traditional manner, and when he set out to pursue science more systematically it was through the accepted channel of study at Edinburgh's famous medical school. Charles's interest in scientific enquiry was indeed to take off during the next two years, though this was no thanks to a school he found mired in inertia and a course that had become outdated to the point of irrelevance. Rather, it was to the conversations he had with friends he made at the university, and to the specimens he collected along the coast of the nearby Firth of Forth. In 1827, he dropped out—much to the disgust of his father Robert, who told him: "You care for nothing but shooting, dogs and rat-catching and you will be a disgrace to yourself and all your family!"

*Above: Darwin's grandfathers, Josiah Wedgwood (top) and Erasmus Darwin (center). Left: Even as a youngster, Darwin was fascinated by zoology. This 1838 illustration shows Surrey Zoological Gardens.*

## An Unworthy Trade

Edinburgh in the eighteenth century had been one of the world's foremost centers for medicine, but that pre-eminence had been purchased at a price. There was a general taboo on "trade" for the gentry, and no occupation could be more obviously unpleasant than medicine, given the need to dissect and dig about in dead bodies by way of training.

Such study was more than messy: a previous Charles Darwin, the *Beagle* voyager's uncle, had died from a disease he'd contracted while cutting into a baby's corpse. And there was bad company to be kept as well: the shortage of cadavers had to be met by buying from professional bodysnatchers or "resurrectionists." In 1827, just after Darwin himself had left the city, William Burke and William Hare were just embarking on a series of fifteen murders in which they killed homeless men and women specifically for sale to leading city surgeon Robert Knox.

But the squeamish stigma attached to medical research was only an extreme version of the genteel prejudice against science and technology in general. If Britain's Industrial Revolution had led the world, it had been brought about not by the country's traditional ruling caste but by a new middle class of which the Darwins were a part.

# Evolution of an Idea

Rat-catching was no career for an English gentleman: Darwin's next move was to go to Cambridge to train as an Anglican clergyman. In that church and in those times, this decision did not necessarily suggest any burning sense of religious vocation: it would have been more a matter of social respectability. Even so, it seems ironic,

*Above: A period illustration of Edinburgh, Scotland, where Darwin studied at the prestigious medical school.*

in the light of Darwin's subsequent reputation, but he had always been orthodox, if not impassioned, in his religious views. (Years later, indeed, he would recall how some of his fellow officers on the *Beagle* had laughed at him for quoting the Bible as an irrefutable authority on some moral question.) Times were already changing, though: the thinkers of the eighteenth-century Enlightenment had called all sorts of certainties into question, and even where traditional assumptions had not been exploded they were often quietly softening.

So it was with Biblically based Creationism. Carried to its logical conclusion, as it had been by James Ussher, Archbishop of Armagh, in the seventeenth century, this suggested an extraordinarily youthful Earth. Adding up all the biblical begats and stated lifespans, Ussher had carefully calculated that the creation had taken place on October 22, 4004 BC. Advances in geological knowledge had for a time been making such literalism look doubtful, and few serious scientists now insisted on so tight a timeline. The discovery of different rock strata, some containing fossils, hinted at the possibility of a plurality of creations, though this could to some degree be accommodated in what became known as "Catastrophe Theory." This account met the Bible halfway, as it were, suggesting that fossils represented the remains of a first creation swept away by one or more catastrophic events, along the lines of Noah's Flood.

By Darwin's day, however, this view too was becoming untenable. The naturalist's nightly reading as the *Beagle* headed south from Devonport, in fact, would be Charles Lyell's *Principles of Geology* (1830). This book argued that the world had taken form gradually through a single continuous (or "uniformitarian") creation from its first beginnings, a complex of forces pushing up landmasses on the one hand and eroding them on the other. Darwin was exhilarated at how beautifully Lyell's theories accounted for the creation—the one problem was the simply staggering lengths of time which were involved. Time and again on his travels, though, we see Darwin finding apparent confirmation of a creation measured out not in centuries but in millions of years. The full significance of such a timescale was not to dawn on him for a while yet, but it was of course a prerequisite for any credible theory of evolution.

# The *Beagle* Beckons

Chief among the mental challenges Darwin's theories confront us with, perhaps, is that of accepting that so apparently ordered a creation could really have come about by an eons-long catalog of haphazard chances. Yet sheer luck played a major part in Darwin's own career: he had not been either the first or second choice

*Below: This Currier & Ives print of 1875 was entitled "The Animal Creation."*

## Evolution in the Air

Charles Darwin is often credited with the "discovery" of evolution, but his real achievement was to come up with an explanation of how it might occur by "natural selection." Individual variations in animals or plants proved either well- or ill-adapted to the environment in which they had to make their way: those that were favored thrived, and their characteristics reinforced through reproduction.

But the general sense that some sort of evolutionary process must have taken place, with microscopic forms gradually developing in size and sophistication over many generations, had already been established for some time. Charles's own grandfather Erasmus Darwin had given it poetic expression in his *Temple of Nature* (1802):

*Organic life beneath the shoreless waves*
*Was born and nurs'd in Ocean's pearly caves;*
*First forms minute, unseen by spheric glass,*
*Move on the mud, or pierce the watery mass;*
*Then as successive generations bloom,*
*New powers acquire and larger limbs assume.*

It was all very well for the idea of evolution to ring true for enlightened minds: the problem was identifying the mechanism by which these changes might be brought about. In 1809, the French scientist Jean Baptiste Lamarck had introduced his theory of "transmutation": roughly, animals' physical forms altered slightly in accordance to how far different parts of their bodies were used; these modifications were passed on and their effects amplified over time. Thus the beak of the wading bird grew very slightly over years of probing in the mud for worms or crustaceans: over time distinct species like the curlew and sandpiper evolved. It was an ingenious theory, but it failed to convince.

**Right:** *An engraving of a Fuegian mother and her child. In December 1832 Darwin noted in his journal that Fuegians were "abject and miserable creatures."*

of naturalist to accompany the *Beagle* expedition—the story of modern science might have been very different.

With him or without him, though, the voyage would have taken place: the British Admiralty had sent a series of such survey vessels out to chart coastlines and reefs around the world. The *Beagle* had itself been used to take soundings around South America and Tierra del Fuego in 1829–30; this new expedition was to help complete the work which had been begun then. An officer of the Royal Navy since 1818, and a flag lieutenant on that first expedition, Robert FitzRoy had been promoted to the captaincy in mid-voyage after the death of expedition commander Pringle Stokes. As commander for this second voyage, he brought with him a wealth of experience: he also brought a curious company of passengers.

## Captain of the Beagle

Robert FitzRoy was a man of decency and high principles, if, perhaps, a bit unbending in his attitudes. He was a man of impressive intelligence too, one of the acknowledged pioneers of scientific metereology. Darwin had great respect for FitzRoy and spent long hours in conversation with him in the course of their voyage together: the captain was certainly an important influence on his developing ideas. Despite this, their differences remained profound: though rocked by the evidence they saw of the Earth's antiquity, FitzRoy would never accept the evolutionary theories of his younger friend. Darwin respected his former captain, though he feared for his long-term welfare given the intensity of his occasional plunges into depression: he had good reason; FitzRoy committed suicide in 1865.

During the *Beagle*'s visit of 1830, natives of Tierra del Fuego had stolen a whaleboat: an angry Captain FitzRoy had taken a number of Fuegians hostage in reprisal. He had ended up taking them back to England to convert them to Christianity and generally "civilize" them, so they could ultimately be restored to their homeland and bring the Christian message to their countrymen and -women. Such high-handedness was in keeping with the time: it would never have occurred to anyone in Britain that this abduction had been anything but benign. It made for an odd company aboard the *Beagle*, though: had he known how eccentric it was to be, Charles's father Robert would only have felt confirmed in his disapproval. He was convinced that this was just another pointless escapade in the life of a young man who ought to be settling down to something steady.

# Setting Sail

*"I look forward with the greatest of pleasure to spending a few weeks in this most quiet and most beautiful spot. What can be imagined more delightful than to watch Nature in its grandest form in the regions of the Tropics?"*

*Previous pages:* A colorful macaw in the Brazilian rainforest. **Left:** The Atlantic islands can be clearly seen on this map of 1754. **Below:** HMS Beagle as shown in a contemporary engraving.

Several have paid the penalty for insolence, by sitting for eight or nine hours in heavy chains. Whilst in this state, their conduct was like children, abusing every body and thing but themselves, and the next moment nearly crying.

"It is an unfortunate beginning," the young naturalist reflected, a tad sanctimoniously, but then he too was capable of abrupt and unaccountable changes of mood. "Dined in gun-room," he continued equably, "and had a pleasant evening." It's ironic that he should have switched so suddenly, when he had just been taking the "thoughtless sailors" to task for what he saw as their childish inconsistency. Darwin displayed the pomposity of the newly minted university graduate as well as the English gentleman's remoteness from the realities of life.

The incident was telling: it shows us, right at the outset, some of the limitations of one of modernity's greatest minds. If Darwin was a scientific genius, he was also an Englishman of his time and social class; his education had left him with much to learn. The crew's casual attitude to the endeavor before it was also a useful reminder that an odyssey that was one day to assume a near-legendary status was at the time just another in a series of surveying tours. This was to be no "voyage of discovery" in the traditional sense; no new continents were to be found; nor would there be much

"After having been twice driven back by heavy southwestern gales, Her Majesty's ship *Beagle*, a ten-gun brig, under the command of Captain Fitz Roy, RN [Royal Navy], sailed from Devonport on the 27th of December, 1831." Thus the official version as later given to readers of Darwin's published account of the voyage: his own private journal is more forthcoming. December 26, it reports, had been "a beautiful day, and an excellent one for sailing." However:

The opportunity has been lost owing to the drunkedness and absence of nearly the whole crew. The ship has been all day in state of anarchy…such a scene proves how absolutely necessary strict discipline is amongst such thoughtless beings as sailors.

adventure as conventionally defined. While Darwin was setting forth into the big wide world to make a name for himself, others were merely trying to get by.

Ultimately, the reverberations of the voyage would far outreach Darwin's ambitions to put together an eye-catching portfolio of research; they show no signs of dying down even now. So how did this ever-so-slightly absurd young man come to change the course of scientific history? In a way, it could be argued, his ingenuousness was his greatest asset: if he could be conventional in his judgments, he had an open-minded receptiveness to new ideas. Above all, perhaps, he had an unspoiled sense of wonder. This was responsive not only to such obvious marvels as the marine iguana or the formation of the Andes but to miracles of an altogether more mundane sort. Just a few weeks earlier (November 23), in Devonport, watching as preparations for the voyage were made, he had noted the awe-inspiring efficiency of the *Beagle*'s provisioning.

All the stores are completed and yesterday between 5 and 6 thousand canisters of preserved meat were

*Above: A Toco toucan shows off its plumage in the rainforest of Brazil: Darwin was overwhelmed by the fecundity and color of the tropical scene. Below: Fishing boats leaving Rio de Janeiro, in an early photograph.*

stowed away. Not one inch of room is lost, the hold would contain scarcely another bag of bread.

And if Darwin could be pompous on occasion, he also showed an engagingly self-deprecating sense of humor and was not only ready but almost eager to acknowledge the limits of his knowledge:

My notions of the inside of a ship were about as indefinite as those of some men on the inside of a man, viz a large cavity containing air, water and food mingled in hopeless confusion.

This was the young man who first embarked on HMS *Beagle*, setting out on a voyage that would change his life—and transform the state of science. It would be an exaggeration to suggest that his destined greatness was already apparent—but there were intriguing signs that he might be at least a little out of the ordinary.

# To Tenerife, and On

The voyage started routinely enough, the *Beagle* tacking out of harbor with some difficulty around 11 a.m.: out in the English Channel, though, it soon caught a "light breeze" to send it scudding southward.

On the 6th of January we reached Teneriffe, but were prevented landing, by fears of our bringing the cholera: the next morning we saw the sun rise behind the rugged outline of the Grand Canary island, and suddenly illuminate the Peak of Teneriffe, whilst the lower parts were veiled in fleecy clouds. This was the first of many delightful days never to be forgotten. On the 16th of January, 1832, we anchored at Porto Praya, in St. Jago, the chief island of the Cape de Verd archipelago…. The neighbourhood of Porto Praya, viewed from the sea, wears a desolate aspect. The volcanic fires of a past age, and the scorching heat of a tropical sun, have in most places rendered the soil unfit for vegetation. The country rises in successive steps of table-land, interspersed with some truncated conical hills, and the horizon is bounded by an irregular chain of more lofty mountains.

Not until January 19 did Darwin manage to snatch time for a walk ashore. He was so thrilled to be setting foot on such emphatically foreign soil that he could hardly keep hold of his scientific objectivity.

## "The Misery is Excessive"

Even before reaching the Canary Islands, Darwin had made the first great discovery of his trip—that he was a hopeless, helpless martyr to seasickness, and seemed destined to remain so. "I will now give all the dear-bought experience I have gained about seasickness," he confided to his private journal on 29 December (by which time the *Beagle* was in the Bay of Biscay, with England only 380 miles astern):

In first place the misery is excessive and far exceeds what a person would suppose who had never been at sea more than a few days. I found the only relief to be in a horizontal position: but that it must never be forgotten that the more you combat with an enemy the sooner he will yield.

The "enemy" was never to yield, as it turned out: Darwin would go almost five years without finding his sea legs, even moderate swells reducing him to abject wretchedness. Fortunately for him, the voyage was in large part to be taken up by a series of lengthy excursions ashore: otherwise it is hard to imagine how he would ever have survived.

The scene, as beheld through the hazy atmosphere of this climate, is one of great interest; if, indeed, a person, fresh from sea, and who has just walked, for the first time, in a grove of cocoa-nut trees, can be a judge of anything but his own happiness. The island would generally be considered as very uninteresting, but to anyone accustomed only to an English landscape, the novel aspect of an utterly sterile land possesses a grandeur which more

*Left: The "rugged outline of the Grand Canary island" with the "Peak of Teneriffe" at its center are seen "veiled in fleecy clouds" in this engraving.*

vegetation might spoil. A single green leaf can scarcely be discovered over wide tracts of the lava plains; yet flocks of goats, together with a few cows, contrive to exist. It rains very seldom, but during a short portion of the year heavy torrents fall, and immediately afterwards a light vegetation springs out of every crevice. This soon withers; and upon such naturally formed hay the animals live. It had not now rained for an entire year.

*Above: A tufted-ear marmoset bestraddles a branch, just one of the wonderful creatures still to be seen in the hills around Rio de Janeiro.*

## Chameleons of the Sea

On January 28, Darwin spent the day on the shore, among the island's rock pools, in which "a great number of curious and beautiful animals" were to be found. "I was much interested," he says, "by watching the habits of an octopus, or cuttlefish."

These animals were not easily caught...they darted tail first, with the rapidity of an arrow...at the same instant discolouring the water with a dark chestnut-brown ink. These animals also escape detection by a very extraordinary, chameleon-like power of changing their colour. They appear to vary their tints according to the nature of the ground over which they pass: when in deep water, their general shade was brownish purple, but when placed on the land, or in shallow water, this dark tint changed into one of a yellowish green.

Cephalopods take their coloring from special cells in their skin called *chromatophores*. While each has only a single pigment, its expands and contracts with great rapidity in response to neural signals, altering the overall effect and enabling the animal to change color at astounding speed.

# "A Deeper Pleasure"

There could hardly have been a starker contrast between the bleak sterility of the Cape Verde Islands and the scene that greeted Darwin when, on February 29, he went ashore in Bahia, Brazil. "The day has passed delightfully," he says.

Delight itself, however, is a weak term to express the feelings of a naturalist who, for the first time, has wandered by himself in a Brazilian forest. The elegance of the grasses, the novelty of the parasitical plants, the beauty of the flowers, the glossy green of the foliage, but above all the general luxuriance of the vegetation, filled me with admiration. A most paradoxical mixture of sound and silence pervades the shady parts of the wood. The noise from the insects is so loud, that it may be heard even in a vessel anchored several hundred yards from the shore; yet within the recesses of the forest a universal silence appears to reign. To a person fond of natural history, such a day as this brings with it a deeper pleasure than he can ever hope to experience again. After wandering about for some hours, I returned to the landing-place; but, before reaching it, I was overtaken by a tropical storm. I tried to find shelter under a tree, which was so thick that it would never have been penetrated by common English rain; but here, in a couple of minutes, a little torrent flowed down the trunk. It is to this violence of the rain that we must attribute the verdure at the bottom of the thickest woods: if the showers were like those of a colder climate, the greater part would be absorbed or evaporated before it reached the ground.

The *Beagle* spent much of March surveying stretches of the Bahia coast, including the Abrolhos archipelago, a few miles offshore. By the end of the month, though, they were sailing down to Rio. "All hands employed in making April Fools," notes Darwin in his private journal for April 1.

## The Wrong Wood

Not many nations can have been named for a tree, though as it happens Brazil received its name as the result of a case of mistaken identity. So called because its sought-after hardwood glowed with the color of an ember (*brasa*), the brasil (*Caesalpiana sappan*) was actually native to the East Indies. But that is precisely where the first Portuguese seafarers to land here believed they were. *Caesalpiana echinata*, the tree the Portuguese found here, though related, is not the same—but then if continents can be confused, two tree species scarcely signify.

The first Portuguese colonists came to Brazil at the start of the sixteenth century. Signed in Spain in 1494, in the immediate aftermath of Columbus's first voyage and under the supervision of Pope Alexander I, the Treaty of Tordesillas had given Portugal authority over newly discovered territories lying to the east of a line roughly corresponding with that of longitude 48º W. Areas to the west of this line would belong to Spain.

## The Eccentric Empire

The Portuguese had to enforce their title to Brazil against efforts by both the Dutch and the French to supplant them, but by 1700 their status as colonial rulers was generally acknowledged. The capital of the colony, long at Salvador, Bahia, was moved south to Rio in 1763, and it was here that the Portuguese king and court fled in 1808 when Napoleon's French armies invaded their home country. Rio thus became capital of what was nominally a United Kingdom of Portugal and Brazil, though Portugal proper was under French control.

In 1821, King Jão VI felt it was at last safe to return to Europe: he left Brazil under the authority of his son, Crown Prince Pedro. But viceregency wasn't enough for Pedro: hardly was his father's back turned when, in 1822, he declared Brazil an independent "empire" (on what basis he called it that isn't clear), and himself Emperor Pedro I. Just the year before the *Beagle*'s visit, Pedro had abdicated in favor of his own son, Pedro II, despite the fact that the boy was only six years old.

At midnight nearly all the watch below was called up in their shirts: carpenters for a leak; quartermasters that a mast was sprung; midshipmen to reef topsails. All turned in to their hammocks again, some growling, some laughing. The hook was too easily baited for me not to be caught: Sullivan cried out, 'Darwin, did you ever see a grampus [a kind of whale]? Bear a hand then!' I accordingly rushed out in a transport of enthusiasm, and was received with a roar of laughter by the whole watch.

They arrived in Rio on April 4, though, "the winds being light," Darwin's private journal records,

We did not pass under the Sugar Loaf till after dinner; our slow cruize was enlivened by the changing prospect of the mountains, sometimes enveloped by white clouds, sometimes brightened by the sun, the wild and stony peaks presented new scenes. When within the harbor the light was not good, but like to a good picture this evening's view prepared the mind for the morrow's enjoyment. In most glorious style did the little *Beagle* enter the port.

Next day the party went ashore: "The morning has been for me very fertile in plans," notes Darwin:

I look forward with the greatest of pleasure to spending a few weeks in this most quiet and most beautiful spot. What can be imagined more delightful than to watch Nature in its grandest form in the regions of the Tropics?

# Up-country

Having made the acquaintance of an Englishman who owned a *fazenda*, or plantation, some way up the coast, Darwin agreed to join him on a journey to visit this estate for a few weeks. By April 8, this excursion was under way. "Our party amounted to seven," Darwin subsequently recorded:

The first stage was very interesting. The day was powerfully hot, and as we passed through the woods, everything was motionless, excepting the large and brilliant butterflies, which lazily fluttered about. The view seen when crossing the hills behind Praia Grande was most beautiful; the colours were intense, and the prevailing tint a dark blue; the sky and the calm waters of the bay vied with each other in splendour. After passing through some cultivated country, we entered a forest, which in the grandeur of all its parts could not be exceeded. We arrived by midday at Ithacaia; this small village is situated on a plain, and round the central house are the huts of the negroes. These, from their regular form and position, reminded me of the drawings of the Hottentot habitations in Southern Africa. As the moon rose

## *Rio de Janeiro*

Portuguese navigator Goncalo Coelho was the first European to visit the inlet on which Rio was to be sited, when he sailed down this coast in January 1502. He concluded—quite mistakenly—that the open waters of Guanabara Bay were an estuary—hence the name he gave it, *Rio de Janeiro*, or "River of January."

The place remained unoccupied until the 1560s, when the Portuguese built a fort here as part of their ongoing struggle with the French. It replaced Salvador as Brazilian capital in 1763, and by Darwin's time had more than 100,000 inhabitants.

Rio lost its status as Brazil's biggest city some time ago to Sao Paulo, which, with more than 11 million people, is today almost twice its size. In terms of political influence it has lost out too, surrendering its capital status to the purpose-built Amazonian city of Brasilia in 1960. But for most of the world (and for most Brazilians) it is still the quintessentially Brazilian city, with its carnival, beaches, lively streetlife and stunning views.

early, we determined to start the same evening for our sleeping-place at the Lagoa Marica. As it was growing dark we passed under one of the massive, bare, and steep hills of granite which are so common in this country. This spot is notorious from having been, for a long time, the residence of some runaway slaves, who, by cultivating a little ground near the top, contrived to eke out a subsistence. At length they were discovered, and a party of soldiers being sent, the whole were seized with the exception of one old woman, who, sooner than again be led into slavery, dashed herself to pieces from the summit of the mountain. In a Roman matron this would have been called the noble love of freedom: in a poor negress it is mere brutal obstinacy.

### Free Spirits

With appalling conditions to be endured on the *fazendas*, and a vast hinterland in which to hide, it was to be expected that many slaves would take the chance to escape. Having done so, many came together in settled communities called *quilombos*, in which the social and ritual orders of Africa held sway.

The most famous of these, not too far to the north of Bahia at Palmares, Pernambuco, had been nothing less than an African republic in the Americas, its population eventually passing the 20,000 mark. Established around 1610, it had endured for almost a century, surviving over twenty attacks before it was put down.

Most such communities were much smaller, but even so they were regarded as a real threat to security and attacked without pity by the colonial authorities wherever found. It wasn't just that the *quilombadas* mounted raids on nearby *fazendas* and small towns, but that the very presence of the *quilombos* encouraged slaves to attempt escape.

# On the *Fazenda*

On April 13, says Darwin, "after three days' travelling, we arrived at Socego, the estate of Senhor Manuel Figuireda, a relation of one of our party."

*"The profusion of food showed itself at dinner, where, if the tables did not groan, the guests surely did."*

The house was simple, and, though like a barn in form, was well suited to the climate. In the sitting-room gilded chairs and sofas were oddly contrasted with the whitewashed walls, thatched roof, and windows without glass. The house, together with the granaries, the stables, and workshops for the blacks, who had been taught various trades, formed a rude kind of quadrangle; in the centre of which a large pile of coffee was drying. These buildings stand on a little hill, overlooking the cultivated ground, and surrounded on every side by a wall of dark green luxuriant forest. The chief produce of this part of the country is coffee. Each tree is supposed to yield annually, on an average, two pounds; but some give as much as eight. Mandioca [manioc] or cassada [cassava] is likewise cultivated in great quantity. Every part of this plant is useful; the leaves and stalks are eaten by the horses, and the roots are ground into a pulp, which, when pressed dry and baked, forms the farinha, the principal article of sustenance in the Brazils. It is a curious, though well-known fact, that the juice of this most nutritious plant is highly poisonous. A few years ago a cow died at this *fazenda*, in consequence of having drunk some of it. Senhor Figuireda told me that he had planted, the year before, one bag of *feijao* or beans, and three of rice; the former of which produced eighty, and the latter three hundred and twenty fold. The pasturage supports a fine stock of cattle, and the woods are so full of game that a deer had been killed on each of the three previous days. This profusion of food showed itself at dinner, where, if the tables did not groan, the guests surely did; for each person is expected to eat of every dish. One day, having, as I thought, nicely calculated so that nothing should go away untasted, to my utter dismay a roast turkey and a pig appeared in all their substantial reality. During the meals, it was the employment of a man to drive out of the room sundry old hounds, and dozens of little black children, which crawled in together, at every opportunity. As long as the idea of slavery could be banished, there was something exceedingly fascinating in this simple and patriarchal style of living: it was such a perfect retirement and independence from the rest of the world....

As soon as any stranger is seen arriving, a large bell is set tolling, and generally some small cannon are fired. The event is thus announced to the rocks and woods, but to nothing else. One morning I walked out an hour before daylight to admire the solemn stillness of the scene; at last, the silence was broken by the morning hymn, raised on high by the whole body of the blacks; and in this manner their daily work is generally begun. On such *fazendas* as these, I have no doubt the slaves pass happy and contented lives. On Saturday and Sunday they work for themselves, and in this fertile climate the labour of two days is sufficient to support a man and his family for the whole week.

## "Am I Not a Man and a Brother?"

Charles Darwin's reaction to the institution of slavery should come as no surprise given his strong familial links with the English abolitionist movement. His maternal grandfather, the ceramics manufacturer Josiah Wedgwood, had been among the most passionate campaigners in this cause. He it had been who designed and produced the famous medallion or seal of the emancipationists. It showed an African, kneeling in shackles and gazing up imploringly: around the edge an inscription of Wedgwood's own devising asked rhetorically, "Am I Not a Man and a Brother?"

One of Wedgwood's closest friends and supporters had been Charles's paternal grandfather, Erasmus Darwin: together the two had exercised a profound influence on late eighteenth-century reformist thought. That influence had extended beyond their own shores: they had kept up a regular correspondence with leading American thinkers of their time, including Thomas Jefferson and Benjamin Franklin.

A rosy picture, but just how "happy and contented" could a slave's life really be? A few days later, Darwin would have cause to wonder. It was then that, during a visit to a neighboring *fazenda* from April 14, he would see the implications for a system under which even individuals of "humanity and good feeling" accustomed themselves to treating their fellow men and women as possessions.

While staying at this estate, I was very nearly being an eye-witness to one of those atrocious acts which can only take place in a slave country. Owing to a quarrel and a lawsuit, the owner was on the point of taking all the women and children from the male slaves, and selling them separately at the public auction at Rio. Interest, and not any feeling of compassion, prevented this act. Indeed, I do not believe the inhumanity of separating thirty families, who had lived together for many years, even occurred to the owner. Yet I will pledge myself, that in humanity and good feeling he was superior to the common run of men. It may be said there exists no limit to the blindness of interest and selfish habit. I may mention one very trifling anecdote, which at the time struck me more forcibly than any story of cruelty. I was crossing a ferry with a negro, who was uncommonly stupid. In endeavoring to make him understand, I talked loud, and made signs, in doing which I passed my hand near his face. He, I suppose, thought I was in a passion, and was going to strike him; for instantly, with a frightened look and half-shut eyes, he dropped his hands. I shall never forget my feelings of surprise, disgust, and shame, at seeing a great powerful man afraid even to ward off a blow, directed, as he thought, at his face. This man had been trained to a degradation lower than the slavery of the most helpless animal.

# A Risky Road

On April 19, the party left the Socego *fazenda*.

During the two first days, we retraced our steps. It was very wearisome work, as the road generally ran across a glaring hot sandy plain, not far from the coast.... On the third day we took a different line, and passed through the gay little village of Madre de Deos. This is one of the principal lines of road in Brazil; yet it was in so bad a state that no wheeled vehicle, excepting the clumsy bullock-wagon, could pass along. In our whole journey we did not cross a single bridge built of stone; and those made of logs of wood were frequently so much out of repair, that it was necessary to go on one side to avoid them. All distances are inaccurately known. The road is often marked by crosses, in the place of milestones, to signify where human blood has been spilled. On the evening of the 23rd we arrived at Rio, having finished our pleasant little excursion.

Such scathing observations on the shortcomings of all non–British-administered colonies were to be a recurrent feature of Darwin's account of his world voyage.

## The Corcovado and Christ

On May 25, Darwin set out with a couple of the *Beagle*'s officers to walk to the very top of the Corcovado, Rio's most celebrated mountain. As he notes in his private journal,

At every corner alternate and most beautiful views were presented to us. At length we commenced ascending the steep sides, which are universally to the very summit clothed by a thick forest.... We soon gained the peak and beheld that view, which perhaps excepting those in Europe, is the most celebrated in the world.

The view from its summit may have been celebrated, but Corcovado itself looked rather different, since as yet it lacked what has become its most famous feature. The giant statue of the *Cristo Redentor*—Christ the Redeemer—with its outstretched hands has become Rio's most universally recognized emblem, but at this time it was still a century away. Standing almost a hundred feet tall, it was designed by Polish sculptor Paul Landowski in 1926, and construction was completed in 1931.

# "Teeming with Life"

Darwin found the sheer fecundity of the tropics all but overwhelming.

During the remainder of my stay at Rio, I resided in a cottage at Botofogo Bay. It was impossible to wish for anything more delightful than thus to spend some weeks in so magnificent a country. In England any person fond of natural history enjoys in his walks a great advantage, by always having something to attract his attention; but in these fertile climates, teeming with life, the attractions are so numerous, that he is scarcely able to walk at all....

The climate, during the months of May and June, or the beginning of winter, was delightful. The mean temperature, from observations taken at nine o'clock, both morning and evening, was only 72 degrees. It often rained heavily, but the drying southerly winds soon again rendered the walks pleasant. One morning, in the course of six hours, 1.6 inches of rain fell. As this storm passed over the forests which surround the Corcovado, the sound produced by the drops pattering on the countless multitude of leaves was very remarkable, it could be heard at the distance of a quarter of a mile, and was like the rushing of a great body of water. After the hotter days, it was delicious to sit quietly in the garden and watch the evening pass into night. Nature, in these climes, chooses her vocalists from more humble performers than in Europe. A

*"It was delicious to sit in the garden and watch the evening pass into night."*

small frog of the genus *Hyla* sits on a blade of grass about an inch above the surface of the water, and sends forth a pleasing chirp: when several are together they sing in harmony on different notes. I had some difficulty in catching a specimen of this frog.... Various cicidae and crickets, at the same time, keep up a ceaseless shrill cry, but which, softened by the distance, is not unpleasant. Every evening after dark this great concert commenced; and often have I sat listening to it, until my attention has been drawn away by some curious passing insect...

Nothing had prepared Darwin for the spectacular show the tropics would put on: there might be finer landscapes, but there could be none with more living color.

Following a pathway, I entered a noble forest, and from a height of five or six hundred feet, one of those splendid views was presented, which are so common on every side of Rio. At this elevation the landscape attains its most brilliant tint; and every form, every shade, so completely surpasses in magnificence all that the European has ever beheld in his own country, that he knows not how to express his feelings. The general effect frequently recalled to my mind the gayest scenery of the opera-house or the great theatres.

*Left: The mountains of Rio rear up dramatically in this engraving made in 1890.* **Above:** *Thick forest cloaks the Corcovado to this day.*

# On to the Pampas

*"Well may we affirm that every part of the world is habitable! Whether lakes of brine, or those subterranean ones hidden beneath volcanic mountains…, and even the surface of perpetual snow—all support organic beings."*

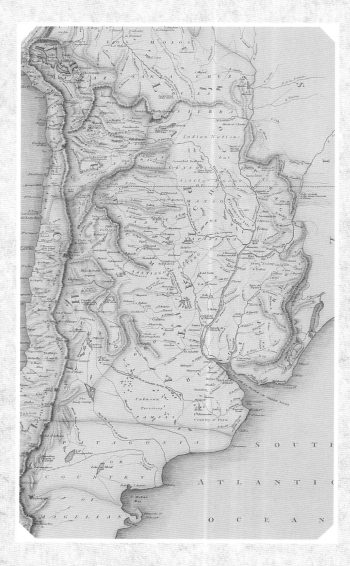

my journal which refer to the same districts without always attending to the order in which we visited them."

First, then, we follow him in his wanderings over the open grasslands of the Banda Oriental ("Eastern Strip," now Uruguay) and on into Buenos Aires Province. Though Darwin clearly felt like an explorer, this area was already comparatively well settled; it was a wealthy ranching region, indeed. Yet it remained unknown to outsiders for the most part, and while remoteness is always relative, it was still way off the "mental map" of most Europeans.

Of Englishmen in particular: as far as they were concerned, colonization by Anglo-Saxons might confer civilization, but a Spanish or Portuguese presence did little to lift a wilderness out of its native savagery. Darwin himself was not entirely above expressing prejudice of this sort: in this respect he was very much a man of his country and his time. In reality the open pampas, arid and austere, hardly lent themselves to intensive agricultural development. As across much of the North American West, cattle ranching offered a way for vast areas of otherwise marginal lands to be made productive. But to eyes accustomed to the neat and tidy fields and pastures of rural Shropshire and an English countryside that had been domesticated over many centuries, the pampas must have seemed substantially "unimproved."

The word "pampas" comes from a native Quichoan word that simply means "space," and that is very much how it appeared to Europeans. In its endless monotony and apparent featurelessness it seemed a topographical vacuum—more an absence than an actual landscape. To an enquiring mind like Darwin's, though, this emptiness was full of exciting surprises, from animals and birds to geological discoveries.

From teeming jungle to barren badlands, the next two years of Darwin's travels would take him by both sea and land on a looping, digressive journey to the end of the world. The pampas of Uruguay and Argentina were largely mysterious to most foreigners; as for Patagonia, that was a place apart. His progress was haphazard: the *Beagle* spent many months tacking back and forth up and down the southeastern coast of the continent, busy about the various scientific and cartographical tasks set for her by the Admiralty. There is little point in recording these comings and goings in literal detail. Darwin himself took significant—but sensible—chronological liberties in his own account. "To prevent useless repetitions," he says, "I will extract those parts of

Like that other "empty" vastness, the North American Plains, the pampas already had a history: native peoples had lived and hunted here for countless generations. More recently, white ranchers had gained title to these lands—and backed up their claims with violence and bloodshed on a shocking scale. Yet real and intriguing as the historical parallels between Argentina and the United States undoubtedly are, they were about to come to an end with General Rosas's rise to power. This particular founding father was no democrat but a dictator in the making, one of the first in a long line of Latin American strongmen, or *caudillos*. But while he may have been a monster, he was capable of great charm, and it seems to have been this aspect of his character that he displayed in his dealings with Darwin.

Yet the young naturalist did not in any case make great claims to political insight or historical knowledge: what interested him most was the country, its flora and fauna, both now and in the past. He was as at least as fascinated by Argentina's emergent coastline as he was by its emergent nationhood; its scenery excited him more than its power struggles.

*Above:* To the west, the pampas ease gently upward to the eastern slopes of the Cordillera: here peaflowers clothe a hillside above Lake Nahuel Huapi.
*Below:* The region's people appeared obstinately alien to nineteenth-century European eyes.

# Striking Anchor

The *Beagle*'s voyage southward resumed on July 5, 1832, as Darwin recorded in his journal for that day.

In the morning we got under way, and stood out of the splendid harbour of Rio de Janeiro. In our passage to the Plata, we saw nothing particular, excepting on one day a great shoal of porpoises, many hundreds in number. The whole sea was in places furrowed by them; and a most extraordinary spectacle was presented, as hundreds, proceeding together by jumps, in which their whole bodies were exposed, thus cut the water. When the ship was running nine knots an hour, these animals could cross and recross the bows with the greatest of ease, and then dash away right ahead. As soon as we entered the estuary of the Plata, the weather was very unsettled. One dark night we were surrounded by numerous seals and penguins, which made such strange noises, that the officer on watch reported he could hear the cattle bellowing on shore. On a second night we witnessed a splendid scene of natural fireworks; the mast-head and yard-arm-ends

*Above: Montevideo was a sleepy little town when Darwin came here in 1832, but by 1890 it was the bustling capital of the Republic of Uruguay.*

shone with St. Elmo's light; and the form of the vane could almost be traced, as if it had been rubbed with phosphorus. The sea was so highly luminous, that the tracks of the penguins were marked by a fiery wake, and the darkness of the sky was momentarily illuminated by the most vivid lightning.

## Son et Lumière

The weird show of sound and light described in this entry by Darwin must have been an extraordinarily eerie experience, though he was sufficiently the scientist to play its impact down. The sounds he heard are easily explained: Darwin himself said that they were the calls of seals and penguins. St Elmo's Fire, as it is generally called, is a sort of benign lightning, an electrical discharge from the clouds that finds a route to earth through a ship's rigging. Phosphorescence in the sea occurs when microscopic dinoflagellate algae are disturbed by anything from the bow of a ship to the passage of a penguin: an internal chemical reaction produces a glow of light.

# A One-horse Town

On July 26, he records, "We anchored at Montevideo," now the capital of Uruguay, but the *Beagle* would spend longer a few miles farther east, off Maldonado. Darwin was frankly underwhelmed:

It is a most quiet, forlorn, little town; built, as is universally the case in these countries, with the streets running at right angles to each other, and having in the middle a large plaza or square, which, from its size, renders the scantiness of the population more evident. It possesses scarcely any trade; the exports being confined to a few hides and living cattle. The inhabitants are chiefly landowners, together with a few shopkeepers and the necessary tradesmen, such as blacksmiths and carpenters, who do nearly all the business for a circuit of fifty miles round.... The scenery is very uninteresting; there is scarcely a house, an enclosed piece of ground, or even a tree, to give it an air of cheerfulness.

Magnanimously enough, however, he was prepared to look on the bright side:

Yet, after being imprisoned for some time in a ship, there is a charm in the unconfined feeling of walking over boundless plains of turf. Moreover, if your view is limited to a small space, many objects possess beauty. Some of the smaller birds are brilliantly colored; and the bright green sward, browsed short by the cattle, is ornamented by dwarf flowers, among which a plant, looking like the daisy, claimed the place of an old friend. What would a florist say to whole tracts, so thickly covered by the *Verbena melindres*, as, even at a distance, to appear of the most gaudy scarlet?

## Beautiful Verbena

At once lovely and easy to care for, verbena has become a beloved standby for modern gardeners, though it had only recently been introduced to Britain in Darwin's day. Hence his excitement at encountering wide areas covered with a bright red carpet of what he was accustomed to seeing as a sought-after bedding plant. Verbena has evolved a great deal down the decades: though the garden variety is descended from the *Verbena melindres* Darwin saw, it would be much hybridized and "improved" in the generations that followed.

# The Back of Beyond

Before leaving Maldonado, Darwin made a brief foray to the Polanco River, seventy miles to the north. The journey took him into the depths of darkest Banda Oriental. He wasn't quite greeted as a god, but still had the sense of being in a place that had been completely bypassed by civilization:

On the first night we slept at a retired little country-house; and there I soon found out that I possessed two or three articles, especially a pocket compass, which created unbounded astonishment. In every house I was asked to show the compass, and by its aid, together with a map, to point out the direction of various places. It excited the liveliest admiration that I, a perfect stranger, should know the road (for direction and road are synonymous in this open country) to places where I had never been. At one house a young woman, who was ill in bed, sent to entreat me to come and show her the compass. If their surprise was great, mine was greater, to find such ignorance among people who possessed their thousands of cattle, and "estancias" of great extent. It can only be accounted for by the circumstance that this retired part of the country is seldom visited by foreigners.

But if Darwin was shocked by the provinciality of the place, there was something romantic, too, about a life led so far from the bland security of civilized society. The next day Darwin and his companions pushed on to the village of Las Minas, and put up for the night at a "*pulperia*, or drinking-shop."

During the evening a great number of gauchos came in to drink spirits and smoke cigars: their appearance is very striking; they are generally tall and handsome,

*Above: A pocket compass like this one was to be Darwin's social passport to the pampas.*

but with a proud and dissolute expression of countenance. They frequently wear their moustaches and long black hair curling down their backs. With their brightly coloured garments, great spurs clanking about their heels, and knives stuck as daggers (and often so used) at their waists, they look a very different race of men from what might be expected from their name of gauchos, or simple countrymen. Their politeness is excessive; they never drink their spirits without expecting you to taste it; but whilst making their exceedingly graceful bow, they seem quite as ready, if occasion offered, to cut your throat. . . .

At night we came to the house of Don Juan Fuentes, a rich landed proprietor, but not personally known to either of my companions. On approaching the house of a stranger, it is usual to follow several little points of etiquette: riding up slowly to the door, the salutation of *Ave Maria* is given, and until somebody comes out and asks you to alight, it is not customary even to get off your horse: the formal answer of the owner is, *sin pecado concebida*—that is, conceived without sin. Having entered the house, some general conversation is kept up for a few minutes, till permission is asked to pass the night there. This is granted as a matter of course. The stranger then takes his meals with the family, and a room is assigned him, where with the horsecloths belonging to his *recado* (or saddle of the Pampas) he makes his bed. . . .

After witnessing the rude wealth displayed in the number of cattle, men, and horses, Don Juan's miserable house was quite curious. The floor consisted of hardened mud, and the windows were without

## Free as a Bird

*My glory it is to live as free*
*As the bird that flies in the sky.*
*I have no nest on this anxious earth*
*Where so much suffering is to be endured.*
*And there is no one to miss or mourn for me*
*When my flight is finally done.*

The gaucho is more quintessentially Argentinean even than the cowboy is American. The poet José Hernández would sum up his mythic qualities in what was to become the national epic, *Martín Fierro* (1872). Its hero's appeal is undeniable, if extremely macho from a modern-day perspective. Meanwhile, the poem's climactic scene—the deadly knife fight in which Martín triumphs over his enemy, a black gaucho—hints at the more sinister racial overtones underlying the gaucho cult.

**Left:** *Dancing with their womenfolk, in this nineteenth-century illustration a group of gauchos cut a benignly rustic figure, but Darwin was more drawn by their air of macho menace.*

glass; the sitting-room boasted only of a few of the roughest chairs and stools, with a couple of tables. The supper, although several strangers were present, consisted of two huge piles, one of roast beef, the other of boiled, with some pieces of pumpkin: besides this latter there was no other vegetable, and not even a morsel of bread. For drinking, a large earthenware jug of water served the whole party. Yet this man was the owner of several square miles of land, of which nearly every acre would produce corn, and, with a little trouble, all the common vegetables. The evening was spent in smoking, with a little impromptu singing, accompanied by the guitar. The signoritas [sic] all sat together in one corner of the room, and did not sup with the men.

# Snarled Up

But the highlight of this visit for Darwin was undoubtedly the opportunity to see the gauchos about their work, and their skill with those two great tools of their trade, the lasso and *bolas*:

So many works have been written about these countries, that it is almost superfluous to describe either the *lazo* or the *bolas*. The *lazo* consists of a very strong, but thin, well-plaited rope, made of raw hide. One end is attached to the broad surcingle, which fastens together the complicated gear of the *recado*, or saddle used in the Pampas; the other is terminated by a small ring of iron or brass, by which a noose can be formed. The gaucho, when he is going to use the *lazo*, keeps a small coil in his bridle-hand, and in the other holds the running noose which is made very large, generally having a diameter of about eight feet. This he whirls round his head, and by the dexterous movement of his wrist keeps the noose open; then, throwing it, he causes it to fall on any particular spot he chooses. The *lazo*, when not used, is tied up in a small coil to the after part of the

*Above: Seen posed as in this early photograph, the mystique of the gaucho as Darwin saw it is lost.*
*Below: A representation of the* bolas.

*recado*. The *bolas*, or balls, are of two kinds: the simplest, which is chiefly used for catching ostriches, consists of two round stones, covered with leather, and united by a thin plaited thong, about eight feet long. The other kind differs only in having three balls united by the thongs to a common centre. The gaucho holds the smallest of the three in his hand, and whirls the other two round and round his head; then, taking aim, sends them like chain shot revolving through the air. The balls no sooner strike any object, than, winding round it, they cross each other, and become firmly hitched. The size and weight of the balls vary, according to the purpose for which they are made: when of stone, although not larger than an apple, they are sent with such force as sometimes to break the leg even of a horse. I have seen the balls made of wood, and as large as a turnip, for the sake of

*Left: Gauchos rope cattle with a cowboy-style lasso in this depiction of a pampas round-up from the nineteenth century.*

catching these animals without injuring them. The balls are sometimes made of iron, and these can be hurled to the greatest distance. The main difficulty in using either *lazo* or *bolas* is to ride so well as to be able at full speed, and while suddenly turning about, to whirl them so steadily round the head, as to take aim: on foot any person would soon learn the art. One day, as I was amusing myself by galloping and whirling the balls round my head, by accident the free one struck a bush, and its revolving motion being thus destroyed, it immediately fell to the ground, and, like magic, caught one hind leg of my horse; the other ball was then jerked out of my hand, and the horse

*"The gauchos roared with laughter; they cried out that they...had never before seen a man caught by himself."*

fairly secured. Luckily he was an old practised animal, and knew what it meant; otherwise he would probably have kicked till he had thrown himself down. The gauchos roared with laughter; they cried out that they had seen every sort of animal caught, but had never before seen a man caught by himself.

# Mice and More

But if he is the picture of ineptness with the *bolas*, Darwin is all businesslike efficiency with the naturalist's notebook:

The order *Rodentia* is here very numerous in species: of mice alone I obtained no less than eight kinds. The largest gnawing animal in the world, the *Hydrochaerus capybara* (the water-hog), is here also common. One which I shot at Montevideo weighed ninety-eight pounds: its length from the end of the snout to

## A Curious Small Animal

The tucutuco (*Ctenomys brasiliensis*)...may be briefly described as a gnawer, with the habits of a mole. It is extremely numerous in some parts of the country, but it is difficult to be procured, and never, I believe, comes out of the ground. It throws up at the mouth of its burrows hillocks of earth like those of the mole, but smaller. Considerable tracts of country are so completely undermined by these animals, that horses in passing over, sink above their fetlocks....Their principal food is the roots of plants, which are the object of their extensive and superficial burrows. This animal is universally known by a very peculiar noise which it makes when beneath the ground. ...The noise consists in a short, but not rough, nasal grunt, which is monotonously repeated about four times in quick succession: the name Tucutuco is given in imitation of the sound.

Darwin was intrigued by the fact that the tucutuco that were captured were invariably blinded by inflammation of the eyes—but why, with their underground existence, had they been equipped with a sense of sight at all?

the stump-like tail was three feet two inches; and its girth three feet eight. These great rodents occasionally frequent the islands in the mouth of the Plata, where the water is quite salt, but are far more abundant on the borders of fresh-water lakes and rivers. Near Maldonado three or four generally live together. In the daytime they either lie among the aquatic plants, or openly feed on the turf plain. When viewed at a distance, from their manner of walking and colour they resemble pigs: but when seated on their haunches, and attentively watching any object with one eye, they reassume the appearance of their congeners, cavies and rabbits. Both the front and side view of their head has quite a ludicrous aspect, from the great depth of their jaw.

> *Above: High above the arid pampas rise the rain-catching hills of Argentina's Lake District. The waters find their way down the Río Negro to the plains below.*

> *"The border of this lake is formed of mud.... The mud is black and has a fetid odour."*

# To the Río Negro

The following July saw the *Beagle* sailing southward down this same coast again, and:

On August the 3rd she arrived off the mouth of the Río Negro. This is the principal river on the whole line of coast between the Strait of Magellan and the Plata. It enters the sea about three hundred miles south of the estuary of the Plata. About fifty years ago, under the old Spanish government, a small colony was established here; and it is still the most southern position (lat. 41 degs.) on this eastern coast of America inhabited by civilized man. ...

During the winter [a nearby *salina*] consists of a shallow lake of brine, which in summer is converted into a field of snow-white salt. The layer near the margin is from four to five inches thick, but towards the centre its thickness increases. This lake was two and a half miles long, and one broad. One of these brilliantly white and level expanses in the midst of the brown and desolate plain offers an extraordinary spectacle. A large quantity of salt is annually drawn from the salina: and great piles, some hundred tons in weight, were lying ready for exportation. The season for working the salinas forms the harvest of Patagones; for on it the prosperity of the place depends. Nearly the whole population encamps on the bank of the river, and the people are employed in drawing out the salt in bullock-waggons, This salt is crystallized in great cubes, and is remarkably pure....

The border of this lake is formed of mud.... The mud is black, and has a fetid odour. I could not at first imagine the cause of this, but I afterwards perceived that the froth which the wind drifted on shore was coloured green, as if by confervae; I attempted to carry home some of this green matter, but from an accident failed. Parts of the lake seen from a short distance appeared of a reddish colour, and this perhaps was owing to some infusorial animalcula. The mud in many places was thrown up by numbers of some kind of worm.... How surprising it is that any creatures should be able to exist in brine, and that they should be crawling among crystals of sulphate of soda and lime! And what becomes of these worms when, during the long summer, the surface is hardened into a solid layer of salt? Flamingos in considerable numbers inhabit this lake, and breed here, throughout Patagonia, in Northern Chile, and at the Galápagos Islands, I met with these birds wherever there were lakes of brine. ...Well may we affirm that every part of the world is habitable! Whether lakes of brine, or those subterranean ones hidden beneath volcanic mountains—warm mineral springs—the wide expanse and depths of the ocean—the upper regions of the atmosphere, and even the surface of perpetual snow—all support organic beings.

From the wonders of the natural world to the mysteries of the human soul, this excursion was to have more than its share of surprises for the young scientist.

Shortly after passing the first spring we came in sight of a famous tree, which the Indians reverence as the altar of Walleechu. It is situated on a high part of the plain; and hence is a landmark visible at a great distance. As soon as a tribe of Indians come in sight of it, they offer their adorations by loud shouts. The tree itself is low, much branched, and thorny: just above the root it has a diameter of about three feet. It stands by itself without any neighbour, and was indeed the first tree we saw; afterwards we met with a few others of the same kind, but they were far from common. Being winter the tree had no leaves, but in their place numberless threads, by which the various offerings, such as cigars, bread, meat, pieces of cloth, etc., had been suspended. Poor Indians, not having anything better, only pull a thread out of their ponchos, and fasten it to the tree. Richer Indians are accustomed to pour spirits and *maté* into a certain hole, and likewise to smoke upwards, thinking thus to afford all possible gratification to Walleechu. To complete the scene, the tree was surrounded by the bleached bones of horses which had been slaughtered as sacrifices. All Indians of every age and sex make their offerings; they then think that their horses will not tire, and that they themselves shall be prosperous.

## The Freakish Flamingo

Few sights in nature are so splendid as that of a flock of flamingos seen in the mass; few so downright strange as that of a single specimen, seen up close. With its stiltlike legs and its downsloped beak, the flamingo is definitely an ornithological eccentric, but in its feeding habits it is stranger still. It is just about unique in finding food in the microscopic algae and crustaceans to be found inhabiting strongly alkaline waters, such as saltpans. It is in these algae, indeed, that are found the pigments that dye their plumage pink. Their extraordinary beaks are designed as suction pumps, which draw in water then force it out through a comblike line of fine plates or *lamellae*, filtering out food like the baleen filaments in the mouth of a whale. Flamingos produce a form of milk to feed their young, which is dyed bright red by the pigment from the algae.

# Getting to Know the General

Latin American history has not exactly been short of strongmen over the last century or so; Argentina has had rather more than its fair share of murderous dictatorships. So it's hard now to recapture the thrill of ingenuous enthusiasm the young Charles Darwin clearly felt toward the country's emerging dictator, General Rosas. His personal charisma was as undeniable as his popularity with his countrymen. Most of all, though, he must have cut an extraordinary, colorful figure compared with Earl Grey and the rest of England's government of the day.

General Rosas intimated a wish to see me; a circumstance which I was afterwards very glad of. He is a man of an extraordinary character, and has a most predominant influence in the country…. He is said to be the owner of seventy-four square leagues of land, and to have about three hundred thousand head of cattle. His estates are admirably managed, and are far more productive of corn than those of others. He first gained his celebrity by his laws for his own *estancias*, and by disciplining several hundred men, so as to resist with success the attacks of the Indians….

General Rosas is also a perfect horseman—an accomplishment of no small consequence. In a country where an assembled army elected its general by the following trial: A troop of unbroken horses being driven into a corral, were let out through a gateway, above which was a cross-bar: it was agreed whoever should drop from the bar on one of these wild animals, as it rushed out, and should be able, without saddle or bridle, not only to ride it, but also to bring it back to the door of the corral, should be their general. The person who succeeded was accordingly elected…. This extraordinary feat has been performed by Rosas.

By these means, and by conforming to the dress and habits of the Gauchos, he has obtained an unbounded popularity in the country,

> *"He is a man of an extraordinary character, and has a most predominant influence."*

## The Great Dictator

Juan Manuel de Rosas was born in 1793 into a leading family of *estancieros* in Argentina's Buenos Aires province. A fabulously wealthy young man, he established himself early as the voice of the country's *federales*—local warlords and mining magnates in the provinces—against the centralizing *unitarios* of urban Buenos Aires. But when, in 1827, he overthrew the *unitario* President Bernardino Rivadivia, his allies quickly found that they had celebrated too soon. Still ostensibly just the Governor of Buenos Aires Province, Rosas was busy consolidating power when Darwin met him in 1833. He would soon make that power absolute and guard it with extreme ruthlessness; in the dreaded *Mazorca* he had the dubious distinction of having established Latin America's first death squads. But he built the prestige of Buenos Aires, and his campaigns against Argentina's native peoples opened up enormous areas for settlement—even if from today's standpoint they come much too close to genocide for comfort. In 1849, he extended his territories northward, incurring the resentment of neighboring states, and in 1852 he was overthrown in a coup with Uruguayan and Brazilian backing. He escaped to England, ironically, where he enjoyed an apparently blameless retirement, eventually dying in 1877.

and in consequence a despotic power. I was assured by an English merchant, that a man who had murdered another, when arrested and questioned concerning his motive, answered, "He spoke disrespectfully of General Rosas, so I killed him." At the end of a week the murderer was at liberty. This doubtless was the act of the general's party, and not of the general himself.

# Evolution Underfoot

Rejoining the *Beagle* once more, Darwin remained ashore at Bahia Blanca, while his shipmates worked to survey the local harbor. He was fascinated by the evidence he saw of this whole coastline's emergence from the ocean: a slow, steady and, surely, extremely protracted process:

Nearer the coast there are some plains formed from the wreck of the upper plain, and from mud, gravel, and sand thrown up by the sea during the slow elevation of the land, of which elevation we have evidence in upraised beds of recent shells, and in rounded pebbles of pumice scattered over the country.

At one site, Punta Alta, he found the fossilized remains of a menagerie of megafauna—including several different giant sloths—another indication of evolution over enormous lengths of time. While Darwin was many years away from his theory of natural selection, his sympathy with the evolutionists' case is already clear.

First, parts of three heads and other bones of the Megatherium [Giant Ground Sloth], the huge dimensions of which are expressed by its name. Secondly, the Megalonyx, a great allied animal. Thirdly, the Scelidotherium, also an allied animal, of which I obtained a nearly perfect skeleton. It must have been as large as a rhinoceros: in the structure of its head it comes according to Mr. Owen, nearest to the Cape Anteater, but in some other respects it approaches to the armadilloes. Fourthly, the Mylodon Darwinii, a closely related genus of little inferior size. Fifthly, another gigantic edental [toothless] quadruped. Sixthly, a large animal, with an osseous coat in compartments, very like that of an armadillo. Seventhly, an extinct kind of horse, to which I shall have again to refer. Eighthly, a tooth of a Pachydermatous [elephant-

*Left: Darwin's fossil finds at Bahia Blanca included remains of several sloths.*

like] animal, probably the same with the Macrauchenia, a huge beast with a long neck like a camel, which I shall also refer to again. Lastly, the Toxodon, perhaps one of the strangest animals ever discovered: in size it equalled an elephant or megatherium, but the structure of its teeth, as Mr. Owen states, proves indisputably that it was intimately related to the Gnawers, the order which, at the present day, includes most of the smallest quadrupeds: in many details it is allied to the Pachydermata: judging from the position of its eyes, ears, and nostrils, it was probably aquatic, like the Dugong and Manatee, to which it is also allied. How wonderfully are the different Orders, at the present time so well separated, blended together in different points of the structure of the Toxodon!

But still stronger as evidence for some sort of evolutionary process, perhaps, was Darwin's discovery of remains which were clearly similar to, but not identical with, modern forms:

## An Unwelcome Presence

We saw also a couple of Zorillos, or skunks—odious animals, which are far from uncommon. In general appearance, the Zorillo resembles a polecat, but it is rather larger, and much thicker in proportion. Conscious of its power, it roams by day about the open plain, and fears neither dog nor man. If a dog is urged to the attack, its courage is instantly checked by a few drops of the fetid oil, which brings on violent sickness.... Whatever is once polluted by it, is for ever useless.

*Right:* Laid out in 1811 to commemorate the revolution of the previous year, the Plaza Mayo was to became the political heart of the Argentine Republic.

At the distance of about thirty miles from Punta Alta, in a cliff of red earth, I found several fragments of bones, some of large size. Among them were the teeth of a gnawer, equalling in size and closely resembling those of the Capybara, whose habits have been described.

# Buenos Aires

On September 20, 1833, Darwin arrived at Buenos Aires having riddern there with a guide from Bahia Blanca. "The outskirts of the city looked quite pretty," he conceded, "with the agave hedges, and groves of olive, peach and willow trees, all just throwing out their fresh green leaves." But after the chaotic (or, to put it more charitably, "organic") medieval streetscapes of the English cities he was used to, it was the sheer rationality of New World urban planning that struck him most:

The city of Buenos Ayres is large, and I should think one of the most regular in the world. Every street is at right angles to the one it crosses, and the parallel ones being equidistant, the houses are collected into solid squares of equal dimensions, which are called quadras. On the other hand, the houses themselves are hollow squares; all the rooms opening into a neat little courtyard. They are generally only one story high, with flat roofs, which are fitted with seats and are much frequented by the inhabitants in summer. In the centre of the town is the Plaza, where the public offices, fortress, cathedral, etc., stand. Here also, the old viceroys, before the revolution, had their palaces. The general assemblage of buildings possesses considerable architectural beauty, although none individually can boast of any.

*"The whole sight is horrible and revolting… the horses and riders are drenched with gore."*

As so often in Argentina, Darwin was unsure whether to be more appalled or excited by the savage scenes enacted every day at the city's cattle market.

The great *corral* where the animals are kept for slaughter to supply food to this beef-eating population, is one of the spectacles best worth seeing. The strength of the horse as compared to that of the bullock is quite astonishing: a man on horseback, having thrown his *lazo* round the horns of a beast, can drag it anywhere he chooses. The animal plowing up the ground with outstretched legs, in vain efforts to resist the force, generally dashes at full speed to one side; but the horse immediately turning to receive the shock, stands so firmly that the bullock is almost thrown down, and it is surprising that their necks are not broken. The struggle is not, however, one of fair strength; the horse's girth being matched against the bullock's extended neck. In a similar manner a man can hold the wildest horse, if caught with the *lazo*, just behind the ears. When the bullock has been dragged to the spot where it is to be slaughtered, the matador with great caution cuts the hamstrings. Then is given the death bellow; a noise more expressive of fierce agony than any I know. I have often distinguished it from a long distance, and have always known that the struggle was then drawing to a close. The whole sight is horrible and revolting: the ground is almost made of bones; and the horses and riders are drenched with gore.

# The Santa Fe Trail

*"I [came] to the conclusion that a horse, which cannot from a comparison of the tooth alone be distinguished from the existing species, lived as a contemporary with the various great monsters that formerly inhabited South America."*

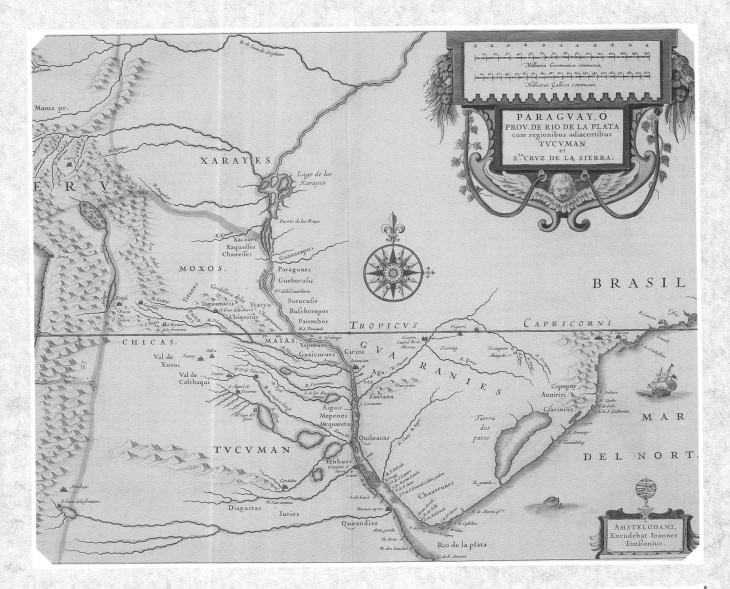

When is a river not a river? When it is the Rìo de la Plata—an estuary without a river to its name. It is an estuary of unusual proportions, though: 180 miles long, and 136 miles across at its widest point. Its name means "River of Silver," a reference to the untold wealth to which it was hoped this vast funnel-shaped inlet would turn out to be the gateway. It certainly could not have been intended as a description of the estuary itself.

Darwin himself would describe this as "[A] poor affair. A wide expanse of muddy water [that] has neither grandeur nor beauty." And no wonder: tidal currents constantly churn up the 2-billion-cubic-foot sediment load deposited here each year by the two rivers that feed the Rìo de la Plata, the Uruguay and the Paraná.

*Previous pages: Argentina is a country of contrasts: this is Tronador, near Bariloche. Above: The neck of the Río de la Plata lies some 10 degrees south of the Tropic of Capricorn, so this map of 1836 makes Darwin's trip upriver appear deceptively short.*

The next stage in Darwin's adventure took him on what he rather lightly called an "excursion" up the latter of these rivers into the interior, as far as the town of Santa Fe. By world standards, the Paraná is an impressive river, with a total length of just under 2,500 miles—approximately the same as the Missouri. Only in the South American context does it slump into comparative anonymity, outclassed as it is in length not only by the Amazon but the Orinoco. In terms of total area drained, however, with a basin extending over 1,197,000 square miles, the Paraná-Paraguay River scores a more impressive fourth in the world rankings. Only the Amazon, the African Congo and Australia's Murray River exceed this statistic; North America's Mississippi/Missouri lags some way behind.

Set against the size of this system as a whole, Darwin's foray upriver would indeed seem no more than an "excursion": to explore the river properly would have meant an epic journey deep into the forests of Brazil. (Strictly speaking, moreover, he did not travel upriver at all but overland—following the course of the river valley and taking to the water only for the return journey downstream.) Santa Fe lies only a short distance upstream, in the Entre Rìos region, so-called because it is literally between two rivers, the Paraná and Uruguay.

As ever, Darwin makes an intriguingly idiosyncratic guide to the country, with his own very particular priorities. Hence we hear that the valley in which nestles the riverside town of Rosario has "immense beds leagues in extent and quite impenetrable, by man or beast" of a certain "thistle-looking plant." For Argentineans, then as now, far from being a mere bed of thistles, Rosario was revered as the "Cradle of the Flag." There, on the bank of the Paraná, General Manuel Belgrano had first raised what would be the country's standard on February 27, 1812, a day destined to resound in the national memory.

But then Darwin often seems surprisingly vague even on scientific subjects: a little farther upriver he notes "a wood of low prickly trees, apparently mimosa." It serves as a useful reminder of how times have changed. The entire *Beagle* project is unthinkable in today's scientific terms. Now, if such a project were undertaken at all it would involve hundreds of scientists with thousands of support staff, and there would have been somebody on hand to give the "prickly trees" their Latin name. Darwin was one of

the last of a dying breed, a "gentleman amateur," omnivorous in his interests, although necessarily limited in the scope of his expertise. At the same time, however, he is humble, perhaps happier than a modern scientist would be to admit to ignorance, and certainly more tolerant of muddle. What rigorous, academically trained scientist today could cope with the idea of an estuary without a river—or come up with something like *The Origin of Species*?

*Top:* "Low prickly trees, apparently mimosa": the attractive plant is native to much of South America, from Mexico to northern Argentina. *Above:* The "Silver River," as seen in a photograph from the early twentieth century.

# Slow Progress

On September 27, recorded Darwin,

In the evening I set out on an excursion to Santa Fe, which is situated nearly three hundred English miles from Buenos Aires, on the banks of the Paraná. The roads in the neighborhood of the city, after the rainy weather, were extraordinarily bad. I should never have thought it possible for a bullock wagon to have crawled along: as it was, they scarcely went at the rate of a mile an hour, and a man was kept ahead, to survey the best line for making the attempt. The bullocks were terribly jaded: it is a great mistake to suppose that with improved roads, and an accelerated rate of traveling, the sufferings of the animals increase in the same proportion. We passed a train of wagons and a troop of beasts on their road to Mendoza. The distance is about 580 geographical miles, and the journey is generally performed in fifty days. These wagons are very long,

narrow, and thatched with reeds; they have only two wheels, the diameter of which in some cases is as much as ten feet. Each is drawn by six bullocks, which are urged on by a goad at least twenty feet long: this is suspended from within the roof; for the wheel bullocks a smaller one is kept; and for the intermediate pair, a point projects at right angles from the middle of the long one.

The whole apparatus looked like some implement of war.

## The Silver River

Spanish navigator Juan Díaz de Solís discovered the Río de la Plata in 1516, having sailed from Lepe, on Spain's southwestern coast, the previous year. It was he who gave it its name, in confident expectation that rich mines would lie upriver, all to be claimed for the greater glory and prosperity of the Spanish monarchy. After that, unfortunately, the omens were not quite so good: Díaz de Solís was killed by natives when he put ashore with a small party. Their shipmates promptly weighed anchor and beat a hasty retreat; it was left to subsequent expeditions to explore the territory further. In the end, the expectations of mineral riches were not to be realized, but the Río de la Plata's hinterland would over time provide a beef bonanza.

*Above: "A train of wagons and a troop of beasts." A convoy sets out across the pampas. Below: 1536: Pedro de Mendoza founding Buenos Aires.*

## Good Order

Santa Fe is a quiet little town, and is kept clean and in good order. The governor's favorite occupation is hunting Indians: a short time since he slaughtered forty-eight, and sold the children at the rate of three or four pounds apiece.

This is as close as the generally upbeat *Voyage of the Beagle* gets to registering the fact that, at the time of Darwin's visit, a white nation was emerging from what amounted to genocide. The informal notes of the *Beagle Diary* are more frank:

The Indians are now so terrified that they offer no resistance even in body; but each escapes as well as he can, neglecting even his wife and children. The soldiers pursue and sabre every man.... This is a dark picture; but how much more shocking is the unquestionable fact that all the women who appear above twenty years old are massacred in cold blood. I ventured to hint that this appeared rather inhuman [and was answered] "Why, what can be done? They breed so...." Everyone here is fully convinced that this is the justest war, because it is against barbarians. Who would believe in this age in a Christian civilized country that such atrocities were committed?

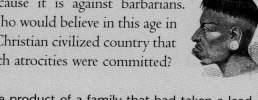

The product of a family that had taken a lead in the abolitionist struggle against the slave trade, Darwin had been brought up with strongly humanitarian instincts. Shocked as he was at what he was witnessing, however, he still felt called upon to support a colonial country's struggle for autonomy. Like many white men of his day, he was confused.

# Folk Medicine

A few days later (October 3–4) Darwin found himself "confined…to my bed by a headache," but even this turned out an occasion for research.

A good-natured old woman, who attended me, wished me to try many odd remedies. A common practice is, to bind an orange-leaf or a bit of black plaster to each temple: and a still more general plan is, to split a bean into halves, moisten them, and place one on each temple, where they will easily adhere. It is not thought proper ever to remove the beans or plaster, but to allow them to drop off, and sometimes, if a man, with patches on his head, is asked, what is the matter? he will answer, "I had a headache the day before yesterday." Many of the remedies used by the people of the country are ludicrously strange, but too disgusting to be mentioned. One of the least nasty is to kill and cut open two puppies and bind them on each side of a broken limb.

Such treatments sound grotesque in an age of scientific medicine, but were by no means restricted to the wilds of the pampas: in the wilder parts of Darwin's native Britain, similar remedies were widely used. The writer John McNeillie reports a cat being killed and lashed to the neck of an injured horse in rural Galloway, in southwestern Scotland, during the 1930s.

*Below: Darwin was shocked at the way Santa Fe's indigenous people were treated by the white settlers.*

# All at Sea

On October 5, Darwin's party:

Crossed the Paraná to Santa Fe Bajada, a town on the opposite shore. The passage took some hours, as the river here consisted of a labyrinth of small streams, separated by low wooded islands.... I was delayed here five days, and employed myself in examining the geology of the surrounding country, which was very interesting. We here see at the bottom of the cliffs, beds containing sharks' teeth and sea-shells of extinct species.... M.A. d'Orbigny found on the banks of the Paraná, at the height of a hundred feet, great beds of an estuary shell, now living a hundred miles lower down nearer the sea; and I found similar shells at a lesser height on the banks of the Uruguay; this shows that just before the pampas was slowly elevated into dry land, the water covering it was brackish. Below Buenos Aires there are upraised beds of sea-shells of existing species, which also proves that the period of elevation of the pampas was within the recent period.

The crucial point in this passage was that this was yet more evidence of enormous changes taking place over enormous lengths of time, evidence reinforced by Darwin's discovery of further fossil Toxodon teeth in these deposits. Alongside them in the mud, however, lay something of still more significance:

A tooth, which I discovered by one point projecting from the side of a bank, interested me much, for I at once perceived that it had belonged to a horse. Feeling much surprised at this, I carefully examined its geological position, and was compelled to come to the conclusion that a horse, which cannot from a comparison of the tooth alone be distinguished from the existing species, lived as a contemporary with the various great monsters that formerly inhabited South America.... Certainly it is a marvellous event in the history of animals that a native kind should have disappeared to be succeeded in after ages by the countless herds introduced with the Spanish colonist!

*Above:* Even in fossilized form, the grinding molars in this mastodon skull are unmistakable: Darwin made a number of exciting finds in his travels on the pampas.
*Left:* Damp-loving arrayán trees crowd the banks and islands of several Argentinean rivers.

## Natural History and the Horse

Modern paleontology confirms that the horse was indeed native to the Americas, even though it disappeared during the Ice Age and had to be reintroduced by the conquistadors. Some of the strongest evidence is found in North America, at the Hagerman Fossil Beds of Idaho. Here abundant traces have been found of horses coexisting with mastodons—like the toxodon, a form of pachyderm. As conditions became colder and more arid, horses are believed to have drifted away northward and over the Beringia land bridge to Eurasia, while the bulkier mastodons, unable to either migrate or adapt, became extinct. Fossil camelids have been found in Idaho too: they are also believed to have migrated out of North America, some going north and west to Eurasia, the ancestors of modern camels. Others headed south into the Andean region of South America, where we now know them as llamas, alpacas and guanaco.

# The Rìos Run Dry

Cataclysmic events were not necessarily confined to the primeval past, as Darwin was to learn in the course of his journey through the Entre Rìos region.

While traveling through the country, I received several vivid descriptions of the effects of a late great drought; and the account of this may throw some light on the cases where vast numbers of animals of all kinds have been embedded together. The period included between the years 1827 and 1830 is called the *gran seco*, or the great drought. During this time so little rain fell that the vegetation, even to the thistles, failed; the brooks were dried up, and the whole country assumed the appearance of a dusty high road. This was especially the case in the northern part of the province of Buenos Aires and the southern part of Santa Fe. Very great numbers of birds, wild animals, cattle, and horses perished from the want of food and

*"So little rain fell that the vegetation failed; the brooks dried up, and the whole country assumed the appearance of a dusty high road."*

water. A man told me that the deer used to come into his courtyard to the well, which he had been obliged to dig to supply his own family with water; and that the partridges had hardly strength to fly away when pursued. The lowest estimation of the loss of cattle in the province of Buenos Aires alone, was taken at one million head. A proprietor at San Pedro had previously to these years 20,000 cattle; at the end not one remained. San Pedro is situated in the middle of the finest country; and even now abounds again with animals; yet during the latter part of the *gran seco*, live cattle were brought in vessels for the consumption of the inhabitants. The animals roamed from their *estancias*, and, wandering far southward, were mingled together in such multitudes, that a government commission was sent from Buenos Aires to settle the disputes of the owners. Sir Woodbine Parish informed me of another and very curious source of dispute; the ground being so long dry, such quantities of dust were blown about, that in this open country the landmarks became obliterated, and people could not tell the limits of their estates.

I was informed by an eye-witness that the cattle in herds of thousands rushed into the Paraná, and being exhausted by hunger they were unable to crawl up the muddy banks, and thus were drowned. The arm of the river which runs by San Pedro was so full of putrid carcasses, that the master of a vessel told me that the smell rendered it quite impassable. Without doubt several hundred thousand animals thus perished in the river: their bodies when putrid were seen floating down the stream; and many in all probability were deposited in the estuary of the Plata.

*Above: The open pampas, empty and apparently unproductive. Below: As grazing land for cattle, these grasslands underpinned the prosperity of a new nation.*

## A Bad Boy

Every December—midsummer in the Pacific waters off the coast of Peru—an apparently trivial change in temperature has far-reaching climatic and ecological consequences. The normally frigid Peru Current is temporarily suppressed as warm water spills east from this localized "hotspot." Every seven years or so, for as yet unexplained reasons, the effects of this warming are greatly amplified. In extreme cases, fish stocks collapse, causing grave problems, while wind and rainfall patterns ashore are thrown into confusion. Sometimes torrential downpours cause flash floods; at other times, catastrophic droughts: there's no knowing quite what the results will be. Known as *El Niño*—"the child"—because it corresponds with Christmas, the nativity of Jesus, the phenomenon has attracted great attention in recent years, since its impact has been noted indirectly all around the world. But in the boy's backyard, in South America, many of the most severe effects have been felt: the drought of 1827–30 was an El Niño event.

# About Turn

"I had intended to push my excursion further," noted Darwin, but on October 12, "not being quite well,"

I was compelled to return by a *balandra*or one-masted vessel of about a hundred tons burden, which was bound for Buenos Aires. As the weather was not fair, we moored early in the day to a branch of a tree on one of the islands. The Paraná is full of islands, which undergo a constant round of decay and renovation. In the memory of the master, several large ones had disappeared, and others again had been formed and protected by vegetation.

Is it too far-fetched to find here a recurrence of the idea that would eventually come to dominate Darwin's scientific life—the view that, far from being a fixed *fait accompli*, creation was a process of endless change? But, if Darwin began to muse on this as he scrambled about these islands' "numerous willow trees and [other trees] bound together by a great variety of creeping plants," the realization that this amounted to a "thick jungle" prompted more pressing concerns.

These thickets afford a retreat for carpinchos and jaguars. The fear of the latter animal quite destroyed all pleasure in scrambling through the woods. This evening I had not proceeded a hundred yards before, finding indubitable signs of the tiger, I was obliged to come back.

## El Tigre

Today the jaguar is assumed to be a beast of the deepest Amazon rainforest, but it was once far more wide-ranging. There was ample testimony to its presence in the luxuriant undergrowth that covered the islands of the Paraná, as Darwin observed:

The jaguar is a much more dangerous animal than is generally supposed: they have killed several woodcutters.... There is a man now in the Bajada who, coming up from below at night time, was seized by a tiger, but he escaped with the loss of use of one arm. ...A few years since a very large one entered a church at Santa Fe. Two padres entering one after the other were killed, a third, coming to see what was the cause of their delay, escaped with difficulty. The beast was killed by unroofing one corner of the room and firing at it.

## "A Very Extraordinary Bird"

In his diary for October 15, 1833, Darwin recorded "a very extraordinary bird," what he called the "scissor-beak":

The lower mandible is as flat and elastic as an ivory paper-cutter; it is an inch and a half longer than the upper. With its mouth wide open, and the lower mandible immersed some depth in the water, it flies rapidly up and down the stream. Thus ploughing the surface, it occasionally seizes a small fish.

American ornithologists know *Rynchops nigra* as the black skimmer, or razor-billed shearwater, a species widespread in the coastal regions and swamps of the southern states. By any name, though, it is indeed a "very extraordinary bird."

# Anglo-Saxon Attitudes

At times, Darwin seems a caricature of the Englishman abroad, comically aghast at the incompetence of foreigners. Hence the remarks he made in the course of his journey back downstream from Santa Fe, on October 18–19:

We continued slowly to sail down the noble stream: the current helped us but little. We met, during our descent, very few vessels. One of the best gifts of nature, in so grand a channel of communication, seems here wilfully thrown away—a river in which ships might navigate from a temperate country, as surprisingly abundant in certain productions as destitute of others, to another possessing a tropical

## The "Scissor-Tail"

Not to be confused with the scissor-beak (not likely to be, in actual fact) was what the Argentineans apparently called the scissor-tail, *Tyrannus savana*, known to modern birders as the Fork-tailed flycatcher. Darwin describes it as:

A bird with a forked tail, terminated by two long feathers…[It] is very common near Buenos Aires. It commonly sits on a branch of the ombu tree, near a house, and thence takes a short flight in pursuit of insects, and returns to the same spot. When on the wing it presents in its manner of flight and generall appearance a caricature-likeness of the common swallow. It has the power of turning very shortly in the air, and in so doing opens and shuts its tail, sometimes in a horizontal or lateral and sometimes in a vertical direction, just like a pair of scissors.

## Blood Sacrifice

By the standards of today's scientists, Darwin's ways often seem astonishingly cavalier and casual. Notwithstanding that, it is remarkable the lengths to which the spirit of enquiry would take him on occasion. "The evenings are quite tropical; the thermometer 79°," he noted in his diary for October 15, 1833. "An abundance of fireflies, and the mosquitoes very troublesome." But just *how* troublesome, exactly? What could any self-respecting scientist do but conduct an experiment?

I exposed my hand for five minutes; it was black with them: I do not think there could have been less than fifty, all busy with sucking.

climate, and a soil which…is perhaps unequalled in fertility in any part of the world. How different would have been the aspect of this river if English colonists had by good fortune first sailed up the Plata! What noble towns would now have occupied its shores!

That swipe at the Spanish off his chest, he makes the rather more reasonable point, supported by history, that tyranny is inherently unstable.

Till the death of Francia, the Dictator of Paraguay, these two countries must remain distinct, as if placed on opposite sides of the globe. And when the old bloody-minded tyrant is gone to his long account, Paraguay will be torn by revolutions, violent in proportion to the previous unnatural calm. That country will have to learn, like every other South American state, that a republic cannot succeed till it contains a certain body of men imbued with the principles of justice and honour.

*Above:* In the absence of any real ethnographical information or understanding, the nineteenth-century imagination could run riot: here "cannabilistic" Paraguayans prepare for a feast.

# Under Way Again

When Darwin returned to the shores of the Rìo de la Plata, he found himself a virtual prisoner because a violent revolution had resulted in an embargo of the port, effectively grounding the *Beagle*. However, Darwin used his "connections" to General Rosas (who was shortly to seize power) to obtain permission to set sail again from Las Conchas, where the party had been detained for two weeks. And so, on November 14, 1833, they set out.

We left Montevideo in the afternoon. I intended to proceed to Colonia del Sacramiento, situated on the northern bank of the Plata and opposite to Buenos Aires, and thence, following up the Uruguay, to the village of Mercedes on the Rìo Negro (one of the many rivers of this name in South America), and from this point to return direct to Montevideo. We slept at the house of my guide at Canelones. In the morning we rose early, in the hopes of being able to ride a good distance; but it was a vain attempt, for all the rivers were flooded. We passed in boats the streams of Canelones, Santa Lucìa, and San Josè, and thus lost much time. On a former excursion I crossed the Lucìa near its mouth, and I was surprised to observe how easily our horses, although not used to swim, passed over a width of at least six hundred yards. On mentioning this at Montevideo, I was told that a vessel containing some mountebanks and their horses, being wrecked in the Plata, one horse swam seven miles to the shore.

The sight of a man and a horse crossing a river brings out an unexpectedly Whitmanesque side to Darwin's character, frank in its admiration for unconstrained physicality and the uncovered physique.

In the course of the day I was amused by the dexterity with which a gaucho forced a restive horse to swim a river. He stripped off his clothes, and jumping on its back, rode into the water till it was out of its depth; then slipping off over the crupper, he caught hold of the tail, and as often as the horse turned round the man frightened it back by splashing water in its face. As soon as the horse touched the bottom on the other side, the man pulled himself on, and was firmly seated, bridle in hand, before the horse gained the bank. A naked man on a naked horse is a fine spectacle; I had no idea how well the two animals suited each other.

The tail of a horse is a very useful appendage; I have passed a river in a boat with four people in it, which was ferried across in the same way as the gaucho. If a man and horse have to cross a broad river, the best plan is for the man to catch hold of the pommel or mane, and help himself with the other arm.

# Of Condescension and Combs

Darwin soon recovered his poise, and some of that old English condescension:

In the evening we proceeded on our road towards Mercedes on the Rìo Negro. At night we asked permission to sleep at an *estancia* at which we happened to arrive. It was a very large estate, being ten leagues square, and the owner is one of the greatest landowners in the country. His nephew had charge of it, and with him there was a captain in the army, who the other day ran away from Buenos Aires. Considering their station, their conversation was rather amusing. They expressed, as was usual, unbounded astonishment at the globe being round, and could scarcely credit that a hole would, if deep enough, come out on the other side. They had, however, heard of a country where there were six months of light and six of darkness, and where the inhabitants were very tall and thin! They were curious about the price and condition of horses and cattle in England. Upon finding out we did not catch our animals with the lassoo, they cried out, "Ah, then, you use nothing but the bolas"; the idea of an enclosed country was quite new to them. The captain at last said, he had one question to ask me, which he should be very much obliged if I would answer with all truth. I trembled to think how deeply scientific it would be: it was, "Whether the ladies of Buenos Aires were not the handsomest in the world." I replied, like a renegade, "Charmingly so." He added, "I have one other question: Do ladies in any other part of the world wear such large combs?" I solemnly assured him that they did not. They were absolutely delighted. The captain exclaimed, "Look there! a man who has seen half the world says it is the case; we always thought so, but now we know it!" My excellent judgment in combs and beauty procured me a most hospitable reception; the captain forced me to take his bed, and he would sleep on his *recado*.

*Above: The other Argentina, a land of quiet lakes and distant hills.*
*Left: Oddly unsettling in its uninterrupted emptiness, the open pampas stretches away beneath an endless sky.*

## La Peineta

The *peineta,* or "Spanish comb," was indeed Andalucian in origin, and still a relatively new fashion in the Argentina of the 1830s. Tortoiseshell combs were worn in combination with the *mantilla,* or veil—a cynic would say, as a means of defeating its original object. With the foundational support of the comb, towering edifices of tumbling locks could be constructed, raising the edges of the veil high above the face. The end result was thus the merest, most alluring hint of modesty, without any actual concealment.

*Above:* "There are many feast days," noted Darwin with all the severity a Protestant Englishman could muster—but he had a sneaking regard for the gauchos' love of life.

# Of Ethics and Animals

The English are famously—even notoriously—a nation of animal lovers: Darwin could never get used to the heedless ways of the pampas.

Animals are so abundant in these countries, that humanity and self-interest are not closely united; therefore I fear it is that the former is here scarcely known. One day, riding in the pampas with a very respectable *estanciero,* my horse, being tired, lagged behind. The man often shouted to me to spur him. When I remonstrated that it was a pity, for the horse was quite exhausted, he cried out, "Why not?—never mind—spur him—it is my horse." I had then some difficulty in making him comprehend that it was for the horse's sake, and not on his account, that I did not choose to use my spurs. He exclaimed, with a look of great surprise, "Ah, Don Carlos, *qué cosa!*" It was clear that such an idea had never before entered his head.

The Argentinean approach was to see animals as a force of nature to be dominated, and, if need be, wrestled into submission; paradoxically, though, this could produce a sense of man and beast in perfect harmony.

The gauchos are well known to be perfect riders The idea of being thrown, let the horse do what it likes; never enters their head. Their criterion of a good rider is, a man who can manage an untamed colt, or who, if his horse falls, alights on his own feet, or can perform other such exploits. I have heard of a man betting that he would throw his horse down twenty times, and that nineteen times he would not fall himself. I recollect seeing a gaucho riding a very stubborn horse, which three times successively reared so high as to fall backwards with great violence. The man judged with uncommon coolness the proper moment for slipping off, not an instant before or after the right time; and as soon as the horse got up, the man jumped on his back, and at last they started at a gallop. The gaucho never appears to exert any muscular force.

*Below: Gauchos could turn their herding skills to anything: in this nineteenth-century image they can be seen slaughtering the birds on a farm that raised rheas, or Argentinean ostriches. Opposite, top: "The polite and dignified manners pervading every rank of life...." A Dover engraving of Paraguay's "higher" class.*

# The Code of the Gaucho

As we have already seen, Darwin was fascinated by the gaucho figure. The gaucho attitude to life simultaneously enthralled and appalled him:

*"In fighting, each party tries to mark the face of his adversary by slashing his nose or eyes; as is often attested by deep and horrid-looking scars."*

During the last six months I have had an opportunity of seeing a little of the character of the inhabitants of these provinces. The gauchos, or countrymen, are very superior to those who reside in the towns. The gaucho is invariably most obliging, polite, and hospitable: I did not meet with even one instance of rudeness or inhospitality. He is modest, both respecting himself and country, but at the same time a spirited, bold fellow. On the other hand, many robberies are committed, and there is much bloodshed: the habit of constantly wearing the knife is the chief cause of the latter. It is lamentable to hear how many lives are lost in trifling quarrels. In fighting, each party tries to mark the face of his adversary by slashing his nose or eyes; as is often attested by deep and horrid-looking scars. Robberies are a natural consequence of universal gambling, much drinking, and extreme indolence. At Mercedes I asked two men why they did not work. One gravely said the days were too long; the other that he was too poor. The number of horses and the profusion of food are the destruction of all industry. Moreover, there are so many feast-days; and again, nothing can succeed without it be begun when the moon is on the increase; so that half the month is lost from these two causes.

Police and justice are quite inefficient. If a man who is poor commits murder and is taken, he will be imprisoned, and perhaps even shot; but if he is rich and has friends, he may rely on it no very severe consequence will ensue. It is curious that the most respectable inhabitants of the country invariably assist a murderer to escape: they seem to think that the individual sins against the government, and not against the people. A traveler has no protection besides his firearms; and the constant habit of carrying them is the main check to more frequent robberies.

**Darwin was prepared to grant the humble gaucho a certain latitude that he was not prepared to concede to his "betters":**

The character of the higher and more educated classes who reside in the towns, partakes, but perhaps in a lesser degree, of the good parts of the gaucho, but is, I fear, stained by many vices of which he is free. Sensuality, mockery of all religion, and the grossest corruption, are far from uncommon. Nearly every public officer can be bribed. The head man in the post office sold forged government franks. The governor and prime minister openly combined to plunder the state. Justice, where gold came into play, was hardly expected by any one. I knew an Englishman, who went to the Chief Justice (he told me, that not then understanding the ways of the place, he trembled as he entered the room), and said, "Sir, I have come to offer you two hundred (paper) dollars (value about five pounds sterling) if you will arrest before a certain time a man who has cheated me. I know it is against the law, but my lawyer (naming him) recommended me to take this step." The Chief Justice smiled acquiescence, thanked him, and the man before night was safe in prison. With this entire want of principle in many of the leading men, with the country full of ill-paid turbulent officers, the people yet hope that a democratic form of government can succeed!

*"Sensuality, mockery of all religion, and the grossest corruption, are far from uncommon."*

**But even where these higher echelons of society were concerned, all credit to Darwin, he was himself prepared to give credit where it was due.**

On first entering society in these countries, two or three features strike one as particularly remarkable. The polite and dignified manners pervading every rank of life, the excellent taste displayed by the women in their dresses, and the equality amongst all ranks. At the Rio Colorado some men who kept the humblest shops used to dine with General Rosas. A son of a major at Bahia Blanca gained his livelihood by making paper cigars, and he wished to accompany me, as guide or servant, to Buenos Aires, but his father objected on the score of the danger alone. Many officers in the army can neither read nor write, yet all meet in society as equals. In Entre Rìos, the Sala consisted of only six representatives. One of them kept a common shop, and evidently was not degraded by the office. All this is what would be expected in a new country; nevertheless the absence of gentlemen by profession appears to an Englishman something strange.

**Finally, as though whipping himself up into a veritable paroxysm of broad-minded tolerance, Darwin ended up bestowing a measure of magnanimous praise on the region's former (and Britain's rival) colonial power.**

When speaking of these countries, the manner in which they have been brought up by their unnatural parent, Spain, should always be borne in mind. On the whole, perhaps, more credit is due for what has been done, than blame for that which may be deficient. It is impossible to doubt but that the extreme liberalism of these countries must ultimately lead to good results. The very general toleration of foreign religions, the regard paid to the means of education, the freedom of the press, the facilities offered to all foreigners, and especially, as I am bound to add, to every one professing the humblest pretensions to science, should be recollected with gratitude by those who have visited Spanish South America.

# In Patagonia

*"It is impossible to reflect without the deepest astonishment on the changed state of this continent. Formerly it must have swarmed with great monsters…but now we find only the tapir, guanaco, armadillo, and capybara; mere pygmies compared to the antecedent races."*

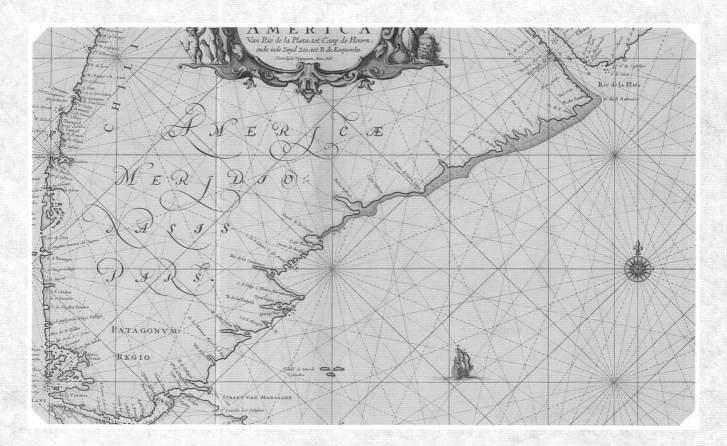

"In calling up images of the past," Darwin would write at the very end of his voyage, "I find the plains of Patagonia most frequently cross before my eyes. Yet these plains are pronounced by all most wretched and useless."

"All" here has to include the great naturalist himself, whom we catch referring to "wretched-looking" country around Port Desire in his diary for December 24, 1833. In fairness to Darwin, he was prepared to wrestle honestly with what he clearly saw as an almost philosophical "Patagonia problem." These plains, he said,

[Are] only characterized by negative possessions—without habitations, without water, without trees, without mountains, they support merely a few dwarf plants. Why then, and the case is not peculiar to myself, do these arid wastes take so firm possession of my memory? Why have not the still more level, greener and fertile pampas, which are so serviceable to mankind, produced an equal impression? I can scarcely analyse these feelings. But it must be partly owing to the free scope given to the imagination.

*Previous pages: Seen here at Cuernos del Paine, the majestic heights of the Western Cordillera would call to Darwin across the empty spaces of Patagonia. Above: What we now call Argentina, as revealed by a map of 1666. Below: A Tehuelche mother and daughter.*

Darwin was surely onto something here: this Patagonia is a place of negatives, an antilandscape, an emptiness the individual imagination feels compelled to fill. This is precisely what happens in British writer Bruce Chatwin's "autobiografictional" account of his own wanderings *In Patagonia*, which has helped put the region back on the intellectual map since its publication in 1977. Chatwin's book, only nominally a travelogue, is notoriously sketchy about what Patagonia actually looks like, and many of the people and communities he encountered have objected indignantly to their portrayal in its pages. But then, justifiably or not, what Chatwin saw in Patagonia was an infinity of space in which he could unpack and explore his own selfhood.

Those modern inhabitants of the region who took exception to what they saw as Chatwin's free-and-easy way with the facts will not necessarily be comforted to know that they are heirs to a long tradition. The first Europeans to land here, the men who came this way with Magellan in 1520, swore blind on their return that Patagonia was a land of giants. Antonio Pigafetta, the expedition's chronicler, and as its cartographer supposedly a man of science, solemnly reports that, when he and his companions came ashore at Puerto San Julián (Darwin's Port St. Julian), they met a native who towered over them to such an extent that their heads only just came up to his waist.

The Tehuelche, as these people came to be known—or the Tsonekas, as they called themselves—could not afford to let their Patagonia be so fantastical a place. They were still hunter-gatherers in Darwin's day, a people to whom the landscape could hardly have been more real, the source—however grudging at times—of their livelihood. Their existence had been affected in complex ways by the coming of the white man. Hunting had been easier since the introduction of the horse. Travel, too, was simpler, including the trip to Punta Arenas and other European outposts, where the Tehuelche made their way at intervals taking hides and other goods with which to trade. On the other hand, European colonists were affronted at the presence of the Tehuelche in a region they believed to have been created by God specifically to be settled by themselves.

Already by the time of Darwin's visit, there had been clear signs of trouble in Patagonia. By the 1870s, however, the region would be the scene of systematic genocide of the sort that had already taken place on the pampas to the north.

*Left: Native Patagonians pursue rhea with* bolas *in the shadow of the mountains.* ***Above:*** *Ferdinand Magellan (c.1480–1521).* ***Top:*** *The red fox of the Andean foothills.*

# Going Ashore

On December 23, reports Darwin, "We arrived at Port Desire [Deseado], on the coast of Patagonia."

The creek runs for about twenty miles inland, with an irregular width. The *Beagle* anchored a few miles within the entrance, in front of the ruins of an old Spanish settlement.

The same evening I went on shore. The first landing in any new country is very interesting, and especially when, as in this case, the whole aspect bears the stamp of a marked and individual character. At the height of between two and three hundred feet above some masses of porphyry a wide plain extends, which is truly characteristic of

*"In every other direction the horizon is indistinct from the trembling mirage which seems to rise from the heated surface."*

Patagonia. The surface is quite level, and is composed of well-rounded shingle mixed with a whitish earth. Here and there scattered tufts of brown wiry grass are supported, and still more rarely, some low thorny bushes. The weather is dry and pleasant, and the fine blue sky is but seldom obscured. When standing in the middle of one of these desert plains and looking towards the interior, the view is generally bounded by the escarpment of another plain, rather higher, but equally level and desolate; and in every other direction the horizon is indistinct from the trembling mirage which seems to rise from the heated surface.

The plains are traversed by many broad, flat-bottomed valleys, and in these the bushes grow rather more abundantly. The present drainage of the country

---

## Seagoing Spiders

Before the *Beagle*'s arrival in Patagonia, Darwin took the opportunity to note "a few observations made at sea":

On several occasions, when the *Beagle* has been within the mouth of the Plata, the rigging has been coated with the web of the Gossamer Spider. ...Vast numbers of a small spider, about one-tenth of an inch in length, and of a dusky red colour, were attached to the webs. The little spider, when first coming in contact with the rigging, was always seated on a single thread, and not on the flocculent mass. This latter seems merely to be produced by the entanglement of the single threads. ...The little aeronaut as soon as it arrived on board was very active, running about, sometimes letting itself fall, and then reascending the same thread; sometimes employing itself in making a small and very irregular mesh in the corners between the ropes. It could run with facility on the surface of the water. ...While watching some that were suspended by a single thread, I several times observed that the slightest breath of air bore them away out of sight, in a horizontal line.

There are more than 3,500 different species in the *Linyphiidae* family, collectively known as "sheetweb" or "dwarf" spiders, and as "money spiders," from a traditional belief that has endured despite the disappointments of generations that if one lands on you, a sum of money will come your way. They are small but their aviational exploits are extraordinary. Their habit of "ballooning," borne aloft by their thread on even the merest wisp of wind, has been a source of fascination to scientists. A large-scale study showed that, in favorable conditions, spiders could cover an average of twenty miles in a six-hour period, and they have been found floating at altitudes greater than 14,000 feet.

is quite insufficient to excavate such large channels. In some of the valleys, ancient, stunted trees, growing in the very centre of the dry watercourse, seem as if placed to prove how long a time had elapsed, since any flood had passed that way. We have evidence, from shells lying on the surface, that the plains of gravel have been elevated within a recent epoch above the level of the sea; and we must look to that period for the excavation of the valleys by the slowly retiring waters. From the dryness of the climate, a man may walk for days without finding a single drop of water. Even at the base of the porphyry hills, there are only a few small wells containing but little water, and that rather saline and half putrid.

*Above:* Port Desire's harbor facilities are not quite as desirable as this map of 1599 makes out.
*Below, left:* "Level and desolate": Patagonia. *Below, right:* "Not uncommon": black-faced ibis in Patagonia.

Despite the unpromising setting, there had been attempts to colonize the country, but these had run up against the harshness of the climate and the hostility of the Tehuelche.

In such a country the fate of the Spanish settlement was soon decided; the dryness of the climate during the greater part of the year, and the occasional hostile attacks of the wandering Indians, compelled the colonists to desert their half-finished buildings. …The result of all the attempts to colonize this side of America south of 41 degrees, has been miserable. Port Famine expresses by its name the lingering and extreme sufferings of several hundred wretched people, of whom one alone survived to relate their misfortunes.

*"Port Famine expresses by its name the lingering and extreme sufferings of several hundred people, of whom one alone survived to relate their misfortunes."*

Soon, Darwin turned his attentions to scientific matters, though at first found less to detain him than might have been expected:

The zoology of Patagonia is as limited as its flora. On the arid plains a few black beetles (*Heteromera*) might be seen slowly crawling about, and occasionally a lizard darted from side to side. Of birds we have three carrion hawks and in the valleys a few finches and insect-feeders. An ibis (*Theristicus melanops*—a species said to be found in central Africa) is not uncommon…: in their stomachs I found grasshoppers, cicadae, small lizards, and even scorpions. At one time of the year these birds go in flocks, at another in pairs, their cry is very loud and singular, like the neighing of the guanaco.

# The Guanaco

## *Camelid King*

The giant Tehuelche allegedly encountered by Magellan's men three hundred years before Darwin's visit was said to have worn the skin of a local animal, which had "the head and ears of a mule, body of a camel, deer legs and the tail of a horse"—presumably, a guanaco. A distinctive beast, the guanaco is a relation of the vicuña and of the domesticated llama and alpaca: it is a slightly more distant relative of the Old World dromedary and camel. Though it lacks their most obvious oddity, the hump, it shares one of the most robust digestive systems in the animal kingdom. The guanaco's three stomachs can squeeze the sustenance out of the most unpromising vegetation and, as Darwin saw, screen out the toxins from the most brackish water. Like the camel, it can cope with the dramatic daily swings of temperature to be found in desert climates; it is well equipped for survival in other ways too. Thanks to a long gestation period (345 days) the infant guanaco can stand up within a few minutes of being born and outrun a man before it is even half an hour old. At the time of Columbus, it is estimated that there may have been up to 35 million guanaco roaming wild in South America; today there are only a few hundred thousand.

The guanaco caught Darwin's imagination rather more than the rest of the region's fauna put together:

The guanaco, which by some naturalists is considered as the same animal with the llama, but in its wild state, is the South American representative of the camel of the East. In size it may be compared to an ass, mounted on taller legs, and with a very long neck. The guanaco abounds over the whole of the temperate parts of the continent, from the wooded islands of Tierra del Fuego, through Patagonia, the hilly parts of La Plata, Chile, even to the Cordillera of Peru. Although preferring an elevated site, it yields in this respect to its relative the Vicuna. On the plains of Southern Patagonia we saw them in greater numbers than in any other part. Generally they go in small herds, from half a dozen to thirty together, but on the banks of the Santa Cruz we saw one herd which must have contained at least five hundred. ...

On the mountains of Tierra del Fuego, I have more than once seen a guanaco, on being approached, not only neigh and squeal, but prance and leap about in the most ridiculous manner, apparently in defiance. ... These animals are very easily domesticated, and I have seen some thus kept in northern Patagonia...though not under any restraint. They are in this state very

bold, and readily attack a man by striking him from behind with both knees. It is asserted that the motive for these attacks is jealousy on account of their females. The wild guanacos, however, have no idea of defence; even a single dog will secure one of these large animals, till the huntsman can come up. . . .

The guanacos appear to have favourite spots for lying down to die. On the banks of the St. Cruz, in certain circumscribed spaces, which were generally bushy and all near the river, the ground was actually white with bones. On one such spot I counted between ten and twenty heads. I particularly examined the bones; they did not appear, as some scattered ones which I had seen, gnawed or broken, as if dragged together by beasts of prey. The animals in most cases must have crawled, before dying, beneath and amongst the bushes. . . . I do not at all understand the reason of this, but I may observe, that the wounded guanacos at the Santa Cruz invariably walked towards the river. At St. Jago in the Cape de Verd Islands, I remember having seen in a ravine a retired corner covered with bones of the goat; we at the time exclaimed that it was the burial ground of all the goats in the island. I mention these trifling circumstances, because in certain cases they might explain the occurrence of a number of uninjured bones in a cave, or buried under alluvial accumulations; and likewise the cause why certain animals are more commonly embedded than others in sedimentary deposits.

## Coast of Cruelty

Just up the coast from Puerto San Julián, where the *Beagle* arrived on January 9, 1834, two of Magellan's men had led a mutiny against him in 1520. He had had their bodies dismembered and displayed on stakes upon the shore. Far from home and entirely dependent on what may be a fragile personal authority, the commander of the voyage of exploration is unlikely to deal leniently with challenges of this kind. Just over half a century later, in 1578, as he set about repeating Magellan's party's circumnavigation of the globe, Francis Drake also reproduced his precursor's punishment. When he came to suspect one of his own party, Thomas Doughty, of planning a mutiny against him, Drake beheaded him on the beach beside the gibbet that Magellan had erected. The message to his watching men was only too clear.

# "The Geology is Interesting"

"The geology of Patagonia is interesting," wrote Darwin, as ever obviously underplaying his excitement. Some way inland from the coastline extended what amounted to a fossilized seashore.

*Left: Dust to dust: the skull of a guanaco lies bleached by the Patagonian sun. Opposite: The Tehuelche of Patagonia had clothed themselves in guanaco hide for many centuries.*

Differently from Europe, where the tertiary formations appear to have accumulated in bays, here along hundreds of miles of coast we have one great deposit, including many tertiary shells, all apparently extinct. The most common shell is a massive gigantic oyster, sometimes even a foot in diameter. These beds are covered by others of a peculiar soft white stone, including much gypsum, and resembling chalk, but really of a pumiceous nature. It is highly remarkable, from being composed, to at least one-tenth of its bulk, of *Infusoria* [a type of single-celled organism]. Professor Ehrenberg has already ascertained in it thirty oceanic forms. This bed extends for 500 miles along the coast, and probably for a considerably greater distance. At Port St. Julian its thickness is more than 800 feet! These white beds are everywhere capped by a mass of gravel, forming probably one of the largest beds of shingle in the world: it certainly extends from near the Rio Colorado to between 600 and 700 nautical miles southward, at Santa Cruz (a river a little south of St. Julian), it reaches to the foot of the Cordillera; half way up the river, its thickness is more than 200 feet; it probably everywhere extends to this great chain, whence the well-rounded pebbles of porphyry have been derived: we may consider its average breadth as 200 miles, and its average thickness as about 50 feet. If this great bed of pebbles, without including the mud necessarily derived from their attrition, was piled into a mound, it would form a great mountain chain! When we consider that all these pebbles, countless as the grains of sand in the desert, have been derived from the slow falling of masses of rock on the old coast-lines and banks of rivers, and that these fragments have been dashed into smaller pieces, and that each of them has since been slowly rolled, rounded, and far transported the mind is stupefied in thinking over the long, absolutely necessary, lapse of years. Yet all this gravel has been transported, and probably rounded, subsequently to the deposition of the white

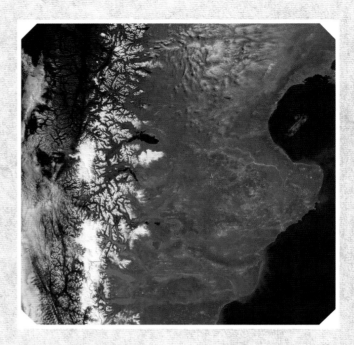

beds, and long subsequently to the underlying beds with the tertiary shells.

Like the gravel itself, some old assumptions about the creation of the earth were being "dashed...and far transported" too: this evidence called into question the idea that the world was only forty centuries old. "Some epoch of extreme violence" might have accounted for such changes, as Darwin acknowledged elsewhere, and the changes indicated here are indeed considerable:

Everything in this southern continent has been effected on a grand scale: the land, from the Río Plata to Tierra del Fuego, a distance of 1,200 miles, has been raised in mass (and in Patagonia to a height of between 300 and 400 feet), within the period of the now existing sea-shells.

But the evidence overwhelmingly points to an incalculably gradual and protracted process, with more violent events interrupting, rather than a single moment of sudden, cataclysmic change.

The old and weathered shells left on the surface of the upraised plain still partially retain their colours. The uprising movement has been interrupted by at least eight long periods of rest, during which the sea ate, deeply back into the land, forming at successive levels the long lines of cliffs, or escarpments, which separate the different plains as they rise like steps one behind the other. The elevatory movement, and the eating-back power of the sea during the periods of rest, have been equable over long lines of coast; for I was astonished to find that the step-like plains stand at nearly corresponding heights at far distant points. The lowest plain is 90 feet high; and the highest, which I ascended near the coast, is 950 feet; and of this, only relics are left in the form of flat gravel-capped hills. The upper plain of Santa Cruz slopes up to a height of 3,000 feet at the foot of the Cordillera. I have said that within the period of existing sea-shells, Patagonia has been upraised 300 to 400 feet: I may add, that within the period when icebergs transported boulders over the upper plain of Santa Cruz, the elevation has been at least 1,500 feet. Nor has Patagonia been affected only by upward movements: the extinct tertiary shells from Port St. Julian and Santa Cruz cannot have lived, according to Professor E. Forbes, in a greater depth of water than from 40 to 250 feet; but they are now covered with sea-deposited strata from 800 to 1,000 feet in thickness: hence the bed of the sea, on which these shells once lived, must have sunk downwards several hundred feet, to allow of the accumulation of the superincumbent strata. What a history of geological changes does the simply constructed coast of Patagonia reveal!

*Right: A toxodon skull of the sort discussed by Darwin.* **Opposite, above:** *Snowbound mountains and open plains: the* Cono Sur *as seen in a twenty-first-century satellite image.* **Opposite, below:** *Living ammonites as envisaged in a nineteenth-century engraving.*

## Kooch's Creation

The Tehuelche told a very different story to account for the creation of their world. In the beginning, they said, there was only an eternal divinity, Kooch. Desperately lonesome in his solitude, he wept copiously for countless eons, forming the ocean; then he sighed, giving birth to the rushing wind. This blew apart the clouds that until now had obscured the earth, letting in light to illuminate the ocean surface. Kooch now created land, an island in the middle of the sea, and stocked it with animals of every kind.

# The Living and the Dead

If thoughts like this occurred, could ideas of evolution be far behind? They were prompted by the discovery of "a group of large bones" in the gravel near Puerto San Julián. These could not be identified at first, but they were afterward identified by London's leading paleontologist, Richard Owen, as "part of an animal allied to the guanaco or llama, but fully as large as the true camel." Darwin was in no doubt as to "the most important result of this discovery":

The confirmation of the law that existing animals have a close relation in form with extinct species. As the guanaco is the characteristic quadruped of Patagonia, and the vicuna of the snow-clad summits of the Cordillera, so in bygone days, this gigantic species of the same family must have been conspicuous on the southern plains. We see this same relation of type between the existing and fossily Ctenomys [tucutuco], between the capybara...and the gigantic Toxodon; and lastly, between the living and extinct Edentata [armadilloes, anteaters, sloths]. At the present day, in South America, there exist probably nineteen species of this order, distributed into several genera; while throughout the rest of the world there are but five. If, then, there is a relation between the living and the dead, we should expect that the Edentata would be numerous in the fossil state. I need only reply by enumerating the megatherium, and the three or four other great species, discovered at Bahia Blanca; the remains of some of which are also abundant over the whole immense territory of La Plata....

It is impossible to reflect without the deepest astonishment on the changed state of this continent. Formerly it must have swarmed with great monsters, like the southern parts of Africa, but now we find only the tapir, guanaco, armadillo, and capybara; mere pigmies compared to the antecedent races.

Darwin wondered why this "succession of races" should have taken place, considering everything from invasion by other species to climate change, yet no single explanation seemed satisfactory. In the end, he was reduced to the suggestion that, whatever the reasons for this might be, every species—like every individual animal—has its allotted lifetime. "All that at present can be said with certainty," he concluded, "is that, as with the individual, so with the species, the house of life has run its course, and is spent."

On April 13, 1834, "the *Beagle* anchored within the mouth of the Santa Cruz... about sixty miles south of Port St. Julian." Thus began perhaps the nearest Darwin would come to an actual journey of exploration.

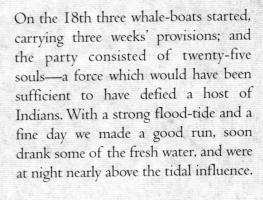

On the 18th three whale-boats started, carrying three weeks' provisions; and the party consisted of twenty-five souls—a force which would have been sufficient to have defied a host of Indians. With a strong flood-tide and a fine day we made a good run, soon drank some of the fresh water, and were at night nearly above the tidal influence.

**April 19th.**—Against so strong a current it was, of course, quite impossible to row or sail: consequently the three boats were fastened together head and stern, two hands left in each, and the rest came on shore to track. As the general arrangements made by Captain FitzRoy were very good for facilitating the work of all, ... I will describe the system. The party including every one, was divided into two spells, each of which hauled at the tracking line alternately for an hour and a half. The officers of each boat lived with, ate the same food, and slept in the same tent with their crew, so that each boat was quite independent of the others. After sunset the first level spot where any bushes were growing, was chosen for our night's lodging. Each of the crew took it in turns to be cook. Immediately the boat was hauled up, the cook made his fire; two others pitched the tent; the coxswain handed the things out of the boat; the rest carried them up to the tents and collected firewood. By this order, in half an hour everything was ready for the night. A watch of two men and an officer was always kept, whose duty it was to look after the boats, keep up the fire, and guard against Indians. During this day we tracked but a short distance, for there were many islets, covered by thorny bushes, and the channels between them were shallow.

*"After sunset the first level spot where any bushes were growing, was chosen for our night's lodging."*

## Feline Variations

The puma or cougar (*Puma concolor*) is to be found all the way down the western Cordillera, from British Columbia southward (hence its popular name, the "mountain lion") extending out into the lower-lying grasslands of southern Brazil's Mato Grosso region, Argentina's pampas, and Patagonia, as noted by Darwin in April 1834. It is even to be found in Amazonia's tropical rainforests, coexisting with the jaguar and ocelot (while a rare variety still clings on in the swamps of Florida). In this particular context, resemblances to these other cats can be seen, the puma's skin showing signs of spotting that are completely absent in specimens found to north and south. There are other differences: the puma of cooler climes grows larger, up to eight feet long, and its fur tends to be thicker in higher terrain—or latitudes. All these variations make sense in adapting the animal to local conditions and provide more evidence against the idea of a fixed, "one-off" creation.

and marks left by the trailing of the *chuzos*, or long spears, were observed on the ground. It was generally thought that the Indians had reconnoitred us during the night. Shortly afterwards we came to a spot where, from the fresh footsteps of men, children, and horses, it was evident that the party had crossed the river.

**April 22nd.**—The country remained the same, and was extremely uninteresting. The complete similarity of the productions throughout Patagonia is one of its most striking characters. The level plains of arid shingle support the same stunted and dwarf plants; and in the valleys the same thorn-bearing bushes grow. Everywhere we see the same birds and insects. Even the very banks of the river and of the clear streamlets which entered it, were scarcely enlivened by a brighter tint of green. The curse of sterility is on the land, and the water flowing over a bed of pebbles partakes of the same curse. Hence the number of waterfowl is very scanty; for there is nothing to support life in the stream of this barren river.

**April 24th.**—Like the navigators of old when approaching an unknown land, we examined and watched for the most trivial sign of a change. The drifted trunk of a tree, or a boulder of primitive rock, was hailed with joy, as if we had seen a forest growing on the flanks of the Cordillera. The top, however, of a heavy bank of clouds, which remained almost constantly in one position, was the most promising sign, and eventually turned out a true harbinger. At first the clouds were mistaken for the mountains themselves, instead of the masses of vapour condensed by their icy summits.

**April 20th.**—Beyond the place where we slept last night, the country is completely *terra incognita*.... We saw in the distance a great smoke, and found the skeleton of a horse, so we knew that Indians were in the neighbourhood. On the next morning (21st) tracks of a party of horse,

*Left: Patagonian warriors fight with spears and shields in a European fantasy of savagery.* **Opposite:** *"Mere pigmies"—especially when infants, like this tapir (above). The full exoticism of the armadillo is captured perfectly in this nineteenth-century painting (below).*

# Condor Country

"The bed of the river became rather narrower," noted Darwin on April 27, "and hence the stream more rapid." The expedition was reaching higher ground, and Darwin's attention turned skyward:

April 27th.—This day I shot a condor. It measured from tip to tip of the wings, eight and a half feet, and from beak to tail, four feet. This bird is known to have a wide geographical range, being found on the west coast of South America, from the Strait of Magellan along the Cordillera as far as eight degrees north of the equator. The steep cliff near the mouth of the Río Negro is its northern limit on the Patagonian coast; and they have there wandered about four hundred miles from the great central line of their habitation in the Andes. Further south, among the bold precipices at the head of Port Desire, the condor is not uncommon; yet only a few stragglers occasionally visit the seacoast. A line of cliff near the mouth of the Santa Cruz is frequented by these birds, and about eighty miles up the river, where the sides of the valley are formed by steep basaltic precipices, the condor reappears. From these facts, it seems that the condors require perpendicular cliffs. In Chile, they haunt, during the greater part of the year, the lower country near the shores of the Pacific, and at night several roost together in one tree; but in the early part of summer, they retire to the most inaccessible parts of the inner Cordillera, there to breed in peace....

When the condors are wheeling in a flock round and round any spot, their flight is beautiful. Except when rising from the ground, I do not recollect ever having seen one of these birds flap its wings. ...As they glided close over my head, I intently watched from an oblique position, the outlines of the separate and great terminal feathers of each wing; and these separate feathers, if there had been the least vibratory movement, would have appeared as if blended together; but they were seen distinct against the blue sky. The head and neck were moved frequently, and apparently with force; and the extended wings seemed to form the fulcrum on which the movements of the neck, body, and tail acted. If the bird wished to descend, the wings were for a moment collapsed; and when again expanded with an altered inclination, the momentum gained by the rapid descent seemed to urge the bird upwards with the even and steady movement of a paper kite. ...It is truly wonderful and beautiful to see so great a bird, hour after hour, without any apparent exertion, wheeling and gliding over mountain and river.

# Distant Peaks

Down on the ground, meanwhile, the grueling climb continued. Finally, two days later:

From some high land we hailed with joy the white summits of the Cordillera, as they were seen occasionally peeping through their dusky envelope of clouds. During the few succeeding days we continued to get on slowly, for we found the river-course very tortuous, and strewed with immense fragments of various ancient slaty rocks, and of granite. The plain bordering the valley had here attained an elevation of about 1,100 feet above the river, and its character was much altered. The well-rounded pebbles of porphyry were mingled with many immense angular fragments of basalt and of primary rocks. The first of these erratic boulders which I noticed, was sixty-seven miles distant from the nearest mountain; another which I measured was five yards square, and projected five feet above the gravel.... The plain here was not quite so level as that nearer the coast, but yet it betrayed no signs of any great violence. Under these circumstances it is, I believe, quite impossible to explain the transportal of these gigantic masses of rock so many miles from their parent-source, on any theory except by that of floating icebergs.

*"A light stomach and an easy digestion are good things to talk about, but very unpleasant in practice."*

**May 4th.**—The river had a winding course, and was very rapid; and the appearance of the country offered no temptation to proceed any further. Everywhere we met with the same productions, and the same dreary landscape. We were now one hundred and forty miles distant from the Atlantic, and about sixty from the nearest arm of the Pacific. The valley in this upper part expanded into a wide basin, bounded on the north and south by the basaltic platforms, and fronted by the long range of the snow-clad Cordillera. But we viewed these grand mountains with regret, for we were obliged to imagine their nature and productions, instead of standing, as we had hoped, on their summits. Besides the useless loss of time which an attempt to ascend the river any higher would have cost us, we had already been for some days on half allowance of bread. This, although really enough for reasonable men, was, after a hard day's march, rather scanty food: a light stomach and an easy digestion are good things to talk about, but very unpleasant in practice.

**May 5th.**—Before sunrise we commenced our descent. We shot down the stream with great rapidity, generally at the rate of ten knots an hour. In this one day we effected what had cost us five-and-a-half hard days' labour in ascending.

On May 8 they were back at the *Beagle*: "Almost everyone is discontented with this expedition," noted Darwin in his journal. His own view, however, was more sanguine. "To me the cruise has been most satisfactory, from affording so excellent a section of the great modern formation of Patagonia." When he said "modern," he was speaking in relative terms, referring to the great seismic shifts that have occurred since the rocks of the region were first formed, the upheaval of the Atlantic coast, and the action of glaciers in gouging out valleys and transporting boulders.

*Below:* "We hailed with joy the white summits of the Cordillera," recorded Darwin on April 29.

# Land of Fire

*"The inanimate works of nature—rock, ice, snow, wind, and water, all warring with each other, yet combined against man—here reigned in absolute sovereignty."*

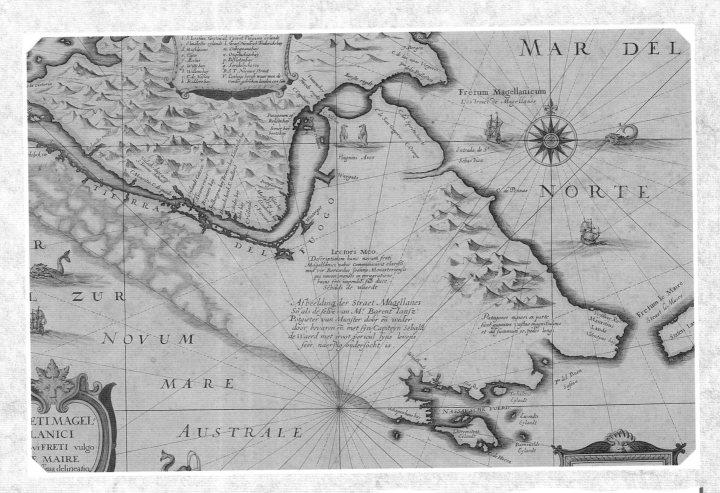

*Previous pages: Black-browed albatrosses incubate their eggs at nests on New Island, in the Falklands.* ***Above:*** *Tierra del Fuego is still substantially* **terra incognita** *on this map dating from 1646.*

agellan named it the "Land of Fire," a grandly evocative title fit for a mysterious island at the outermost limits of the earth. It is something of a let-down, then, to find that his inspiration (if it can be called that) was nothing more heroic than the sight of the natives' cooking fires twinkling on its hillsides as his ships sailed by.

There is no point pretending otherwise: Darwin was disappointed with Tierra del Fuego, a land not of fire so much as of gray skies and unceasing rain. As an Englishman, Darwin would have known a thing or two about dismal weather, but here there seemed no end to the dampness and the chill. The fauna was limited; the flora restricted by climate and isolation alike; the whole place was something of a washout, all in all.

More sombre still, though, was what Darwin saw (or thought he saw) of his fellow humans: the Fuegians shocked him—these were "savages" indeed. They included, noted the naturalist, some of "the most abject and miserable creatures I anywhere beheld": his reactions seem to have been half of pity; half of horrified loathing. The intensity of his response is surely born out of recognition: Darwin saw himself in these otherwise utterly alien beings.

If this section of Darwin's voyage was in some ways a disappointment, it marked a crucial stage in his intellectual journey. This is really apparent only in hindsight, though. Darwin himself would perhaps never quite appreciate fully how he had been affected by what he saw of the Fuegians and their interaction with their compatriots who had been exposed to "civilization."

There is much to make us uncomfortable in Darwin's account of Fuegian life—much, that is, besides the patronizing language with which he and his companions seemed so at ease. Darwin was unselfconscious in his sense of superiority; unabashed in his assumption that the Fuegians were to be regarded as children; unashamed of finding something "ludicrous" in their departures from Anglo-Saxon cultural norms. But he was sufficiently the scientist to see beyond immediate prejudice—albeit dimly: he acknowledged the Fuegians' quickness, even if in condescending terms. Their skills as mimics impressed him even as they occasioned him amusement; he was intrigued by their ability to remember strings of English words.

Ultimately, perhaps, he was more disturbed than anything else by this encounter with his "wild" *alter ego*: "Of individual objects," he would later remark:

No one is more sure to create astonishment than the first sight, in his native haunt, of a real barbarian—of man in his lowest and most savage state. One's mind hurries back over past centuries, and then asks, "Could our progenitors be such as these?" …I do not believe it is possible to describe or paint the difference of savage and civilized man. It is the difference between a wild and tame animal.

From our modern perspective, the passage positively reeks of arrogance: who was he to adjudge one man "savage," another "civilized"? Yet, in fairness, it was precisely because he did see his precursors in these "barbarians" that Darwin reacted with such horror when he met them. As the years went by, and he developed his evolutionary theory, critics would confuse the issue, with their caricatures of the big-jawed and brutish Darwinian "ape-man." But if Darwinism cut humanity down to size, suggesting that it was an animal species like any other, it also highlighted just how far evolution had brought us from those of the other beasts. That, Darwin saw, applied as much to the "lowest and most savage" Fuegian as it did to the most polished product of the English drawing room: that little spark of insight was surely lit in the Land of Fire.

*Above:* The black-throated finch is widespread in Tierra del Fuego. *Below:* Gentoo penguins gather on the shore of Sealion Island in the Falklands.

# "Our First Arrival"

In his journal for December 17, 1832, Darwin described "our first arrival in Tierra del Fuego":

A little after noon we doubled Cape St. Diego, and entered the famous strait of Le Maire. We kept close to the Fuegian shore, but the outline of the rugged, inhospitable Statenland was visible amidst the clouds. In the afternoon we anchored in the Bay of Good Success. While entering we were saluted in a manner becoming the inhabitants of this savage land. A group of Fuegians, partly concealed by the entangled forest, were perched on a wild point overhanging the sea; and as we passed by, they sprang up and waving their tattered cloaks sent forth a loud and sonorous shout. The savages followed the ship, and just before dark we saw their fire, and again heard their wild cry. The harbour consists of a fine piece of water half surrounded by low rounded mountains of clay-slate, which are covered to the water's edge by one dense gloomy forest. A single glance at the landscape was sufficient to show me how widely different it was from anything I had ever beheld. At night it blew a gale of wind, and heavy squalls from the mountains swept past us. It would have been a bad time out at sea, and we, as well as others, may call this Good Success Bay.

*Left:* "I could not believe how wide was the difference between savage and civilized man." Darwin never quite got over the shock of his first encounter with the Fuegians, though he came to recognize the quickness of their perceptions.

## Strait Man

Fernão de Magalhães was born in Portugal around 1480; in 1506 he went as a soldier-explorer to the East Indies. In 1513, when he was serving rather closer to home in Morocco, he sustained a wound that left him lame and unfit to fight. Undaunted, Magalhães was fired with enthusiasm for a scheme to find a westerly route to the Indies: the same project in which Christopher Columbus had been engaged. Columbus had been diverted from his task by one of history's great red herrings, the American continent, but Magalhães was convinced that a way to the East Indies could be found. But King Emanuel of Portugal was uninterested in his plan, so Magalhães turned instead to Charles I of Spain. Hence his hispanicization as "Fernando de Magallanes," from which came the name Ferdinand Magellan, and hence the Spanish flag under which, in 1519, with a five-ship flotilla, he at last set sail.

His voyage took him south and westward down the eastern side of the South American continent, and through the strait which, ever since, has borne his name. He then sailed into a "new" Ocean, which, on account of its tranquility at the time, he called the Pacific, before landing first at the Mariana Islands and then at the Philippines. There he was killed, having unwisely taken sides in a dispute between natives; his second-in-command, Juan Sebastián del Cano completed the journey to the Spice Islands of the Indies and, ultimately, the first circumnavigation of the globe.

[The following day] the Captain sent a party to communicate with the Fuegians. When we came within hail, one of the four natives who were present advanced to receive us, and began to shout most vehemently, wishing to direct us where to land. When we were on shore the party looked rather alarmed, but continued talking and making gestures with great rapidity. It was without exception the most curious and interesting spectacle I ever beheld: I could not have believed how wide was the difference between savage and civilized man: it is greater than between a wild and domesticated animal, inasmuch as in man there is a greater power of improvement. The chief spokesman was old, and appeared to be the head of the family; the three others were powerful young men, about six feet high. The women and children had been sent away...

The old man had a fillet of white feathers tied round his head, which partly confined his black, coarse, and entangled hair. His face was crossed by two broad transverse bars; one, painted bright red, reached from ear to ear and included the upper lip; the other, white like chalk, extended above and parallel to the first, so that even his eyelids were thus coloured. The other two men were ornamented by streaks of black powder, made of charcoal....Their very attitudes were abject, and the expression of their countenances distrustful, surprised, and startled. After we had presented them with some scarlet cloth, which they

*Above: With its spectacular scenery, the Beagle Channel has become a destination for the more enterprising kind of cruise, but conditions can be atrocious even in these comparatively sheltered waters.*

immediately tied round their necks, they became good friends. ... The language of these people, according to our notions, scarcely deserves to be called articulate. Captain Cook has compared it to a man clearing his throat, but no European ever cleared his throat with so many hoarse, guttural, and clicking sounds.

But if Darwin was unimpressed with the Fuegians' language, he could not help being struck by their receptiveness and skill, not just with the spoken word but with every aspect of expression and body language:

*"They are excellent mimics: as often as we coughed or yawned...they immediately imitated us."*

They are excellent mimics: as often as we coughed or yawned, or made any odd motion, they immediately imitated us. Some of our party began to squint and look awry; but one of the young Fuegians (whose whole face was painted black, excepting a white band across his eyes) succeeded in making far more hideous grimaces. They could repeat with perfect correctness each word in any sentence we addressed them, and they remembered such words for some time. Yet we Europeans all know how difficult it is to distinguish apart the sounds in a foreign lan-

*Left: A way of life now gone for ever: two Fuegians with a child in tow go hunting by canoe.*

# A Gloomy Scene

The next day found Darwin on less controversial—but still sticky—ground:

The next day I attempted to penetrate some way into the country. Tierra del Fuego may be described as a mountainous land, partly submerged in the sea, so that deep inlets and bays occupy the place where valleys should exist. The mountain sides, except on the exposed western coast, are covered from the water's edge upwards by one great forest. The trees reach to an elevation of between 1,000 and 1,500 feet, and are succeeded by a band of peat, with minute alpine plants; and this again is succeeded by the line of perpetual snow, which, according to Captain King, in the Strait of Magellan descends to between 3,000 and 4,000 feet. To find an acre of level land in any part of the country is most rare. ...The surface is covered by a thick bed of swampy peat. Even within the forest, the ground is concealed by a mass of slowly putrefying vegetable matter, which, from being soaked with water, yields to the foot....

guage. Which of us, for instance, could follow an American Indian through a sentence of more than three words? All savages appear to possess, to an uncommon degree, this power of mimicry. How can this faculty be explained? Is it a consequence of the more practised habits of perception and keener senses, common to all men in a savage state, as compared with those long civilized? ...

Little accustomed to Europeans as they appeared to be, yet they knew and dreaded our fire-arms; nothing would tempt them to take a gun in their hands. They begged for knives, calling them by the Spanish word "cuchilla." They explained also what they wanted, by acting as if they had a piece of blubber in their mouth, and then pretending to cut instead of tear it.

## *The Yahgan Dictionary*

A generation after Darwin's visit, in 1864, English missionaries came to Tierra del Fuego led by Thomas Bridges, who threw himself into his task with the utmost energy and perseverance. His first son, also Thomas (born 1874) was to grow up wholly dedicated to his homeland and its people. The first Fuegian-born individual of European stock, he started out with a unique advantage when it came to writing down the vocabulary and grammar of the native Yahgan language.

His first objective was to find a means for producing a printed version of the Bible, so that future generations of Yahgan speakers could read the Word of God. But as measles epidemics ravaged a population unprepared by background to resist, it became tragically clear that he was recording a dying tongue. Doomed to disappear it might have been, but it could hardly be said that it was "scarcely...articulate": Bridges' Dictionary recorded 32,000 words in all. In its grammatical structures, it astonished scholars with its complexity and subtlety—in various ways more sophisticated than many a more "civilized" tongue.

I continued slowly to advance for an hour along the broken and rocky banks, and was amply repaid by the grandeur of the scene. The gloomy depth of the ravine well accorded with the universal signs of violence. On every side were lying irregular masses of rock and torn-up trees; other trees, though still erect, were decayed to the heart and ready to fall. The entangled mass of the thriving and the fallen reminded me of the forests within the tropics—yet there was a difference: for in these still solitudes, Death, instead of Life, seemed the predominant spirit.

**Above:** *"From the waterfalls and number of dead trees, I could hardly crawl along,"* Darwin complained. More recent visitors have thrilled at the primeval beauty of the Fuegian scene.

### Everbrown

Unlike Darwin, many visitors to Tierra del Fuego—more fortunate with the weather, perhaps—have found it one of the most thrilling places in the world, its wild isolation only enhancing its natural beauty. But nothing, it seems, could persuade Darwin that this was anything other than a hole.

The trees all belong to one kind, the *Fagus betuloides* [Magallanes beech]; for the number of the other species…is quite inconsiderable. This beech keeps its leaves throughout the year; but its foliage is of a peculiar brownish-green colour, with a tinge of yellow. As the whole landscape is thus coloured, it has a sombre, dull appearance; nor is it often enlivened by the rays of the sun.

# Wigwam Cove

Viewed on the map, Tierra del Fuego is very clearly a continuation of the main South American landmass, which has its termination in the stormy headland of Cape Horn.

**December 21st.**—The *Beagle* got under way: and on the succeeding day, favoured to an uncommon degree by a fine easterly breeze, we closed in with the Barnevelts, and running past Cape Deceit with its stony peaks, about three o'clock doubled the weather-beaten Cape Horn. The evening was calm and bright, and we enjoyed a fine view of the surrounding isles. Cape Horn, however, demanded his tribute, and before night sent us a gale of wind directly in our teeth. We stood out to sea, and on the second day again made the land, when we saw on our weather-bow this notorious promontory in its proper form—veiled in a mist, and its dim outline surrounded by a storm of wind and water. Great black clouds were rolling across the heavens, and squalls of rain, with hail, swept by us with such extreme violence, that the Captain determined to run into Wigwam Cove.

**December 25th.**—Close by the Cove, a pointed hill, called Kater's Peak, rises to the height of 1,700 feet. The surrounding islands all consist of conical masses of greenstone…. The cove takes its name of "Wigwam" from some of the Fuegian habitations; but every bay in the neighbourhood might be so called with equal propriety. The inhabitants, living chiefly upon shell-fish, are obliged constantly to change their place of residence; but they return at intervals to the same spots, as is evident from the piles of old shells, which must often amount to many tons in freight…The Fuegian wigwam resembles, in size and dimensions, a haycock. It merely consists of a few broken branches stuck in the ground, and very imperfectly thatched on one side with a few tufts of grass and rushes. The whole cannot be the work of an hour, and it is only used for a few days.

*"At night, five or six human beings, naked and scarcely protected from the wind and rain … sleep on the wet ground coiled up like animals."*

**Below:** *Choppy waters: Cape Horn has long been notorious for its ferocious storms.*

# "What Pleasure in Life…?"

An encounter "one day on shore near Wollaston Island" led Darwin to question what sort of lives the poorest Fuegians could be said to have:

We pulled alongside a canoe with six Fuegians. These were the most abject and miserable creatures I anywhere beheld. On the east coast the natives, as we have seen, have guanaco cloaks, and on the west they possess seal-skins. Amongst these central tribes the men generally have an otter-skin, or some small scrap about as large as a pocket-handkerchief, which is barely sufficient to cover their backs as low down as their loins. It is laced across the breast by strings, and according as the wind blows, it is shifted from side to side. But these Fuegians in the canoe were quite naked, and even one full-grown woman was absolutely so. It was raining heavily, and the fresh water, together with the spray, trickled down her body. In another harbour not far distant, a woman, who was suckling a recently-born child, came one day alongside the vessel, and remained there out of mere curiosity, whilst the sleet fell and thawed on her naked bosom, and on the skin of her naked baby! These poor wretches were stunted in their growth, their hideous faces bedaubed with

white paint, their skins filthy and greasy, their hair entangled, their voices discordant, and their gestures violent. Viewing such men, one can hardly make one's self believe that they are fellow-creatures, and inhabitants of the same world. It is a common subject of conjecture what pleasure in life some of the lower animals can enjoy: how much more reasonably the same question may be asked with respect to these barbarians! At night, five or six human beings, naked and scarcely protected from the wind and rain, sleep on the wet ground coiled up like animals. Whenever it is low water, winter or summer, night or day, they must rise to pick shell-fish from the rocks; and the women either dive to collect sea-eggs, or sit patiently in their canoes, and with a baited hair-line without any hook, jerk out little fish. If a seal is killed, or the floating carcass of a putrid whale is discovered, it is a feast; and such miserable food is assisted by a few tasteless berries and fungi.

# A Utopia of Impoverishment

Darwin's name would later be taken in vain by a motley crew of aggressively *laissez-faire* thinkers who believed the strong should thrive and the weakest go to the wall. Their views travestied those of Darwin, who made few comments in this area, though what he saw in Tierra del Fuego prompted the following thought:

The perfect equality among the individuals composing the Fuegian tribes must for a long time retard their civilization. As we see those animals, whose instinct compels them to live in society and obey a chief, are most capable of improvement, so is it with the races of mankind. Whether we look at it as a cause or a consequence, the more civilized always have the most artificial governments. For instance, the inhabitants of Otaheite, who, when first discovered, were governed by hereditary kings, had arrived at a far higher grade than another

*Above: Clouds scud across the sky above a landscape of snowy mountain and thick forest, as seen from the waters of the Beagle Channel.*

branch of the same people, the New Zealanders—who, although benefited by being compelled to turn their attention to agriculture, were republicans in the most absolute sense. In Tierra del Fuego, until some chief shall arise with power sufficient to secure any acquired advantage, such as the domesticated animals, it seems scarcely possible that the political state of the country can be improved. At present, even a piece of cloth given to one is torn into shreds and distributed; and no one individual becomes richer than another. On the other hand, it is difficult to understand how a chief can arise till there is property of some sort by which he might manifest his superiority and increase his power.

By sharing so willingly, Darwin felt, the Fuegians condemned themselves to everlasting poverty, and continuing status as—in his view—the most primitive people in the world.

I believe, in this extreme part of South America, man exists in a lower state of improvement than in any other part of the world. The South Sea Islanders, of the two races inhabiting the Pacific, are comparatively civilized. The Esquimau in his subterranean hut, enjoys some of the comforts of life, and in his canoe, when fully equipped, manifests much skill. Some of the tribes of Southern Africa prowling about in search of roots, and living concealed on the wild and arid plains, are sufficiently wretched. The Australian, in the simplicity of the arts of life, comes nearest the Fuegian: he can, however, boast of his boomerang, his spear and throwing-stick, his method of climbing trees, of tracking animals, and of hunting.

It was, insisted Darwin, a matter of social organization, rather than one of intellectual capability or aptitude.

Although the Australian may be superior in acquirements, it by no means follows that he is likewise superior in mental capacity: indeed, from what I saw of the Fuegians when on board and from what I have read of the Australians, I should think the case was exactly the reverse.

# The Falklands

"On March 1st, 1833, and again on March 16th, 1834, the *Beagle* anchored in Berkeley Sound, in East Falkland Island," wrote Darwin. He went on to give his British readers a handy introduction to their least-known—and perhaps least desirable—imperial possession.

## The Fight for the Falklands

The Falklands were originally occupied by French colonists from the port of Saint Malo—hence their later Spanish name, *Las Malvinas*. They were indeed to be fought over with what was often to seem a quite disproportionate passion, one such confrontation occasioning the famous observation of the great eighteenth-century English sage Dr. Samuel Johnson that "Patriotism is the last refuge of the scoundrel." It was with a similar spirit of skepticism that, 150 years after Darwin's visit, the great Argentinean writer Jorge Luis Borges would regard his country's 1980s war with Great Britain over the islands. It was, he said, "two bald men fighting over a comb."

The generals of Argentina's military government could hardly have been more wrong if they had been hoping to boost their flagging prestige by mounting their invasion of the islands in 1982. Rather, it was British premier Margaret Thatcher, until then languishing in the opinion polls, who gained a new lease of political life from the episode. To the junta's apparent amazement, she dispatched a task force to the South Atlantic and had the islands taken back by force.

If the war had its farcical aspects, it produced some real benefits, notably the ignominious collapse of Argentina's military regime. Both Britain and a newly democratic Argentina have been involved in amicable discussions over fishing rights in the region, and over what appear to be considerable reserves of natural gas and oil.

This archipelago is situated in nearly the same latitude with the mouth of the Strait of Magellan; it covers a space of one hundred and twenty by sixty geographical miles, and is little more than half the size of Ireland. After the possession of these miserable islands had been contested by France, Spain, and England, they were left uninhabited. The government of Buenos Ayres then sold them to a private individual, but likewise used them, as old Spain had done before, for a penal settlement. England claimed her right and seized them. The Englishman who was left in charge of the flag was consequently murdered. A British officer was next sent, unsupported by any power: and when we arrived we found him in charge of a population, of which rather more than half were runaway rebels and murderers.

The theatre is worthy of the scenes acted on it. An undulating land, with a desolate and wretched aspect, is everywhere covered by a peaty soil and wiry grass, of one monotonous brown colour. Here and there a peak or ridge of grey quartz rock breaks through the smooth surface. ...The only quadruped native to the island is a large wolflike fox (*Canis antarcticus*), which is common to both East and West Falkland. I have no doubt it is a peculiar species and confined to this archipelago; because many sealers, gauchos, and Indians, who have visited these islands, all maintain that no such animal is found in any part of South America....

*Opposite:* King penguins survey the scene before them with a fittingly regal air at a colony on Volunteer Point in the eastern Falklands. *Above:* A flash of snowy white against an azure sky, backlit by the sun, a South American tern is seen in flight above the Falklands.

## Fated to Extinction

Darwin's fears for the Falklands fox, or warrah, would prove all too justified. The decision to develop the island economy by encouraging large-scale sheep farming effectively doomed it. Inevitably it was branded, if not a danger, then at least a pest. Its own incorrigible curiosity and boldness didn't help. The authorities sealed its fate by offering a bounty for every one killed. The last known warrah was shot in 1876.

These wolves are well known from Byron's account of their tameness and curiosity, which the sailors, who ran into the water to avoid them, mistook for fierceness. To this day their manners remain the same. They have been observed to enter a tent, and actually pull some meat from beneath the head of a sleeping seaman. The gauchos also have frequently in the evening killed them by holding out a piece of meat in one hand, and in the other a knife ready to stick them. As far as I am aware, there is no other instance in any part of the world, of so small a mass of broken land, distant from a continent, possessing so large an aboriginal quadruped peculiar to itself. Their numbers have rapidly decreased; they are already banished from that half of the island which lies to the eastward of the neck of land between St. Salvador Bay and Berkeley Sound. Within a very few years after these islands shall have become regularly settled, in all probability this fox will be classed with the dodo, as an animal which has perished from the face of the earth.

## The Bird That Brays

Another day, having placed myself between a penguin and the water, I was much amused by watching its habits. It was a brave bird; and till reaching the sea, it regularly fought and drove me backwards…. This bird is commonly called the jackass penguin, from its habit, while on shore, of throwing its head backwards, and making a loud strange noise, very like the braying of an ass; but while at sea, and undisturbed, its note is very deep and solemn, and is often heard in the night-time. In diving, its little wings are used as fins; but on the land, as front legs.

The bird known in the Falklands as the Jackass penguin is actually the Magellanic penguin (*Spheniscus magellanicus*), the true Jackass (*Spheniscus demersus*) being confined to the southwestern coast of Africa.

# Most Ludicrous

June 1 found the expedition back in the Magellan Strait, anchoring at Port Famine. Darwin was unimpressed.

It was now the beginning of winter, and I never saw a more cheerless prospect; the dusky woods, piebald with snow, could be only seen indistinctly, through a drizzling hazy atmosphere. We were, however, lucky in getting two fine days. On one of these, Mount Sarmiento, a distant mountain 6,800 feet high, presented a very noble spectacle. I was frequently surprised in the scenery of Tierra del Fuego, at the little apparent elevation of mountains really lofty. I suspect it is owing to a cause which would not at first be imagined, namely, that the whole mass, from the summit to the water's edge, is generally in full view.

But if the scenery did nothing for him for the most part, he was still less impressed by its inhabitants, who attacked the expedition in what was a dismally undignified farce.

During our stay at Port Famine, the Fuegians twice came and plagued us. As there were many instruments, clothes, and men on shore, it was thought necessary to frighten them away. The first time a few great guns were fired, when they were far distant. It was most ludicrous to watch through a glass the Indians, as often as the shot struck the water, take up stones, and, as a bold defiance, throw them towards the ship, though about a mile and a half distant! A boat was sent with orders to fire a few musket-shots wide of them. The Fuegians hid themselves behind the trees, and for every discharge of the muskets they fired their arrows; all, however, fell short of the boat, and the officer as he pointed at them laughed. This made the Fuegians frantic with passion, and they shook their mantles in vain rage. At last, seeing the balls cut and strike the trees, they ran away, and we were left in peace and quietness.

*Opposite: It may not be much to look at, but kelp sustains an ecosystem of great richness and diversity.*

## Port Famine

In March 1584, at the start of the southern fall, the Spanish navigator Sarmiento de Gamboa put ashore on the coast some way south of Punta Arenas, now in Chile. In the first flush of patriotic optimism, he gave it the imposing title of Rey Don Felipe II de España, "King Philip II of Spain," but it was not by that name that it would be remembered. As winter began to bite, and provisions proved inadequate, the colonists realized that their plight was desperate: Sarmiento was forced to brave mountainous seas to sail north to Rio for fresh supplies.

Having obtained the stocks he needed, he set off southward once more—soon to be caught up by a tropical storm and shipwrecked. He set sail yet again in a fresh vessel, but this time his new crew mutinied—and then his ship was captured by the English. Taken back to London, he told his story to Sir Walter Raleigh and Queen Elizabeth I, who allowed him to return to Spain. But before he could make it home, he was captured by French Protestant Huguenots, and was unable to raise the ransom they demanded to secure his freedom.

In 1587, the British buccaneer Thomas Cavendish put into Rey Don Felipe and found fifteen survivors still alive, though in fearful condition. Despite being close to death from starvation, all except one refused to board his Protestant ship. Cavendish renamed the place "Port Famine," or Puerto del Hambre: the city was abandoned, but its ruins may still be seen.

# Consider the Kelp

And if distant prospects were sublime, the scenery at close hand was nothing to write home about. Nor was there much to detain even a naturalist as determinedly receptive and open-minded as Darwin himself. "I have already mentioned the sombre and dull character of the evergreen forests," he comments, clearly underwhelmed, going on to add that "the zoology of Tierra del Fuego…is very poor." A complete waste of biological space, then? Not quite, he is willing to concede: "There is one marine production which, from its importance, is worthy of a particular history."

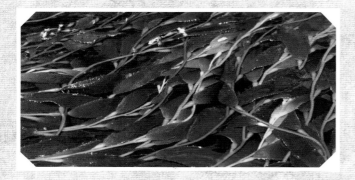

It is the kelp, or *Macrocystis pyrifera*. This plant grows on every rock from low-water mark to a great depth, both on the outer coast and within the channels. I believe, during the voyages of the *Adventure* and *Beagle*, not one rock near the surface was discovered which was not buoyed by this floating weed. The good service it thus affords to vessels navigating near this stormy land is evident; and it certainly has saved many a one from being wrecked. I know few things more surprising than to see this plant flourishing amidst those great breakers of the western ocean, which no mass of rock, let it be ever so hard, can long resist. The stem is round, slimy, and smooth, and seldom has a diameter of so much as an inch. A few taken together are sufficiently strong to support the weight of the large loose stones, to which in the inland channels they grow attached; and yet some of these stones were so heavy that when drawn to the surface, they could scarcely be lifted…. Captain Fitz Roy, moreover, found it growing up from the greater depth of 45 fathoms. The beds of this seaweed, even when of not great breadth, make excellent natural floating breakwaters. It is quite curious to see, in an exposed harbour, how soon the waves from the open sea, as they travel through the straggling stems, sink in height, and pass into smooth water.

The number of living creatures of all Orders, whose existence intimately depends on the kelp, is wonderful. A great volume might be written, describing the inhabitants of one of these beds of sea-weed. Almost all the leaves, excepting those that float on the surface, are so thickly incrusted with corallines as to be of a white colour. We find exquisitely delicate structures, some inhabited by simple hydra-like polypi, others by more organized kinds, and beautiful compound Ascidiae. On the leaves, also, various patelliform shells, Trochi, uncovered molluscs, and some bivalves are attached. Innumerable crustacea frequent every part of the plant. On shaking the great entangled roots, a pile of small fish, shells, cuttle-fish, crabs of all orders, sea-eggs, star-fish, beautiful *Holuthuriae*, *Planariae*, and crawling nereidous animals of a multitude of forms, all fall out together. Often as I recurred to a branch of the kelp, I never failed to discover animals of new and curious structures.

*"These vast piles of snow…never melt, and seem destined to last as long as the world holds together."*

If the tropical rainforest is today's gold standard for biodiversity, in Darwin's view, the kelp bore that comparison:

I can only compare these great aquatic forests of the southern hemisphere with the terrestrial ones in the intertropical regions. Yet if… a forest was destroyed, I do not believe nearly so many species of animals would perish as would here, from the destruction of the kelp. Amidst the leaves of this plant numerous species of fish live, which nowhere else could find food or shelter; with their destruction the … birds, the otters, seals, and porpoises, would soon perish; and lastly, the Fuegian savage, the miserable lord of this miserable land, would redouble his cannibal feast, decrease in numbers, and perhaps cease to exist.

# Farewell

Despite the call of the kelp, Darwin was not displeased when time came to go. As he noted in his journal, June 8:

We weighed anchor early in the morning and left Port Famine. Captain FitzRoy determined to leave the Strait of Magellan by the Magdalen Channel, which had not long been discovered. Our course lay due south…. The wind was fair, but the atmosphere was very thick; so that we missed much curious scenery. The dark ragged clouds were rapidly driven over the mountains, from their summits nearly down to their bases. The glimpses which we caught through the dusky mass were highly interesting: jagged points, cones of snow, blue glaciers, strong outlines, marked on a lurid sky, were seen at different distances and heights. In the midst of such scenery we anchored at Cape Turn, close to Mount Sarmiento, which was then hidden in the clouds. At the base of the lofty and almost perpendicular sides of our little cove there was one deserted wigwam, and it alone reminded us that man sometimes wandered into these desolate regions. But it would be difficult to imagine a scene where he

## *Macrocystis Pyrifera*

Apart from its sheer size, there is nothing so much to look at in the kelp seen singly. Its stem binds it as tightly as possible to the seabed, while its waving "blade" floats upward, straining after light. It is in the mass that the kelp forest is able to sustain the astonishing biodiversity that Darwin described in such ecstatic terms. Modern marine biology has relatively little to add to Darwin's account—except that it is now enlivened by stunning underwater photography. There is also a more detailed understanding of how the whole ecosystem works, from the plankton larvae and other organisms that teem in the sluggish waters and rotting debris of the forest floor to the fish, birds and mammals that form the apex of the system.

seemed to have fewer claims or less authority. The inanimate works of nature—rock, ice, snow, wind, and water, all warring with each other, yet combined against man—here reigned in absolute sovereignty.

**June 9th.**—In the morning we were delighted by seeing the veil of mist gradually rise from Sarmiento, and display it to our view. This mountain... has an altitude of 6,800 feet. Its base... is clothed by dusky woods, and above this a field of snow extends to the summit. These vast piles of snow, which never melt, and seem destined to last as long as the world holds together, present a noble and even sublime spectacle. The outline of the mountain was admirably clear and defined. Owing to the abundance of light reflected from the white and glittering surface, no shadows were cast on any part; and those lines which intersected the sky could alone be distinguished: hence the mass stood out in the boldest relief. Several glaciers descended in a winding course from the upper great expanse of snow to the sea-coast: they may be likened to great frozen Niagaras....By night we reached the western part of the channel; but the water was so deep that no anchorage could be found.

**June 10th.**—In the morning we made the best of our way into the open Pacific. The western coast generally consists of low, rounded, quite barren hills of granite and greenstone. Sir J. Narborough called one part South Desolation, because it is "so desolate a land to behold": and well indeed might he say so.

*Above:* A glacier grinds its inexorable way down to the Beagle Channel. *Below:* The coast of Tierra del Fuego is one of the wildest, and most beautiful, in the world.

Outside the main islands, there are numberless scattered rocks on which the long swell of the open ocean incessantly rages. We passed out between the East and West Furies; and a little farther northward there are so many breakers that the sea is called the Milky Way. One sight of such a coast is enough to make a landsman dream for a week about shipwrecks, peril, and death; and with this sight we bade farewell for ever to Tierra del Fuego.

# An Englishman's Paradise

*"Who can avoid wondering at the force which has upheaved these mountains, and even more so at the countless ages which it must have required to have broken through, removed, and levelled whole masses of them?"*

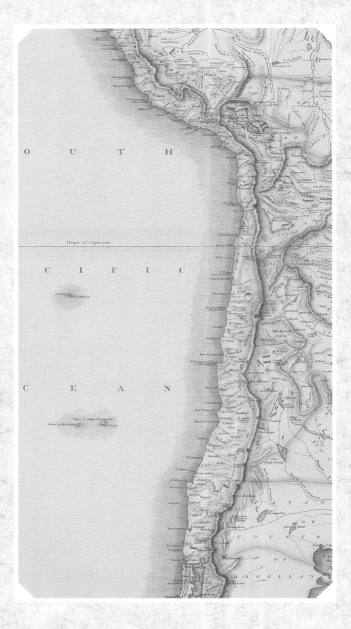

whom they are addressed. For what it is worth, though, Austen herself seems to have approved of them. The great author died in 1817, when Darwin was only eight: what she would have made of his later theories can only be imagined. But it is not difficult to imagine her liking the earnest, slightly gauche young man Darwin was at this time—or that stubbornly prosaic streak that is to be found in many of his descriptions.

Ever since Eirik the Red named Greenland, colonists have been talking up their finds: we saw the same with Juan Díaz de Solís and his Río de la Plata. The name of the central Chilean city of Valparaíso famously comes from the Spanish for "Vale of Paradise"—but whose idea of heaven was it really? In an age when Romanticism still held sway, did any red-blooded man have any business finding it quite as blessed a scene as Darwin did? Granted, Tierra del Fuego would have tested anyone's allegiance to "crooked, twisted, blasted trees," and Darwin was entitled to enjoy the improvement in the weather. But his sense of well-being went beyond this, it is clear: he responded to the air of order and industry he detected in a country he deemed "more civilized" than Argentina.

I n Jane Austen's novel *Sense and Sensibility*, published at the height of literary and artistic Romanticism in 1811, Edward Ferrars makes a damaging admission. "I like a fine prospect," he admits, "but not on picturesque principles. I do not like crooked, twisted, blasted trees. I admire them much more if they are tall, straight, and flourishing. I do not like ruined, tattered cottages. I am not fond of nettles or thistles, or heath blossoms. I have more pleasure in a snug farmhouse than a watchtower—and a troop of tidy, happy villagers please me better than the finest banditti in the world." His words outrage young Marianne Dashwood, the confirmed Romantic to

And what clearer indicator of civilization could there be, for an Englishman of Darwin's generation and class, than the presence of a chap from the Old School? In all seriousness, the fact that his old friend Richard Corfield was in Valparaíso would turn out to be a stroke of luck, especially when Darwin was subsequently taken ill. But Corfield—a thriving merchant—was also a representative of a British community in the city that was already considerable and growing all the time.

Britain's first imperial golden age had ended by the end of the eighteenth century—American Independence had seen to that. Its second, when the *Pax Britannica* prevailed over an empire on which the sun never set, was as yet a distant prospect in Darwin's day. Thanks to its industrial revolution, though, Britain was buoyant; the Napoleonic Wars had built its military strength and it was well on the way to being the colonial power in India. As the influence of the Spanish Empire slowly faded, there were openings to be found in Latin America—particularly in the countries of the *Cono Sur*, or "Southern Cone." However bloody the history behind the fact, Uruguay, Argentina and Chile were "whiter" than their neighbors to the north, their lands more amenable to European-style exploitation. Though never explicitly imperial holdings, these three countries all became centers for British investment and acquired a certain Anglo-Saxon tone. Amiable yet unadventurous, Darwin may have been as improbable an empire-builder as he was an explorer, but the *Beagle* expedition was clearly part (albeit a small one) of a quasi-imperialist project. Charting these coasts, visiting their ports, and meeting and greeting local dignitaries, Darwin and his companions were doing their bit to boost Britain's profile in the region.

*Above: Santiago de Chile, as shown in a drawing made in 1890. Left: The serene features of this young Araucanian girl give no hint of the implacable resistance her people would offer to the Spanish colonists—or of the brutality with which they would eventually be put down.*

# "Delightful"

On 23 July, 1834, the *Beagle* arrived at Valparaíso, "the chief seaport of Chile," as Darwin explains.

When morning came, everything appeared delightful. After Tierra del Fuego, the climate felt quite delicious—the atmosphere so dry, and the heavens so clear and blue with the sun shining brightly, that all nature seemed sparkling with life. The view from the anchorage is very pretty. The town is built at the very foot of a range of hills, about 1,600 feet high, and rather steep. ...In a northwesterly direction there are some fine glimpses of the Andes: but these mountains appear much grander when viewed from the neighbouring hills: the great distance at which they are situated can then more readily be perceived. The volcano of Aconcagua is particularly magnificent. This huge and irregularly conical mass has an elevation greater than that of Chimborazo; for, from measurements made by the officers in the *Beagle*, its height is no less than 23,000 feet. The Cordillera, however, viewed from this point, owe the greater part of their beauty to the atmosphere through which they are seen. When the sun was setting in the Pacific, it was admirable to watch how clearly their rugged outlines could be distinguished, yet how varied and how delicate were the shades of their colour.

"The immediate neighbourhood of Valparaíso is not very productive to the naturalist," reported Darwin:

During the long summer the wind blows steadily from the southward, and a little off shore, so that rain never falls; during the three winter months, however, it is sufficiently abundant. The vegetation in consequence is very scanty: except in some deep valleys, there are no trees, and only a little grass and a few low bushes are scattered over the less steep parts of the hills. When we reflect, that at the distance of 350 miles to the south, this side of the Andes is completely hidden by one impenetrable forest, the contrast is very remarkable. I took several long walks while collecting objects

## Valparaíso

Valparaíso was quietly booming when Darwin arrived in 1834, though the good times had been three centuries in coming. As the first major port of call for vessels that had made the difficult passage around Cape Horn, this was a place of crucial strategic importance. The opening of the Panama Canal in 1914 would change all that, however, and Valparaíso would once again subside into merely regional significance, though it has arguably had a disproportionate influence on the life of the country as a whole. Chile's main naval base as well as a mercantile port, Valparaíso has a strong military tradition—and a strong tradition of staging military coups. In 1891, naval officers with clerical backing overthrew the reformist liberal government of José Manuel Balmaceda. History was to repeat itself almost a century later, in 1973, when the elected government of Salvador Allende was overthrown by Valparaíso-born Augusto Pinochet, a general supported by senior naval officers based in the city.

## The Stone Sentinel

"No less than 23,000 feet"? Modern estimates suggest the *Beagle*'s officers were exaggerating, though not by much: at 22,840 feet, Aconcagua is the highest peak in the Americas. Though a volcano, as Darwin said, it is a dormant one, with no historical record of any eruption—despite hearsay reports of one a little later during Darwin's visit to the region. Technically, it is what is known to vulcanologists as a "composite volcano," its slopes formed from alternating layers of blast-projected cinder and solidified lava flows. For all that it is such a dominant feature of the Valparaíso skyline, Aconcagua actually stands in the far northwest of Argentina's Mendoza province. It was first successfully scaled in 1897.

of natural history. ...There are many very beautiful flowers; and, as in most other dry climates, the plants and shrubs possess strong and peculiar odours—even one's clothes by brushing through them became scented. I did not cease from wonder at finding each succeeding day as fine as the foregoing. What a difference does climate make in the enjoyment of life! How opposite are the sensations when viewing black mountains half enveloped in clouds, and seeing another range through the light blue haze of a fine day! The one for a time may be very sublime; the other is all gaiety and happy life.

*"What a difference does climate make in the enjoyment of life!"*

Tierra del Fuego had obviously never stood a chance! Along with its other amenities, moreover, Valparaíso had important geological strata to be studied in pursuit of what was clearly becoming a consuming interest:

**August 14th.**—I set out on a riding excursion, for the purpose of geologizing the basal parts of the Andes, which alone at this time of the year are not shut up by the winter snow. Our first day's ride was northward along the seacoast. After dark we reached the Hacienda of Quintero, the estate which formerly belonged to Lord Cochrane. My

## An Independent Nation

Darwin sometimes made a maddeningly idiosyncratic guide. His historic sense was haphazard, some things catching his imagination, others simply passing him by. One of these last is the matter of Chile having only within the previous sixteen years succeeded in achieving its independence from the Spanish Empire. Up until 1818, the country had been a district of the Viceroyalty of Peru—not even a province in its own right. The fight for independence had been led by Bernardo O'Higgins, the illegitimate son of an Irish-born Spanish official.

It had been an epic struggle: O'Higgins and his army had been put to flight by Spanish forces and compelled to withdraw to safety over the passes of the high Andes. There, however, they had received the assistance of Argentina's liberator, Jose San Martín, and his army: striking back, they had broken the Spanish at Chacabuco.

Once in power, O'Higgins had shown himself to be that contradictory thing, a benevolent despot, imposing liberal tolerance with an iron hand. In 1823, he had been deposed and driven into exile by conservative and clerical interests, but by now Chile's independence was firmly established.

*Below: Wherever you are in Chile, the Cordillera looms up, a dominant presence: here we see the Andes just south of Santiago in aerial view.*

object in coming here was to see the great beds of shells, which stand some yards above the level of the sea, and are burnt for lime. The proofs of the elevation of this whole line of coast are unequivocal: at the height of a few hundred feet old-looking shells are numerous, and I found some at 1,300 feet. These shells either lie loose on the surface, or are embedded in a reddish-black vegetable mould. I was much surprised to find under the microscope that this vegetable mould is really marine mud, full of minute particles of organic bodies.

Again, evidence of uplift—and surely, to judge by appearances, all taking place over an enormous period of time.

# A "Patchwork Valley"

On August 15, Darwin recorded, "We returned towards the valley of Quillota." He was moved almost to poetry by what he saw:

The country was exceedingly pleasant; just such as poets would call pastoral: green open lawns, separated by small valleys with rivulets, and the cottages, we may suppose of the shepherds, scattered on the hill-sides. We were obliged to cross the ridge of the

**Right:** *Picturesque they may be, but Chile's valleys are by no means always as idyllic as Darwin found. This stand of firs testifies to decades of unforgiving winds.*

Chilicauquen. At its base there were many fine evergreen forest-trees, but these flourished only in the ravines, where there was running water. Any person who had seen only the country near Valparaíso, would never have imagined that there had been such picturesque spots in Chile. As soon as we reached the brow of the Sierra, the valley of Quillota was immediately under our feet. The prospect was one of remarkable artificial luxuriance. The valley is very broad and quite flat, and is thus easily irrigated in all parts. The little square gardens are crowded with orange and olive trees, and every sort of vegetable. On each side huge bare mountains rise, and this from the contrast renders the patchwork valley the more pleasing. Whoever called Valparaíso the "Valley of Paradise" must have been thinking of Quillota....

*"Whoever called Valparaíso the 'Valley of Paradise' must have been thinking of Quillota."*

**It is striking that what so moved Darwin was not a scene of wilderness but one of "artificial luxuriance"—nature harnessed to human ends.**

Chile, as may be seen in the maps, is a narrow strip of land between the Cordillera and the Pacific; and this strip is itself traversed by several mountain-lines, which in this part run parallel to the great range. Between these outer lines and the main Cordillera, a succession of level basins, generally opening into each other by narrow passages, extend far to the southward: in these, the principal towns are situated, as San Felipe, Santiago, San Fernando. These basins or plains, together with the transverse flat valleys (like that of Quillota) which connect them with the coast, I have no doubt are the bottoms of ancient inlets and deep bays, such as at the present day intersect every part

## Hummingbirds

"Two species of humming-birds are common," observed Darwin.

*Trochilus forficatus* is found over a space of 2,500 miles on the west coast, from the hot dry country of Lima, to the forests of Tierra del Fuego— where it may be seen flitting about in snow-storms. ...When this species migrates in the summer southward, it is replaced by the arrival of another species coming from the north. This second kind (*Trochilus gigas*) is a very large bird for the delicate family to which it belongs: when on the wing its appearance is singular....Whilst hovering over a flower, it flaps its wings with a very slow and powerful movement, totally different from that vibratory one common to most of the species, which produces the humming noise.... Although flying from flower to flower in search of food, its stomach generally contained abundant remains of insects, which I suspect are much more the object of its search than honey.

of Tierra del Fuego and the western coast. Chile must formerly have resembled the latter country in the configuration of its land and water. The resemblance was occasionally shown strikingly when a level fog-bank covered, as with a mantle, all the lower parts of the country: the white vapour curling into the ravines, beautifully represented little coves and bays; and here and there a solitary hillock peeping

*Above:* Chilean guasos marshal their cattle in this early-twentieth-century scene. **Opposite, below:** "The orchards produce an overflowing abundance."

## The Guaso vs the Gaucho

Darwin did have a more romantic side, as evidenced earlier in his South American travels in his frank admiration of the Argentinean gaucho. He was to be disappointed, however, in his Chilean equivalent.

The guasos of Chile…are, however, a very different set of beings. Chile is the more civilized of the two countries, and the inhabitants, in consequence, have lost much individual character. Gradations in rank are much more strongly marked: the guaso does not by any means consider every man his equal… The gaucho, although he may be a cutthroat, is a gentleman; the guaso is in few respects better, but at the same time a vulgar, ordinary fellow…The gaucho seems part of his horse, and scorns to exert himself except when on his back: the guaso may be hired to work as a labourer in the fields…

The guaso was a hireling, then, a man to be despised, where the gaucho was, in Martín Fierro's phrase, "free as the bird." As we saw in his disparagement of the primitive egalitarianism of Fuegian life, Darwin felt inequalities of rank and fortune were essential to the advancement of society. Without such progress, he believed, humanity was doomed to remain mired in ignorance and squalor, but he clearly regretted the servility that went hand in hand with civilization.

up, showed that it had formerly stood there as an islet. The contrast of these flat valleys and basins with the irregular mountains, gave the scenery a character which to me was new and very interesting.

From the natural slope to seaward of these plains, they are very easily irrigated, and in consequence singularly fertile. Without this process the land would produce scarcely anything, for during the whole summer the sky is cloudless. The mountains and hills are dotted over with bushes and low trees, and excepting these the vegetation is very scanty. Each landowner in the valley possesses a certain portion of hill-country, where his half-wild cattle, in considerable numbers, manage to find sufficient pasture. Once every year there is a grand "rodeo," when all the cattle are driven down, counted, and marked, and a certain number separated to be fattened in the irrigated fields. Wheat is extensively cultivated, and a good deal of Indian corn: a kind of bean is, however, the staple article of food for the common labourers. The orchards produce an overflowing abundance of peaches, figs, and grapes.

# An Excursion

The following day, Darwin continued,

The mayor-domo of the Hacienda was good enough to give me a guide and fresh horses; and in the morning we set out to ascend the Campana, or Bell Mountain, which is 6,400 feet high. The paths were very bad, but both the geology and scenery amply repaid the trouble. We reached by the evening, a spring called the Agua del Guanaco, which is situated at a great height. This must be an old name, for it is very many years since a guanaco drank its waters. … We unsaddled our horses near the spring, and prepared to pass the night. The evening was fine, and the atmosphere so clear, that the masts of the vessels at anchor in the bay of Valparaiso, although no less than twenty-six geographical miles distant, could be distinguished clearly as little black streaks. …

The setting of the sun was glorious; the valleys being black whilst the snowy peaks of the Andes yet retained a ruby tint. When it was dark, we made a fire beneath a little arbour of bamboos, fried our *charqui* (or dried slips of beef), took our maté, and were quite comfortable. There is an inexpressible charm in thus living in the open air. The evening was calm and still; the shrill noise of the mountain bizcacha, and the faint cry of a goatsucker, were occasionally to be heard. Besides these, few birds, or even insects, frequent these dry, parched mountains.

**August 17th.**—In the morning we climbed up the rough mass of greenstone which crowns the summit. …We spent the day on the summit, and I never enjoyed one more thoroughly. Chile, bounded by the Andes and the Pacific, was seen as in a map. The pleasure from the scenery, in itself beautiful, was heightened

*"The setting of the sun was glorious; the valleys being black whilst the snowy peaks of the Andes yet retained a ruby tint."*

## The Maté Ceremony

One thing that gauchos and guasos had in common was a taste for maté, a refreshing drink still popular in parts of Brazil and throughout the *Cono Sur*. An infusion of the leaves and stems of the *Ilex paraguarensis* tree, it has a mildly stimulant effect, thanks to the theine (caffeine) it contains. Strictly speaking, the "maté" was not the drink itself, but the hollowed-out gourd from which it was sucked through a metal spout known as the *bombilla*. It was—still is, in many situations—passed round all those present, taken just as seriously as the British did their tea.

by the many reflections which arose from the mere view of the Campana range with its lesser parallel ones, and of the broad valley of Quillota directly intersecting them. Who can avoid wondering at the force which has upheaved these mountains, and even more so at the countless ages which it must have required to have broken through, removed, and levelled whole masses of them? It is well in this case to call to mind the vast shingle and sedimentary beds of Patagonia, which, if heaped on the Cordillera, would increase its height by so many thousand feet.

When in that country, I wondered how any mountain chain could have supplied such masses, and not have been utterly obliterated. We must not now reverse the wonder, and doubt whether all-powerful time can grind down mountains—even the gigantic Cordillera—into gravel and mud.

All the gravel and shingle deposits of Patagonia, Darwin realized, must originally have been washed down eastward from atop these heights: of what colossal size must these mountains once have been?

## Of Copper and Cacti

On the evening of August 18, Darwin and his party arrived at the mines of Jajuel, where they were to stay for the next five days.

These mines are of copper, and the ore is all shipped to Swansea [in the UK's southern Wales], to be smelted. Hence the mines have an aspect singularly quiet, as compared to those in England: here no smoke, furnaces, or great steam-engines, disturb the solitude of the surrounding mountains....

He felt considerable sympathy for the men who worked the mine.

The labouring men work very hard.... During summer and winter they begin when it is light, and leave off at dark. ...The miners who work in the mine itself...come down from their bleak habitations only once in every fortnight or three weeks.

The cacti, "or rather *opuntias,* were here very numerous," Darwin noted while at Jajuel. "I measured one of a spherical figure, which, including the spines, was six feet and four inches in circumference...."

# On to Santiago

**August 27th.**—After crossing many low hills we descended into the small land-locked plain of Guitron. In the basins, such as this one, which are elevated from one thousand to two thousand feet above the sea, two species of acacia, which are stunted in their forms, and stand wide apart from each other, grow in large numbers. These trees are never found near the sea-coast; and this gives another characteristic feature to the scenery of these basins. We crossed a low ridge which separates Guitron from the great plain on which Santiago stands. The view was here pre-eminently striking: the dead level surface, covered in parts by woods of acacia, and with the city in the distance, abutting horizontally against the base of the Andes, whose snowy peaks were bright with the evening sun. At the first glance...it was quite evident that the plain represented the extent of a former inland sea. As soon as we gained the level road we pushed our horses into a gallop, and reached the city before it was dark.

I stayed a week in Santiago, and enjoyed myself very much. In the morning I rode to various places on the plain, and in the evening dined with several of the English merchants, whose hospitality at this place is well known. A never-failing source of pleasure was to ascend the little hillock of rock (St. Lucia) which projects in the middle of the city. The scenery certainly is most striking, and, as I have said, very peculiar. ...Of the town I have nothing to say in detail: it is not so fine or so large as Buenos Ayres, but is built after the same model. I arrived here by a circuit to the north; so I resolved to return to Valparaiso by a rather longer excursion to the south of the direct road.

**September 5th.**—By the middle of the day we arrived at one of the suspension bridges, made of hide, which cross the Maypu, a large turbulent river a few leagues southward of Santiago. These bridges are very poor affairs. The road, following the curvature of the suspending ropes, is made of bundles of sticks placed close together. It...oscillated rather fearfully, even with the weight of a man leading his horse.

## Bridging History

Given the fearful oscillations he had endured, it is perhaps not surprising that Darwin should speak disparagingly of the suspension bridges in the mountains, but, "poor affairs" or not, these structures were historical monuments of some antiquity. Though (more or less) maintained in the centuries since, they had originally been built under the aegis of the Incan Empire—and in many cases by their predecessors perhaps five hundred years before. They were key points in an Incan road network that extended through some 25,000 miles in all, from Chile and Argentina all the way to Ecuador.

**September 6th.**—We proceeded due south, and slept at Rancagua. The road passed over the level but narrow plain, bounded on one side by lofty hills, and on the other by the Cordillera. The next day we turned up the valley of the Rio Cachapual, in which the hot-baths of Cauquenes, long celebrated for their medicinal properties, are situated. The suspension bridges, in the less frequented parts, are generally taken down during the winter when the rivers are low. Such was the case in this valley, and we were therefore obliged to cross the stream on horseback. This is rather disagreeable, for the foaming water, though not deep, rushes so quickly over the bed of large rounded stones, that one's head becomes quite confused, and it is difficult even to perceive whether the horse is moving onward or standing still. In summer, when the snow melts, the torrents are quite impassable....

The mineral springs of Cauquenes burst forth on a line of dislocation, crossing a mass of stratified rock, the whole of which betrays the action of heat. A considerable quantity of gas is continually escaping from the same orifices with the water. Though the springs are only a few yards apart, they have very different temperature; and this appears to be the result of an unequal mixture of cold water: for those with the lowest temperature have scarcely any mineral taste.

## Santiago de Chile

Santiago got short shrift in Darwin's account: it was Chile's capital city after all, though at this stage it was still somewhat overshadowed by Valparaíso. But Darwin's dismissiveness was unjust. Santiago had been established almost 300 years before, in 1541, by Pedro de Valdivia, a veteran of Francisco Pizarro's Peruvian campaign. Its history very nearly ended within two years of its foundation, its colonists only narrowly avoiding annihilation by Chile's warlike Araucanian people. The native attacks continued on and off for generations, in fact, and Santiago grew only slowly. By the time Chile won her independence in 1818 it was a place to be reckoned with, and from that time on it began to expand apace.

# Bandit Country

One day during his stay at Cauquenes, Darwin "rode up the valley to the farthest inhabited spot."

Shortly above that point, the Cachapual divides into two deep tremendous ravines, which penetrate directly into the great range. I scrambled up a peaked mountain, probably more than six thousand feet high. Here, as indeed everywhere else, scenes of the highest interest presented themselves. It was by one of these ravines, that Pincheira entered Chile and ravaged the neighbouring country. ...He was a renegade half-caste Spaniard, who collected a great body of Indians together and established himself by a stream in the Pampas, which place none of the forces sent after him could ever discover. From this point he used to sally forth, and crossing the Cordillera by passes hitherto unattempted, he ravaged the farm-houses and drove the cattle to his secret rendezvous. Pincheira was a capital horseman, and he made all around him equally good, for he invariably shot any one who hesitated to follow him. It was against this man, and other wandering Indian tribes, that Rosas waged the war of extermination.

*Below: They seem amiable enough in this early photograph, but the Araucanians were persistent rebels against Chile's Spanish colonizers: not until 1883 were they finally subdued.*

## The Royalist Revolutionary

Jose Antonio Pincheira is believed to have been born around 1801: by the time he was a teenager he and his brothers Antonio, Santos and Pablo were leading a band of brigands in the lonely lands to the south of the Maule River. Jose Antonio's espousal of the monarchist principle seems to have been largely opportunistic, if truth be told, after he fell in with a remnant of the Spanish force that had just been smashed by O'Higgins and San Martín. Whatever his motives, though, he was to prove a courageous and resourceful guerrilla leader, resisting the armies of both Argentina and Chile for fifteen years. He had finally been cornered in the mountains by Chilean forces, just two years previously; he capitulated on the promise of an official pardon. At the time of Darwin's writing he was living quietly in the city of Concepción, where he was finally to die in 1850.

**September 13th.**—We left the baths of Cauquenes, and, rejoining the main road, slept at the Rio Clara. From this place we rode to the town of San Fernando. Before arriving there, the last land-locked basin had expanded into a great plain, which extended so far to the south, that the snowy summits of the more distant Andes were seen as if above the horizon of the sea. San Fernando is forty leagues from Santiago; and it was my farthest point southward; for we here turned at right angles towards the coast. We slept at the gold-mines of Yaquil, which are worked by Mr. Nixon, an American gentleman, to whose kindness I was much indebted during the four days I stayed at his house. The next morning we rode to the mines, which are situated at the distance of some leagues, near the summit of a lofty hill. On the way we had a glimpse of the lake Tagua-tagua, celebrated for its floating islands... They are composed of the stalks of various dead plants intertwined together, and on the surface of which other living ones take root. Their form is generally circular, and their thickness from four to six feet, of which the greater part is immersed in the water. As the wind blows, they pass from one side of the lake to the other, and often carry cattle and horses as passengers.

Darwin was now taken ill, and was taken back to Valparaíso in some discomfort. He remained there until the end of October, "an inmate in Mr. Corfield's house, whose kindness to me I do not know how to express." He ended his account of his stay in Valparaíso with his observations on two of the region's most distinctive birds:

Of birds, two species of the genus *Pteroptochos*...are perhaps the most conspicuous. ...The Turco is not uncommon. It lives on the ground, sheltered among the thickets which are scattered over the dry and sterile hills. With its tail erect, and stilt-like legs, it may be seen every now and then popping from one bush to another with uncommon quickness. It really requires little imagination to believe that the bird is ashamed of itself, and is aware of its most ridiculous figure. On first seeing it, one is tempted to exclaim, "A vilely stuffed specimen has escaped from some museum, and has come to life again!"

The second species (or *Pteroptochos albicollis*) is allied to the first in its general form. It is called Tapaculo, or "cover your posterior," and well does the shameless little bird deserve its name; for it carries its tail more than erect, that is, inclined backwards towards its head. It is very common, and frequents the bottoms of hedge-rows, and the bushes scattered over the barren hills, where scarcely another bird can exist. In its general manner...it bears a close resemblance to the Turco; but its appearance is not quite so ridiculous. The Tapaculo is an active bird, and continually making a noise: these noises are various and strangely odd; some are like the cooing of doves, others like the bubbling of water, and many defy all similes. The country people say it changes its cry five times in the year— according to some change of season, I suppose.

*Left:* Those same colossal forces that created the Cordillera over so many million years laid down the rich mineral deposits on which the economy of modern Chile has been built. *Above:* Taken ill in Chile, Darwin found in a friend in need in Mr Corfield; in Valparaíso (seen here in 1893) he found a home from home. *Top:* A rainstorm shows Nordenskjold Lake in an especially dramatic light: the Chilean Andes can boast some of the loveliest scenery in the world.

# The Broken Land

*"It is a bitter and humiliating thing to see works, which have cost man so much time and labour, overthrown in one minute...we have scarcely beheld, since leaving England, any sight so deeply interesting."*

*Previous pages: Even as the Andes were forced upward by geotectonic forces, they were ground down by glaciation: Chile's Laguna San Rafael is famous for its "icefields."* **Left:** *Southern Chile's interrupted coastline is revealed in this 1866 map.* **Below:** *The Andes form a dramatic backdrop to the Chilean scene.*

far the largest of these, but there are myriad more in the Chonos Archipelago to the south. With time on his hands, Darwin not only had time to survey the region's wildlife but to muse on the means by which these "emerald islands" had been created.

"The broken land," he more than once called the Chonos Archipelago, though the label might be applied to the region as a whole. A glance at the map of South America clearly shows what seems to have been a continuous coastline, constantly interrupted by expanses of open water. Though he would not have been making any value judgment, Darwin's expression does imply a previous "unbroken" state—when these islets, perhaps, were the hilltops of a rugged landscape. It implies, in other words, a sense that the world might not always be as it currently presents itself, that creation might be a process rather than a one-off *fiat* or *fait accompli.*

The next stage of the expedition saw the *Beagle* turning completely on its tracks and sailing southward, retracing its earlier course down the coast of Chile. This part of the country is magnificent, though still comparatively little known in the world outside, a place of awesome grandeur and breathtaking beauty. Here are to be found fjords and islets like those that line Alaska's Pacific coast, the snow-capped Andes a stunning backdrop to every scene.

But the crew of the *Beagle* had not come here to enjoy the view. FitzRoy's men were busy surveying the coast and charting inshore waters. There was a lot for them to do: successive glaciations have gouged out deep inlets in this jagged coastline, while subsequent sea-level rises have created scores of offshore islands. At getting on for twice the size of Long Island, Chiloé is by

We tend conventionally to think in terms of a world whose geography has been established once and for all, each area allocated its appropriate flora and fauna. Even evolutionary thinking as popularly understood helps perpetuate such assumptions, with its notion of "niches," the adaptation of species to particular environments. Here is the desert with its cactus and camels; here, the Arctic waste with its polar bears—colored for camouflage; here, the rainforest, teeming with appropriately exotic life. How well creation works, each animal and plant with its allotted place—evidence, surely, of control by some all-powerful intelligence.

In Chile, however, Darwin found himself confronted by the suggestion of something altogether different: a creation apparently fixed in one form, but subsequently "broken" into another. It was by no means the first such evidence he had seen on his travels to date; neither was it in any sense conclusive—he was still some years away from his first real forays into evolutionary theory. In hindsight, however, these and similar

experiences in South America can be seen as helping mentally to prepare the way for Darwin's later theories. The hold of traditional thinking may not have been broken, but it was clearly weakening.

There is another obvious sense in which this was a "broken land": Chile has often been the scene of devastating earthquakes. Darwin, as it happens, was present for one of the worst of these, and deeply moved at the human cost of what he saw. As a scientist, however, he was understandably—if somewhat guiltily—thrilled to have been a witness, and awed at the titanic forces he knew had been involved. He surmised—modern science would say correctly—that such upheavals had been responsible for raising up the whole Cordillera, over what surely had to have been a vast period of time. And not only was the world ancient, but the signs were that it was still unfinished. This was a creation under construction, he realized.

*Above: The Anemone multifada, or cut-leaf anemone, is a familiar sight in the foothills of the Andes. Left: The Romanche Glacier is one of the glories of southern Chile.*

1832 1833 1834 1835 1836 1837

# Sailing South

On November 10, 1834, "the *Beagle* sailed from Valparaíso to the south, for the purpose of surveying the southern part of Chile, the island of Chiloé, and the broken land called the Chonos Archipelago, as far south as the Peninsula of Tres Montes. On the 21st we anchored in the bay of S[an] Carlos, the capital of Chiloé."

This island is about ninety miles long, with a breadth of rather less than thirty. The land is hilly, but not mountainous, and is covered by one great forest, except where a few green patches have been cleared round the thatched cottages. From a distance the view somewhat resembles that of Tierra del Fuego; but the woods, when seen nearer, are incomparably more beautiful. Many kinds of fine evergreen trees, and plants with a tropical character, here take the place of the gloomy beech of the southern shores. In winter the climate is detestable, and in summer it is only a little better. I should think there are few parts of the world, within the temperate regions, where so much rain falls. The winds are very boisterous, and the sky almost always clouded: to have a week of fine weather is something wonderful. It is even difficult to get a single glimpse of the Cordillera: during our first visit, once only the volcano of Osorno stood out in bold relief, and that was before sunrise; it was curious to watch, as the sun rose, the outline gradually fading away in the glare of the eastern sky.

*"The winds are very boisterous, and the sky almost always clouded: to have a week of fine weather is something wonderful."*

**November 26th.**—The day rose splendidly clear. The volcano of Orsono was spouting out volumes of smoke. This most beautiful mountain, formed like a perfect cone, and white with snow, stands out in front of the Cordillera. Another great volcano, with a saddle-shaped summit, also emitted from its immense crater little jets of steam. Subsequently we saw the lofty-peaked Corcovado—well deserving the name of *el famoso Corcovado*. Thus we beheld, from one point of view, three great active volcanoes, each about seven thousand feet high. In addition to this, far to the south, there were other lofty cones covered with snow, which, although not known to be active, must be in their origin volcanic....

**December 1st.**—We steered for the island of Lemuy. I was anxious to examine a reported coal-mine which turned out to be lignite of little value, in the sandstone...of which these islands are composed. When we reached Lemuy we had much difficulty in finding any place to pitch our tents, for it was spring-tide, and the land was wooded down to the water's edge. In a short time we were surrounded by a large

**Left:** *A clump of mistletoe grows in a tree in southern Chile.* **Above:** *The scenery of the Chilean fjords is spellbinding.*

*Right:* The name of Chiloé's Mount Puntiagudo—in Spanish, "sharp point"—needs no explanation: here we see it reflected in the still waters of All Saints' Lake.

group of the nearly pure Indian inhabitants. They were much surprised at our arrival, and said one to the other, "This is the reason we have seen so many parrots lately; the cheucau...has not cried 'beware' for nothing." They were soon anxious for barter. Money was scarcely worth anything, but their eagerness for tobacco was something quite extraordinary. After tobacco, indigo came next in value; then capsicum, old clothes, and gunpowder. The latter article was required for a very innocent purpose: each parish has a public musket, and the gunpowder was wanted for making a noise on their saint or feast days...

During the four succeeding days we continued sailing southward. The general features of the country remained the same, but it was much less thickly inhabited. On the large island of Tanqui there was scarcely one cleared spot, the trees on every side extending their branches over the sea-beach. I one day noticed, growing on the sandstone cliffs, some very fine plants of the panke (*Gunnera scabra*), which somewhat resembles the rhubarb on a gigantic scale. The inhabitants eat the stalks, which are subacid, and tan leather with the roots, and prepare a black dye from them. The leaf is nearly circular, but deeply indented on its margin. I measured one which was nearly eight feet in diameter, and therefore no less than twenty-four in circumference! The stalk is rather more than a yard high, and each plant sends out four or five of these enormous leaves, presenting together a very noble appearance.

## No Man's Land

Chacao, Darwin would discover, was so far from the center of things that its people were vague even as to which country they belonged to.

We had not long bivouacked, before the bare-footed son of the governor came down to reconnoitre us. Seeing the English flag hoisted at the yawl's mast-head, he asked with the utmost indifference, whether it was always to fly at Chacao. In several places the inhabitants were much astonished at the appearance of men-of-war's boats, and hoped and believed it was the forerunner of a Spanish fleet, coming to recover the island from the patriot government of Chile.

# The End of Christendom

On December 6, Darwin recorded, "We reached Caylen, called *el fin del Cristiandad*."

In the morning we stopped for a few minutes at a house on the northern end of Laylec, which was the extreme point of South American Christendom, and a miserable hovel it was. ...These extreme Christians were very poor, and, under the plea of their situation, begged for some tobacco. As a proof of the poverty of these Indians, I may mention that shortly before this, we had met a man, who

## The Prophet of the Forests

The "Cheucau," wrote Darwin, giving this bird its Latin title, *Pteroptochos rubecula*,

Frequents the most gloomy and retired spots within the damp forests. Sometimes, although its cry may be heard close at hand, let a person watch ever so attentively he will not see the cheucau; at other times, let him stand motionless and the red-breasted little bird will approach within a few feet in the most familiar manner. It then busily hops about the entangled mass of rotting cones and branches, with its little tail cocked upwards. The cheucau is held in superstitious fear by the Chilotans, on account of its strange and varied cries. There are three very distinct cries: One is called "chiduco," and is an omen of good; another, "huitreu," which is extremely unfavourable; and a third, which I have forgotten. These words are given in imitation of the noises; and the natives are in some things absolutely governed by them.

had travelled three days and a half on foot, and had as many to return, for the sake of recovering the value of a small axe and a few fish. How very difficult it must be to buy the smallest article, when such trouble is taken to recover so small a debt….

We stayed three days in this harbour, on one of which Captain Fitz Roy, with a party, attempted to ascend to the summit of San Pedro. In vain we tried to gain the summit: the forest was so impenetrable, that no one who has not beheld it can imagine so entangled a mass of dying and dead trunks. …We ultimately gave up the attempt in despair.

**December 10th.**—The yawl and whale-boat, with Mr. Sulivan, proceeded on their survey, but I remained on board the *Beagle*, which the next day left San Pedro for the southward. On the 13th we ran into an opening in the southern part of Guayatecas, or the Chonos Archipelago; and it was fortunate we did so, for on the following day a storm, worthy of Tierra del Fuego, raged with great fury. White massive clouds were piled up against a dark blue sky, and across them black ragged sheets of vapour were rapidly driven. The successive mountain ranges appeared like dim shadows, and the setting sun cast on the woodland a yellow gleam, much like that produced by the flame of spirits of wine. The water was white with the flying spray, and the wind lulled and roared again through the rigging: it was an ominous, sublime scene. During a few minutes there was a bright rainbow, and it was curious to observe the effect of the spray, which being carried along the surface of the water, changed the ordinary semi-circle into a circle—a band of prismatic colours being continued, from both feet of the common arch across the bay, close to the vessel's side: thus forming a distorted, but very nearly entire ring.

*Above: The Velo de la Novia ("Bride's Veil") waterfall is one of many in Chile's Simpson River National Park. Opposite, top: A rainbow arcs above one of the fjords of southern Chile as the sun battles through angry cloud. Opposite, bottom: Beautifully tended wayside shrines are a feature of the Christianized Chilean countryside.*

## Not So Cunning

The ways of the wildlife collectors of the nineteenth century often seem shocking to animal-lovers today, to whom the idea of "naturalists" shooting specimens seems quite wrong. Darwin showed no such squeamish-ness—here, indeed, he proved sufficiently ruthless and cunning to prevail over so proverbially sly a creature as a fox:

In the evening we reached the island of San Pedro, where we found the *Beagle* at anchor. In doubling the point, two of the officers landed to take a round of angles with the theodolite. A fox (*Canis fulvipes*), of a kind said to be peculiar to the island, and very rare in it, and which is a new species, was sitting on the rocks. He was so intently absorbed in watching the work of the officers, that I was able, by quietly walking up behind, to knock him on the head with my geological hammer. This fox, more curious or more scientific, but less wise, than the general-ity of his brethren, is now mounted in the museum of the Zoological Society.

Three days later, "We stood out to sea" and headed northward. And then, on December 30,

We anchored in a snug little cove at the foot of some high hills, near the northern extremity of Tres Montes. After breakfast the next morn-ing, a party ascended one of these mountains, which was 2,400 feet high. The scenery was remarkable The chief part of the range was composed of grand, solid, abrupt masses of granite, which appeared as if they had been coeval with the beginning of the world. The granite was capped with mica-slate, and this in the lapse of ages had been worn into strange finger-shaped points. These two formations, thus differing in their outlines, agree in being almost destitute of vegetation. This barrenness had to our eyes a strange appearance, from having been so long accustomed to the sight of an almost universal for-est of dark-green trees. I took much delight in examining the structure of these mountains. The complicated and lofty ranges bore a noble aspect of durability—equally profitless, however, to man and to all other animals.

# A Happy New Year?

Darwin's account of January 1, 1835, finds him in surprisingly somber mood:

The new year is ushered in with the ceremonies proper to it in these regions. She lays out no false hopes: a heavy north-western gale, with steady rain, bespeaks the rising year. Thank God, we are not destined here to see the end of it, but hope then to be in the Pacific Ocean, where a blue sky tells one there is a heaven—a something beyond the clouds above our heads.

The north-west winds prevailing for the next four days, we only managed to cross a great bay, and then anchored in another secure harbour. I accompanied the Captain in a boat to the head of a deep creek. On the way the number of seals which we saw was quite astonishing: every bit of flat rock, and parts of the beach, were covered with them. They appeared to be of a loving disposition, and lay huddled together, fast asleep, like so many pigs; but even pigs would have been ashamed of their dirt, and of the foul smell which came from them. ...

*"We were amused by the impetuous manner in which the heap of seals, old and young, tumbled into the water."*

We found the water (probably only that of the surface) nearly fresh: this was caused by the number of torrents which, in the form of cascades, came tumbling over the bold granite mountains into the sea. The fresh water attracts the fish, and these bring many terns, gulls, and two kinds of cormorant. We saw also a pair of the beautiful black-necked swans, and several small sea-otters, the fur of which is held in such high estimation. In returning, we were again amused by the impetuous manner in which the heap of seals, old and young, tumbled into the water as the boat passed. They did not remain long under water, but rising, followed us with outstretched necks, expressing great wonder and curiosity.

# Lowe's Harbor

Watching every herd of seals on the rocks here, Darwin noted, were:

the patient but inauspicious eyes of the turkey-buzzard. This disgusting bird, with its bald scarlet head, formed to wallow in putridity, is very common on the west coast, and their attendance on the seals shows on what they rely for their food.

Why such a violent reaction to a bird just doing its best to fill its ecological niche? Is this more evidence of Darwin's feeling out of sorts? This is the naturalist who had felt so enraptured by the flight of the Andean condor—but then he had seen that bird soaring high in the heavens above his head. Really, there is little to be chosen between the two species in terms of ugliness in close-up, nor in terms of effortless elegance in flight.

*Opposite, top: Elephant seals don't so much form colonies as conglomerated masses of heaving blubber and hide. Opposite, left: Stately and calm, a black-necked swan scuds across the waters of a fjord. Below: Sea otters are among the most charming creatures in the world.*

On January 7, "having run up the coast, we anchored near the northern end of the Chonos Archipelago, in Lowe's Harbour, where we remained a week."

The islands were here, as in Chiloe, composed of a stratified, soft, littoral deposit; and the vegetation in consequence was beautifully luxuriant. The woods came down to the sea-beach, just in the manner of an evergreen shrubbery over a gravel walk. . . .
    In the central parts of the Chonos Archipelago (lat. 45°), the forest has very much the same character with that along the whole west coast, for 600 miles southward to Cape Horn. The arborescent grass of Chiloe is not found here; while the beech of Tierra del Fuego grows to a good size, and forms a considerable proportion of the wood; not, however, in the same exclusive manner as it does farther southward. Cryptogamic plants ["lower" plants, including lichen and algae] here find a most congenial climate. In the Strait of Magellan…the country appears too cold and wet to allow of their arriving at perfection; but in these islands, within the forest, the number of species and great abundance of mosses, lichens, and small ferns, is quite extraordinary….
    The zoology of these broken islets of the Chonos Archipelago is, as might have been expected, very poor. Of quadrupeds two aquatic kinds are common. The *Myopotamus coypus* (like a beaver, but with a round tail) is well known from its fine fur, which is an object of trade throughout the tributaries of La Plata. It here, however, exclusively frequents salt water; which same circumstance has been mentioned as sometimes occurring with the great rodent, the Capybara. A small sea-otter is very numerous; this animal does not feed exclusively on fish, but, like the seals, draws a large supply from a small red crab, which swims in shoals near the surface of the water…At one place I caught in a trap a singular little mouse (*Muscus brachiotis*); it appeared common on several of the islets, but the Chilotans at Lowe's Harbour said that it was not found in all. What a

succession of chances, or what changes of level must have been brought into play, thus to spread these small animals throughout this broken archipelago!

Darwin hit on an ingenious explanation to account for the unevenness of this distribution:

It is said that some rapacious birds bring their prey alive to their nests. If so, in the course of centuries, every now and then, one might escape from the young birds. Some such agency is necessary to account for the distribution of the smaller gnawing animals on islands not very near each other.

Darwin was underwhelmed by the variety of birdlife he found down here, though he noted the presence of the cheucau and "an allied species, but larger," the "guid-guid" (*Pteroptochos tarnii*) or "barking bird."

This latter name is well given; for I defy any one at first to feel certain that a small dog is not yelping somewhere in the forest. Just as with the cheucau, a person will sometimes hear the bark close by, but in vain many endeavour by watching, and with still less chance by beating the bushes, to see the bird; yet at other times the guid-guid fearlessly comes near. Its manner of feeding and its general habits are very similar to those of the cheucau.

On the coast, a small dusky-coloured bird (*Opetiorhynchus patagonicus*) is very common. It is remarkable from its quiet habits; it lives entirely on the sea-beach, like a sandpiper. Besides these birds only few others inhabit this broken land. In my rough notes I describe the strange noises, which, although frequently heard within these gloomy forests, yet scarcely disturb the general silence. The yelping of the guid-guid, and the sudden whew-whew of the cheucau, sometimes come from afar off, and sometimes from close at hand; the little black wren of Tierra del Fuego occasionally adds its cry; the creeper (*Oxyurus*) follows the intruder screaming and twittering; the humming-bird may be seen every now and then darting from side to side, and emitting, like an insect, its shrill chirp; lastly,

## Petrels

There may have been relatively few types of bird to be seen ashore, but, notes Darwin:

These southern seas are frequented by several species of Petrels: the largest kind, *Procellaria gigantea*, or nelly (*quebrantahuesos*, or "break bones," of the Spaniards), is a common bird, both in the inland channels and on the open sea. In its habits and manner of flight, there is a very close resemblance with the albatross…The "break-bones" is, however, a rapacious bird, for it was observed by some of the officers at Port St. Antonio chasing a diver, which tried to escape by diving and flying, but was continually struck down, and at last killed by a blow on its head…A second species (*Puffinus cinereus*), which is common to Europe, Cape Horn, and the coast of Peru, is of much smaller size than the *P. gigantea*, but, like it, of a dirty black colour. It generally frequents the inland sounds in very large flocks: I do not think I ever saw so many birds of any other sort together, as I once saw of these behind the island of Chiloe. Hundreds of thousands flew in an irregular line for several hours in one direction. When part of the flock settled on the water the surface was blackened, and a noise proceeded from them as of human beings talking in the distance.

*Right: Perky and alert, the rufous-collared sparrow is to be found from southern Mexico to Tierra del Fuego.*
*Below: Boiling rock; liquid fire: volcanic lava is both of these. No sight on earth could be more infernally awesome.*

# Osorno Erupts

"On January the 15th," noted Darwin, "we sailed from Lowe's Harbour, and three days afterwards anchored a second time in the bay of S[an] Carlos in Chiloé."

from the top of some lofty tree the indistinct but plaintive note of the white-tufted tyrant-flycatcher (*Myiobius*) may be noticed. From the great preponderance in most countries of certain common genera of birds, such as the finches, one feels at first surprised at meeting with the peculiar forms above enumerated, as the commonest birds in any district. In central Chile two of them, namely, the *Oxyurus* and *Scytalopus*, occur, although most rarely. When finding, as in this case, animals which seem to play so insignificant a part in the great scheme of nature, one is apt to wonder why they were created.

*"At midnight the sentry observed something like a large star, which... presented a very magnificent spectacle."*

Why would a conscious creator bother with what were only ever destined to be marginal species? Darwin was still far from dismissing the idea of some "great scheme" of nature, but the idea was clearly presenting him with problems.

But it should always be recollected, that in some other country perhaps they are essential members of society, or at some former period may have been so.

On the night of the 19th the volcano of Osorno was in action. At midnight the sentry observed something like a large star, which gradually increased in size till about three o'clock, when it presented a very magnificent spectacle. By the aid of a glass, dark objects, in constant succession, were seen, in the midst of a great glare of red light, to be thrown up and to fall down. The light was sufficient to cast on the water a long bright reflection. Large masses of molten matter seem very commonly to be cast out of the craters in this part of the Cordillera. I was assured that when the Corcovado is in eruption, great masses are projected upwards and are seen to burst in the air, assuming many fantastical forms, such as trees: their size must be immense, for they can be distinguished from the high land behind S. Carlos, which is no less than ninety-three miles from the Corcovado. In the morning the volcano became tranquil.

I was surprised at hearing afterwards that Aconcagua in Chile, 480 miles northwards, was in action on the same night; and still more surprised to hear that the great eruption of Coseguina (2,700 miles north of Aconcagua), accompanied by an earthquake felt over 1,000 miles, also occurred within six hours of this same time. This coincidence is the more remarkable, as Coseguina had been dormant for twenty-six years; and Aconcagua most rarely shows any signs of action. It is difficult even to conjecture whether this coincidence was accidental, or shows some subterranean connection.

February 4th.—Sailed from Chiloe. During the last week I made several short excursions. One was to examine a great bed of now-existing shells, elevated

350 feet above the level of the sea: from among these shells, large forest trees were growing. Another ride was to P[unta] Huechucucuy. I had with me a guide who knew the country far too well; for he would pertinaciously tell me endless Indian names for every little point, rivulet, and creek. In the same manner as in Tierra del Fuego, the Indian language appears singularly well adapted for attaching names to the most trivial features of the land. I believe every one was glad to say farewell to Chiloe; yet if we could forget the gloom and ceaseless rain of winter, Chiloe might pass for a charming island. There is also something very attractive in the simplicity and humble politeness of the poor inhabitants.

# A Momentous Day

"This day has been memorable in the annals of Valdivia," wrote Darwin on February 20, 1835, for

The most severe earthquake experienced by the oldest inhabitant. I happened to be on shore, and was lying down in the wood to rest myself. It came on suddenly, and lasted two minutes, but the time appeared much longer. The rocking of the ground was very sensible. The undulations appeared to my companion and myself to come from due east, whilst others thought they proceeded from south-west: this shows how difficult it sometimes is to perceive the directions of the

## The Araucanians

During an excursion to Valdivia and the nearby Christian mission of Cudico in mid-February, Darwin met Araucanian people, whom he described as "wild." In fact, the Araucanians are famed for the ferocity with which they resisted colonial rule. That resistance continues today, in the form of a popular protest movement campaigning for a recognition of Araucanian identity. It has also taken up specific causes, such as land rights, and has found itself in coalition with ecological groups attempting to stop damaging timber exploitation and hydro-electric damming schemes. The sense of a people at war has been perpetuated by the Chilean government's readiness to resort to the label "terrorist" for protestors employing overwhelmingly peaceful means.

vibrations. There was no difficulty in standing upright, but the motion made me almost giddy: it was something like the movement of a vessel in a little cross-ripple, or still more like that felt by a person skating over thin ice, which bends under the weight of his body.

A bad earthquake at once destroys our oldest associations: the earth, the very emblem of solidity, has moved beneath our feet like a thin crust over a fluid—one second of time has created in the mind a strange idea of insecurity, which hours of reflection would not have produced. In the forest, as a breeze moved the trees, I felt only the earth tremble, but saw no other effect.

*Left: Araucanian women work at their looms, employing skills their ancestors have possessed since prehistoric times, when Andean weavers produced some of the finest textiles ever seen.*

*Right:* The sun sinks slowly above a vista of calm waters and distant mountains; the sense of tranquility in southern Chile is remarkable.

Captain Fitz Roy and some officers were at the town during the shock, and there the scene was more striking; for although the houses, from being built of wood, did not fall, they were violently shaken, and the boards creaked and rattled together. The people rushed out of doors in the greatest alarm. It is these accompaniments that create that perfect horror of earthquakes, experienced by all who have thus seen, as well as felt, their effects. Within the forest it was a deeply interesting, but by no means an awe-exciting phenomenon.

## The Indian Flanders

Just before the earthquake, the *Beagle* landed near a derelict fort at Niebla. It had been built in 1658, the culmination of a larger complex of fortifications designed to protect the city of Valdivia from attack by both land and sea. From the ocean, this prosperous settlement had already proved vulnerable to raids by privates; from the landward side came the menace of the Mapuche. This people belonged to the wider Araucanian family of tribes who would prove such a challenge to the Spanish conquistadors throughout Chile. So indefatigable was their resistance that Chile acquired the nickname of the "Indian Flanders," after Spain's notoriously restive European possession in what is now northern France and Belgium. Valdivia's other two main forts, Mancera and Corral, can also still be seen: in its heyday the city's defenses were widely admired as masterpieces of military engineering. But they were powerless to defend a system many of whose leading members had decided to dispense with it: in the revolution of 1818 they proved an irrelevance.

And on March 4 they arrived off the coast at Concepción to find a scene of devastation. Darwin was told: "That not a house in Concepcion or Talcahuano (the port) was standing; that seventy villages were destroyed; and that a great wave had almost washed away the ruins of Talcahuano."

Of this latter statement I soon saw abundant proofs—the whole coast being strewed over with timber and furniture as if a thousand ships had been wrecked. ...During my walk round the island, I observed that numerous fragments of rock, which, from the marine productions adhering to them, must recently have been lying in deep water, had been cast up high on the beach; one of these was six feet long, three broad, and two thick.

The island itself [Quiriquina, just offshore] as plainly showed the overwhelming power of the earthquake, as the beach did that of the consequent great wave. The ground in many parts was fissured in north and south lines.... Some of the fissures near the cliffs were a yard wide. Many enormous masses had already fallen on the beach; and the inhabitants thought that when the rains commenced far greater slips would happen. ...I believe this convulsion has been more effectual in lessening the size of the island of Quiriquina, than the ordinary wear-and-tear of the sea and weather during the course of a whole century.

# "A Great Wave"

The next day I landed at Talcahuano, and afterwards rode to Concepcion. Both towns presented the most awful yet interesting spectacle I ever beheld. To a person who had formerly known them, it possibly might have been still more impressive; for the ruins were so mingled together, and the whole scene possessed so little the air of a habitable place, that it was scarcely possible to imagine its former condition. The earthquake commenced at half-past eleven o'clock in the forenoon. If it had happened in the middle of the night, the greater number of the inhabitants (which in this one province must amount to many thousands) must have perished, instead of less than a hundred: as it was, the invariable practice of running out of doors at the first trembling of the ground, alone saved them. In Concepcion each house, or row of houses, stood by itself, a heap or line of ruins; but in Talcahuano, owing to the great wave, little more than one layer of bricks, tiles, and timber with here and there part of a wall left standing, could be distinguished. From this circumstance Concepcion, although not so completely desolated, was a more terrible, and if I may so call it, picturesque sight...It is generally thought that this has been the worst earthquake ever recorded in Chile; but as the very severe ones occur only after long intervals, this cannot easily be known; nor indeed would a much worse shock have made any difference, for the ruin was now complete. Innumerable small tremblings followed the great earthquake, and within the first twelve days no less than three hundred were counted.

*"Innumerable small tremblings followed the great earthquake, and within the first twelve days no less than three hundred were counted."*

Almost as devastating as the earthquake, it seemed, had been the gigantic tsunami that had followed it.

Shortly after the shock, a great wave was seen from the distance of three or four miles, approaching in the middle of the bay with a smooth outline; but along the shore it tore up cottages and trees, as it swept onwards with irresistible force. At the head of the bay it broke in a fearful line of white breakers, which rushed up to a height of 23 vertical feet above the highest spring-tides. Their force must have been prodigious; for at the Fort a cannon with its carriage, estimated at four tons in weight, was moved 15 feet inwards. A schooner was left in the midst of the ruins, 200 yards from the beach. The first wave was followed by two others, which in their retreat carried away a vast wreck of floating objects. In one part of the bay, a ship was pitched high and dry on shore, was carried off, again driven on shore, and again carried off. ... One old woman with a little boy, four or five years old, ran into a boat, but there

*Right: Bystanders flee as a volcano at Antuco, Chile, erupts in this artist's impression of 1835.*

was nobody to row it out: the boat was consequently dashed against an anchor and cut in twain; the old woman was drowned, but the child was picked up some hours afterwards clinging to the wreck. ...It was remarked with much truth, that from the destruction being universal, no one individual was humbled more than another, or could suspect his friends of coldness—that most grievous result of the loss of wealth....

Darwin then turned a skeptical scientist's eye to two accounts of the event, first by his colleague Captain FitzRoy, then by the local "lower orders." He was quick to put down any hint of infernal chemistry in the description given by the former—and as for the latter's account, that left him both amused and intrigued.

The lower orders in Talcahuano thought that the earthquake was caused by some old Indian women, who two years ago, being offended, stopped the volcano of Antuco. This silly belief is curious, because it shows that experience has taught them to observe, that there exists a relation between the suppressed action of the volcanos, and the trembling of the ground.

# Mixed Feelings

Not surprisingly, perhaps, Darwin experienced a range of emotions, from human compassion to a scientist's excitement. And if he was shocked at the human tragedy, he was awed by his sense that he might be witnessing the working out of a geological timetable in which the existence of all humanity—let alone a lifetime—was no more than the blink of an eye.

I have not attempted to give any detailed description of the appearance of Concepcion, for I feel that it is quite impossible to convey the mingled feelings which I experienced. Several of the officers visited it before me, but their strongest language failed to give a just idea of the scene of desolation.

## Why Here?

The world's most powerful recorded earthquake shook Chile in 1960, a jarring 9.5 on the Richter Scale. The cause is essentially simple: the movement of the geotectonic plates that comprise the earth's crust as new rock forms seeps slowly yet steadily through gaps far out in the Pacific floor. Welling up from deep in the earth, this "new" rock is a good deal denser than that from which adjacent continental plates are made. So as, gradually yet inexorably, it runs up against the western side of the American landmass, it pushes downward by a process called "subduction." This in turn causes the continental plate to ride up—the entire Western Cordillera was built this way over millions of years. The process may be gradual, but that does not mean it is smooth: the continental plate resists for long periods, only to shift at intervals with violent upheavals.

It is a bitter and humiliating thing to see works, which have cost man so much time and labour, overthrown in one minute; yet compassion for the inhabitants was almost instantly banished, by the surprise in seeing a state of things produced in a moment of time, which one was accustomed to attribute to a succession of ages. In my opinion, we have scarcely beheld, since leaving England, any sight so deeply interesting.

Darwin reasoned that these phenomena were the local manifestations of a far greater system that was ordering events along this entire coast—and, for that matter, far out at sea.

Modern plate-tectonics theory was as yet unheard of, and the mechanics of mountain building a mystery, but Darwin was thinking along similar lines to the geologists of a later age. The Andes, whose heights seem so awesome, their form apparently fixed for eternity, were actually still being built, earthquake on earthquake and year on year.

# Over the Andes

*"It was like thinking on time, where the minute that now glides past is irrevocable. So it was with these stones; the ocean is their eternity, and each note of that wild music told of one more step towards their destiny."*

heaven and earth: for the Incas, however, they meant much more. Viewed from below, mountains marked points on the skyline by which they could orient themselves both physically and spiritually, for the Incas' relationship with their landscape was intimate. The Andes were awesome in their sheer scale as well: to a people for whom even a rock could resonate with sanctity, the majesty of a mighty peak can only be imagined.

For months a constant presence in the background as the *Beagle* meandered up and down the Chilean coast, the Andes had remained unexplored territory for Darwin. He had felt their mystique, though: he had hoped to attack them from their eastern side as much as a year before when FitzRoy had organized an expedition up the Santa Cruz River. The captain had been forced to abandon that venture, and Darwin had been bitterly disappointed. His few brief forays into the foothills from the Chilean side had only sharpened his curiosity. And, as we have seen, he had speculated unceasingly on the mountains' geological formation, his thinking following strikingly modern lines. The Cordillera, he felt sure, had been forced up very gradually over millions of years, in a series of what he described as "little starts"—though these were experienced by humanity as devastating earthquakes.

In 1995, at 20,700 feet on a snow-swept peak at Nevado Ampato, Peru, the frozen remains of a teenage girl were discovered. She was richly dressed, her red-and-white shawl held in place about her shoulders by silver pins, and the archeologists promptly nicknamed her Juanita. A black alpaca thread tied her long, black pony tail to her waistband; from it hung a tiny box, two miniature drinking cups and a dog or fox, all carved in wood. Beside her were some female figurines dressed much as she was, as well as offerings of coca leaves and corn. She had lain here peacefully for centuries since being sacrificed—killed by a blow to the back of the head.

Similar shrines have been found on several other Andean summits: each peak had its own *apu* or deity, it is thought. Many ancient cultures revered high mountains as meeting-places of

*Above: Machu Picchu was yet to be rediscovered when Darwin made his way over the Andes. Below: The Atacama Desert is one of the most arid spots on Earth.*

It was partly in hopes of testing these theories that Darwin now set out from Valparaíso for a journey that would take him right across the Cordillera to Mendoza in what is now northwestern Argentina. Yet Darwin was excited too, as a traveler and as a naturalist confronted with one of the most extraordinary environments on the globe. At one point on his journey he joked that he was weary of using the description "barren and sterile" in his journal, but this is a superficial view, as he was well aware.

They may look "thin" on the map, but Chile and Peru offer an extraordinary breadth of ecological variety, compressed though this is by the vertical arrangement dictated by the mountains. A flight of 120 miles from the coast of Peru over the Andes, it has been pointed out, crosses more than twenty of the world's thirty-four major ecological zones, including everything from arid desert to tropical rainforest. Darwin's journey took him farther south to end on the pampas, but the principle still applies: he traversed a rapidly changing sequence of climatic and ecological zones. Only the highest *janca*, the belt of bare rock and ice above about 15,500 feet, can really be described as barren, yet this has a profound ecological significance all its own. Though the same succession of climates may be encountered on the eastern slopes of the Cordillera, a completely different flora and fauna is to be found. The high Andes form a biological barrier as impassable as any ocean, Darwin observed. In time, perhaps, he would reflect on this division—and the variety either side of it—when he considered how the different species came into being, and how they could follow such different evolutionary paths.

# Of Terraces and Time

On March 12, 1835, Darwin returned to a familiar theme: his conviction that the Cordillera must have risen up very slowly over many millennia.

All the main valleys in the Cordillera are characterized by having, on both sides, a fringe or terrace of shingle and sand, rudely stratified, and generally of considerable thickness. ...On these fringes the roads are generally carried, for their surfaces are even, and they rise, with a very gentle slope up the valleys: hence, also, they are easily cultivated by irrigation. They may be traced up to a height of between 7,000 and 9,000 feet, where they become hidden by the irregular piles of debris. ...They precisely resemble in composition the matter which the torrents in each valley would deposit, if they were checked in their course by any cause, such as entering a lake or arm of the sea; but the torrents, instead of depositing matter, are now steadily at work wearing away both the solid rock and these alluvial deposits, along the whole line of every main valley and side valley. ...I am convinced that the shingle terraces were accumulated, during the gradual elevation of the Cordillera, by the torrents delivering...their detritus...lower and lower down as the land slowly rose.

*"So was it with these stones; the ocean is their eternity... "*

The spectacle of water running down these valleys moved Darwin to an eloquence approaching poetry:

The rivers which flow in these valleys ought rather to be called mountain-torrents. Their inclination is very great, and their water the colour of mud. The roar which the Maypu made, as it rushed over the great rounded fragments, was like that of the sea. Amidst the din of rushing waters, the noise from the stones, as they rattled one over another, was most distinctly audible even from a distance. This rattling noise, night and day, may be heard along the whole course of the torrent. The sound spoke eloquently to the geologist; the thousands of stones striking against each other that made the one dull uniform sound, were all hurrying in one direction. It was like thinking on time, where the minute that now glides past is irrevocable. So was it with these stones; the ocean is their eternity, and each note of that wild music told of one more step towards their destiny.

It is not possible for the mind to comprehend, except by a slow process, any effect which is produced by a cause repeated so often, that the multiplier itself conveys an idea, not more definite than the savage

*Above: The slopes of the Cordillera are cleft by deep valleys down which rivers rush headlong; here we see the Aconcagua Valley. Left: Santiago is seen against its mountainous backdrop in this early photograph.*

implies when he points to the hairs of his head. As often as I have seen beds of mud, sand, and shingle, accumulated to the thickness of many thousand feet, I have felt inclined to exclaim that causes, such as the present rivers and the present beaches, could never have ground down and produced such masses. But, on the other hand, when listening to the rattling noise of these torrents, and calling to mind that whole races of animals have passed away from the face of the earth, and that during this whole period, night and day, these stones have gone rattling onwards in their course, I have thought to myself, can any mountains, any continent, withstand such waste?

*Above: This track was for centuries the only route between Chile and the Argentinean region of Mendoza.*

# Breathtaking

On the morning of March 21, noted Darwin,

We arrived at the foot of the ridge, that separates the waters flowing into the Pacific and Atlantic Oceans. The road, which as yet had been good with a steady but very gradual ascent, now changed into a steep zigzag track up the great range, dividing the republics of Chile and Mendoza.

About noon we began the tedious ascent of the Peuquenes ridge, and then for the first time experienced some little difficulty in our respiration. The mules would halt every fifty yards, and after resting for a few seconds the poor willing animals started of their own accord again. The short breathing from the rarefied atmosphere is called by the Chilenos *"puna"* and they have most ridiculous notions concerning its origin. Some say "all the waters here have *puna*"; others that "where there is snow there is *puna*"—and this no doubt is true. The only sensation I experienced was a slight tightness across the head and chest, like that felt on leaving a warm room and running quickly in frosty weather. There was some imagination even in this; for upon finding fossil shells on the highest ridge, I entirely forgot the *puna* in my delight. Certainly the exertion of walking was extremely great, and the respiration became deep and laborious: I am told that in Potosi (about 13,000 feet above the sea)

strangers do not become thoroughly accustomed to the atmosphere for an entire year. The inhabitants all recommend onions for the *puna*; as this vegetable has sometimes been given in Europe for pectoral complaints, it may possibly be of real service—for my part I found nothing so good as the fossil shells!

When about half-way up we met a large party with seventy loaded mules. It was interesting to hear the wild cries of the muleteers, and to watch the long descending string of the animals; they appeared so diminutive, there being nothing but the black mountains with which they could be compared. When near the summit, the wind, as generally happens, was impetuous and extremely cold. On each side of the ridge, we had to pass over broad bands of perpetual snow, which were now soon to be covered by a fresh layer. When we reached the crest and looked backwards, a glorious view was presented. The atmosphere resplendently clear; the sky an intense blue; the profound valleys; the wild broken forms: the heaps of ruins, piled up during the lapse of ages; the bright-coloured rocks, contrasted with the quiet mountains of snow, all these together produced a scene no one could have imagined. ...I felt glad that I was alone: it was like watching a thunderstorm, or hearing in full orchestra a chorus of the *Messiah*.

## Indians with Altitude

Today geographers give the name *puna* to those frigid slopes of the Andes extending from around 13,000 to 16,500 feet, just below the permanent snowfields of the *janca* and the peaks themselves. But the word is still used for altitude sickness among the region's inhabitants. At 13,000 feet, the pressure is some 60 percent of its sea-level value, so the lungs and heart have to work far harder for their oxygen. In extreme cases, *puna* can be fatal; generally individuals adjust to altitude over time, but there are indications that the people of the Andes have evolved physiologically over the estimated 800 generations of their presence there. The peoples of this highland zone tend to be shorter and squatter than the lowland tribes, and to have appreciably greater lung capacity.

Having crossed the Peuquenes, we descended into a mountainous country, intermediate between the two main ranges, and then took up our quarters for the night. We were now in the republic of Mendoza. The elevation was probably not under 11,000 feet, and the vegetation in consequence exceedingly scanty. The root of a small scrubby plant served as fuel, but it made a miserable fire, and the wind was piercingly cold …At the place where we slept water necessarily boiled, from the diminished pressure of the atmosphere, at a lower temperature than it does in a less lofty country… Hence the potatoes, after remaining for some hours in the boiling water, were nearly as hard as ever. The pot was left on the fire all night, and next morning it was boiled again, but yet the potatoes were not cooked. I found out this, by overhearing my two companions … they had come to the simple conclusion, "that the cursed pot did not choose to boil potatoes."

**March 22nd.**—After eating our potatoless breakfast, we travelled across the intermediate tract to the foot of the Portillo range. In the middle of summer cattle are brought up here to graze; but they had now all been removed: even the greater number of the Guanacos had decamped, knowing well that if overtaken here by a snow-storm, they would be caught in a trap. We had a fine view of a mass of mountains called Tupungato, the whole clothed with unbroken snow, in the midst of which there was a blue patch, no doubt a glacier—a circumstance of rare occurrence in these mountains.

## Red Snow

On several patches of the snow, I found the *Protococcus nivalis*, or red snow, so well known from the accounts of Arctic navigators. My attention was called to it, by observing the footsteps of the mules stained a pale red, as if their hoofs had been slightly bloody. I at first thought that it was owing to dust blown from the surrounding mountains of red porphyry; for from the magnifying power of the crystals of snow, the groups of these microscopical plants appeared like coarse particles. The snow was coloured only where it had thawed very rapidly, or had been accidentally crushed. A little rubbed on paper gave it a faint rose tinge mingled with a little brick-red. I afterwards scraped some off the paper, and found that it consisted of groups of little spheres in colourless cases, each of the thousandth part of an inch in diameter.

# Continental Divide

On March 23 the party reached the summit and started making its way down the other side. The scene, as Darwin observed, was intriguingly different-yet-the-same:

The descent on the eastern side of the Cordillera is much shorter or steeper than on the Pacific side; in other words, the mountains rise more abruptly from the plains than from the alpine country of Chile. A level and brilliantly white sea of clouds was stretched out beneath our feet, shutting out the view of the equally level Pampas. We soon entered the band of clouds, and did not again emerge from it that day…I was much struck with the marked difference between the vegetation of these eastern valleys and those on the Chilian side: yet the climate, as well as the kind of soil, is nearly the same, and the difference of longitude very trifling. The same remark holds good with the quadrupeds, and in a lesser degree with the birds and insects … This fact is in perfect accordance with the geological history of the Andes; for these mountains have existed as a great barrier since the present races of animals have appeared; and therefore, unless we suppose the same species to have been created in two different places, we ought not to expect any closer similarity between the organic beings on the opposite sides of the Andes than on the opposite shores of the ocean. In both cases, we must leave out of the question those kinds which have been able to cross the barrier, whether of solid rock or salt-water.

## The Republic of Mendoza

Darwin's "Republic of Mendoza," now a province of Argentina, was the base used by José de San Martín for his attack on the power of Spain through its possessions in Bolivia and Peru. From here, in 1817, he set out with his Army of the Andes, making an epic march over the Uspallata Pass to Chile. (This, a few years later, and in less warlike circumstances, would be the route taken by Darwin for his return journey over the mountains back to Valparaíso.) In April 1818, San Martín and his men supplementing Bernardo O'Higgins's Chilean forces were able to deal decisive blows to the royalist army first at Chacabuco and then at the Battle of Maipu. Even then the heroics weren't over: in pursuit of his long-contemplated master plan, San Martín set about organizing a naval fleet for the attack on Lima. This was finally accomplished, an expedition being sent successfully in 1820: Peru too was now freed from Spanish rule.

March 24th.—Early in the morning I climbed up a mountain on one side of the valley, and enjoyed a far extended view over the Pampas. This was a spectacle to which I had always looked forward with interest, but I was disappointed: at the first glance it much resembled a distant view of the ocean, but in the northern parts many irregularities were soon distinguishable. The most striking feature consisted in the rivers, which, facing the rising sun, glittered like silver threads, till lost in the immensity of the distance…

*Left:* The Uspallata Pass, linking Argentina with Chile.

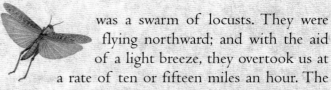

## A Bloodthirsty Bug

That night, attempting to sleep in his lodgings in Luxan, Darwin suffered a more personal insect assault, from "the *benchuca*, a species of Reduvius, the great black bug of the pampas."

It is most disgusting to feel soft wingless insects, about an inch long, crawling over one's body. Before sucking they are quite thin, but afterwards they become round and bloated with blood. ...It was curious to watch its body during the act of sucking, as in less than ten minutes it changed from being as flat as a wafer to a globular form.

But the vinchuca is host to the *Trypanosoma cruzi* parasite, the cause of Chagas' Disease, a condition that attacks the nervous system in much the same way as African Sleeping Sickness, though its worst effects may take decades to develop. It has been suggested that Darwin's collapse of September–October 1834 might have marked the onset of an infection caused by an earlier bite of which he was unaware. This would account for the nervous disorders Darwin did indeed suffer much later in life—but the evidence is inconclusive.

"The sun was exceedingly powerful, and the ride devoid of all interest," remarked Darwin of the two days' journey that took them across the "sterile" plains of Mendoza as far as Luxan. There was a river here, and that meant a welcome sight of fertile, cultivated country. But this farmland, they quickly saw, was under attack from a formidable enemy:

At first we thought that it was smoke from some great fire on the plains; but we soon found that it

was a swarm of locusts. They were flying northward; and with the aid of a light breeze, they overtook us at a rate of ten or fifteen miles an hour. The main body filled the air from a height of twenty feet, to that, as it appeared, of two or three thousand above the ground.... The sky, seen through the advanced guard, appeared like a mezzotinto engraving, but the main body was impervious to sight; they were not, however, so thick together, but that they could escape a stick waved backwards and forwards. When they alighted, they were more numerous than the leaves in the field, and the surface became reddish instead of being green: the swarm having once alighted, the individuals flew from side to side in all directions. ...The poor cottagers in vain attempted by lighting fires, by shouts, and by waving branches to avert the attack.

On March 27 they reached Mendoza itself, and things immediately started looking up:

The country was beautifully cultivated, and resembled Chile. This neighbourhood is celebrated for its fruit; and certainly nothing could appear more flourishing than the vineyards and the orchards of figs, peaches, and olives. We bought water-melons nearly twice as large as a man's head, most deliciously cool and well-flavoured, for a halfpenny apiece; and for the value of threepence, half a wheelbarrowful of peaches. ...The land, as in Chile, owes its fertility entirely to artificial irrigation; and it is really wonderful to observe how extraordinarily productive a barren traversia is thus rendered.

# "A Marvellous Story"

Two days later they turned back, this time heading north to cross the Cordillera by the Uspallata (or Aconcagua) Pass. Here, on March 30, Darwin was to make a remarkable geological discovery.

This range has nearly the same geographical position with respect to the Cordillera, which the gigantic Portillo line has, but it is of a totally different origin: it consists of various kinds of submarine lava, alternating with volcanic sandstones and other remarkable sedimentary deposits; the whole having a very close resemblance to some of the tertiary beds on the shores of the Pacific. From this resemblance I expected to find silicified wood, which is generally characteristic of those formations. I was gratified in a very extraordinary manner. In the central part of the range, at an elevation of about seven thousand feet, I observed on a bare slope some snow-white projecting columns. These were petrified trees, eleven being silicified, and from thirty to forty converted into coarsely crystallized white calcareous spar. They were abruptly broken off, the upright stumps projecting a few feet above the ground. The trunks measured from three to five feet each in circumference. They stood a little way apart from each other, but the whole formed one group. Mr Robert Brown has been kind enough to examine the wood: he says it belongs to the fir tribe, partaking of the character of the Araucarian family,

*"It required little geological practice to interpret the marvellous story which this scene at once unfolded."*

but with some curious points of affinity with the yew. The volcanic sandstone in which the trees were embedded, and from the lower part of which they must have sprung, had accumulated in successive thin layers around their trunks; and the stone yet retained the impression of the bark.

It required little geological practice to interpret the marvellous story which this scene at once unfolded; though I confess I was at first so much astonished that I could scarcely believe the plainest evidence. I saw the spot where a cluster of fine trees once waved their branches on the shores of the Atlantic, when that ocean (now driven back 700 miles) came to the foot of the Andes. I saw that they had sprung from a volcanic soil which had been raised above the level of the sea, and that subsequently this dry land, with its upright trees, had been let down into the depths of the ocean. In these depths, the formerly dry land was covered by sedimentary beds, and these again by enormous streams of submarine lava—one such mass attaining the thickness of a thousand feet; and these deluges of molten stone and aqueous deposits five times alternately had been spread out. The ocean which received such thick masses, must have been profoundly deep; but again the subterranean forces exerted themselves, and I now beheld the bed of that ocean, forming a chain of mountains more than seven thousand feet in height. Nor had those antagonistic forces been dormant, which are always at work wearing down the surface of the land; the great piles of strata had been intersected by many wide valleys, and the trees now changed into silex, were

*Opposite: "This neighbourhood is celebrated for its fruit," noted Darwin. Among its produce were watermelons (left) and olives (right). Above: Petrified wood is formed when dissolved minerals steep the cellular structures of trunks and branches in inundated or buried forests; by slow degrees the entire structure literally turns to stone.*

exposed projecting from the volcanic soil, now changed into rock, whence formerly, in a green and budding state, they had raised their lofty heads. Now, all is utterly irreclaimable and desert; even the lichen cannot adhere to the stony casts of former trees. Vast, and scarcely comprehensible as such changes must ever appear, yet they have all occurred within a period, recent when compared with the history of the Cordillera; and the Cordillera itself is

*Left: A Chilean copper mine, as seen in an early-twentieth-century photograph.*

absolutely modern as compared with many of the fossiliferous strata of Europe and America.

Sadly, souvenir hunters have long since taken the trees of Darwin's extraordinary forest away, but a roadside plaque marks the site on which it stood.

## Different Strokes...

Darwin was flatly unimpressed by the sight of the *Puente del Inca*, a natural bridge formed of stratified tufa from nearby mineral springs gradually undermined by the Cuevas River. Local legend had it that an Incan king had brought his young son to be cured at the springs but was unable to cross the torrent; his warriors had linked arms to make a human bridge over the flood, then been turned to stone. This was not the sort of story to impress Darwin, who declared the famous attraction "a miserable object.... This Inca's bridge is truly a sight not worth seeing."

# "A Peculiar Race"

After crossing the watershed again via a 12,454-foot pass, Darwin's party returned to Valparaìso. On May 4, "we proceeded to Los Hornos, ...where the principal hill was drilled with holes, like a great ants' nest."

The Chilian miners are a peculiar race of men in their habits. Living for weeks together in the most desolate spots, when they descend to the villages on feast-days, there is no excess of extravagance into which they do not run. They sometimes gain a considerable sum, and then... try how soon they can contrive to squander it. They drink excessively, buy quantities of clothes, and in a few days return penniless to their miserable abodes, there to work harder than beasts of burden. This thoughtlessness, as with sailors, is evidently the result of a similar manner of life. ...We met a party of these miners in full costume, carrying the body of one of their companions to be buried. They marched at a very quick trot, four men supporting the corpse. One set having run as hard as they could for about two hundred yards, were relieved by four others, who had previously dashed on ahead on horseback. Thus they proceeded, encouraging each other by wild cries: altogether the scene formed a most strange funeral....

## The Boys from Ballinary

On June 8, Darwin "rode up to Ballenar," a "considerable town [that] takes its name from Ballenagh in Ireland, the birthplace of the family of O'Higgins, who were presidents and generals in Chili." Ambrosio O'Higgins (c.1720–1801) had indeed been born in Ballinary, County Sligo, but, like so many of the sons of the Irish Catholic gentry of the time, had left the country. With English penal laws clamping down firmly on Catholic worship and education, and no prospect of advancement under an aggressively Protestant political order, thousands sought their fortunes as soldiers in the service of the Catholic crowns of continental Europe. Ambrosio was sent to Cadiz, Spain, into the care of an uncle, a Jesuit priest. He joined the Spanish colonial service, making his name by the enthusiasm and flair with which he put down Araucanian rebels. In 1789 he became Governor of Chile and, in 1796, Viceroy of Peru—but history had the last word in the career of his son, who became Chile's heroic liberator.

*Above: A Chilean eel seller standing with his donkey.*

Captain Head has described the wonderful load which the *Apires* [ore carriers], truly beasts of burden, carry up from the deepest mines. I confess I thought the account exaggerated: so that I was glad to take an opportunity of weighing one of the loads, which I picked out by hazard. It required considerable exertion on my part, when standing directly over it, to lift it from the ground.... The *apire* had carried this up eighty perpendicular yards... up notched poles, placed in a zigzag line up the shaft. According to the general regulation, the *apire* is not allowed to halt for breath, except the mine is six hundred feet deep. ...At this time the *apires* were bringing up the usual load twelve times in the day; that is 2,400 pounds from eighty yards deep; and they were employed in the intervals in breaking and picking ore.

## "Barren and Sterile"

"I am tired of repeating the epithets barren and sterile," wrote Darwin in his journal for June 10. The words, he pointed out, are "comparative; I have always applied them to the plains of Patagonia, which can boast of spiny bushes and some tufts of grass; and this is absolute fertility, as compared with northern Chile." But in Coquimbo, two weeks earlier, he had noted:

On the morning of the 17th it rained lightly, the first time this year, for about five hours…It was interesting to watch the effect of this trifling amount of moisture. Twelve hours afterwards the ground appeared as dry as ever; yet after an interval of ten days, all the hills were faintly tinged with green patches; the grass being sparingly scattered in hair-like fibres a full inch in length. Before this shower every part of the surface was bare as on a high road.

In fact, Darwin would discover that rain falls "about once in every two or three years… [and] without snow on the Andes, desolation extends throughout the valley."

These men, excepting from accidents, are healthy, and appear cheerful. Their bodies are not very muscular... Although with a knowledge that the labour was voluntary, it was nevertheless quite revolting to see the state in which they reached the mouth of the mine; their bodies bent forward, leaning with their arms on the steps, their legs bowed, their muscles quivering, the perspiration streaming from their faces over their breasts, their nostrils distended, the corners of their mouth forcibly drawn back, and the expulsion of their breath most laborious.... After staggering to the pile of ore, they emptied the *carpacho* [sack]; in two or three seconds recovering their breath, they wiped the sweat from their brows, and apparently quite fresh descended the mine again at a quick pace. This appears to me a wonderful instance of the amount of labour which habit, for it can be nothing else, will enable a man to endure.

# Curious Machinery

On June 22, they reached the town of Copiapó, whence, four days later, Darwin was off on another foray:

I hired a guide and eight mules to take me into the Cordillera by a different line from my last excursion. As the country was utterly desert, we took a cargo and a half of barley mixed with chopped straw. About two leagues above the town a broad valley called the *Despoblado*, or uninhabited, branches off from that one by which we had arrived. Although a valley of the grandest dimensions, and leading to a pass across the Cordillera, yet it is completely dry, excepting perhaps for a few days during some very rainy winter. The sides of the crumbling mountains were furrowed by scarcely any ravines; and the bottom of the main valley, filled with shingle, was smooth and nearly level. No considerable torrent could ever have flowed down this bed of shingle; for if it had, a great cliff-bounded channel, as in all the southern valleys, would assuredly have been formed.

*"Although a valley of the grandest dimensions...yet it is completely dry."*

**Above:** *Water is the most precious of all resources in Chile's more arid regions: here a donkey hauls a barrel through the desert.*

I feel little doubt that this valley, as well as those mentioned by travellers in Peru, were left in the state we now see them by the waves of the sea, as the land slowly rose. I observed in one place, where the *Despoblado* was joined by a ravine (which in almost any other chain would have been called a grand valley), that its bed, though composed merely of sand and gravel, was higher than that of its tributary. A mere rivulet of water, in the course of an hour, would have cut a channel for itself; but it was evident that ages had passed away, and no such rivulet had drained this great tributary. It was curious to behold the machinery, if such a term may be used, for the drainage, all, with the last trifling exception, perfect, yet without any signs of action. Every one must have remarked how mud-banks, left by the retiring tide, imitate in miniature a country with hill and dale; and here we have the original model in rock, formed as the continent rose during the secular retirement of the ocean, instead of during the ebbing and flowing of the tides. If a shower of rain falls on the mud-bank, when left dry, it deepens the already-formed shallow lines of excavation; and so it is with the rain of successive centuries on the bank of rock and soil, which we call a continent.

The mystery for Darwin was the amount of apparent archeological evidence that this district had perhaps not always been quite so *despoblado*:

I suppose the distance from the river of Copiapo to this spot was at least twenty-five or thirty English miles; in the whole space there was not a single drop of water, the country deserving the name of desert in the strictest sense. Yet about half way we passed some old Indian ruins near Punta Gorda…

I observed Indian ruins in several parts of the Cordillera: the most perfect which I saw, were the Ruinas de Tambillos, in the Uspallata Pass…Tradition says that they were used as halting-places for the Incas, when they crossed the mountains. Traces of Indian habitations have been discovered in many other parts, where it does not appear probable that they were used as mere resting-places, but yet where the land is as utterly unfit for any kind of cultivation….

In this northern part of Chile, within the Cordillera, old Indian houses are said to be especially numerous: by digging amongst the ruins, bits of woollen articles, instruments of precious metals, and heads of Indian corn, are not unfrequently discovered…. I am aware that the Peruvian Indians now frequently inhabit most lofty and bleak situa-

tions; but at Copiapo I was assured by men who had spent their lives in travelling through the Andes, that there were very many (*muchisimas*) buildings at heights so great as almost to border upon the perpetual snow, and in parts where there exist no passes, and where the land produces absolutely nothing, and what is still more extraordinary, where there is no water.

## Incan Infrastructure

The word *tambillo* comes from a hispanicization of the Quechuan *tampu*. This was the name given by the Incas to the waystations they built at intervals throughout a highway network that was one of the unsung glories of the ancient world. There were 25,000 miles of road in all, and hundreds of *tampus*, ranging from small huts to considerable storage depots. Kept fully stocked with supplies for any eventuality, they allowed the rapid movement of large military forces at a moment's notice across an empire that at its height in the sixteenth century, extended from central Chile to Ecuador.

## Nitrate City

Today a lively resort, Iquique (now in Chile, but in Darwin's day, Peru) was once a dismal place indeed, isolated even by South American standards. Its people lived like castaways, caught between the waters of the Pacific and the all-but-total aridity of the Atacama Desert. That they were prepared to live there at all was, as Darwin noted, on account of the trade in nitrates—

sodium nitrate and potassium nitrate (saltpeter). So lucrative was this traffic that in 1879 it precipitated the War of the Pacific, in which victorious Chile took the Atacama as its own. Business boomed and profits soared, though wages remained low for the many thousands of immigrant workers, toiling under nightmarish conditions in the desert, but the industry's days were in any case numbered. During World War I, German scientists succeeded in synthesizing substitutes for natural nitrates, and problems were deepened by the Great Depression of the 1930s. Today the industry endures, but on a very much smaller scale.

# On to Peru

At the beginning of July, Darwin rendezvoused with the *Beagle*, and the expedition continued northward along the coast until July 12, when it reached Iquique.

*Left and below:* Two views of Callao: an illustration of 1655 and a 1924 photograph, showing the once-peaceful bay after its transformation as Lima's seaport.

The town contains about a thousand inhabitants, and stands on a little plain of sand at the foot of a great wall of rock, 2,000 feet in height, here forming the coast. The whole is utterly desert. A light shower of rain falls only once in very many years; and the ravines consequently are filled with detritus, and the mountain-sides covered by piles of fine white sand, even to a height of a thousand feet. ...The aspect of the place was most gloomy; the little port, with its few vessels, and small group of wretched houses, seemed overwhelmed and out of all proportion with the rest of the scene. ...

I hired with difficulty, at the price of four pounds sterling, two mules and a guide to take me to the nitrate of soda works. These are at present the support of Iquique. This salt was first exported in 1830: in one year an amount in value of one hundred thousand pounds sterling, was sent to France and England. It is principally used as a manure and in the manufacture of nitric acid: owing to its deliquescent property it will not serve for gunpowder.

Having made his way inland to visit a saltpeter mine and to marvel—once again—at the bleak sterility of the coastal desert, Darwin rejoined the *Beagle*, and they took to sea once more.

**July 19th.**—We anchored in the Bay of Callao, the seaport of Lima, the capital of Peru. We stayed here six weeks but from the troubled state of public affairs, I saw very little of the country. ...No state in South America, since the declaration of independence, has suffered more from anarchy than Peru. ...

Callao is a filthy, ill-built, small seaport. The inhabitants, both here and at Lima, present every imaginable shade of mixture, between European, Negro, and Indian blood. They appear a depraved, drunken set of people. The atmosphere is loaded with foul smells.... The fortress, which withstood Lord Cochrane's long siege, has an imposing appearance. But the President, during our stay, sold the brass guns, and proceeded to dismantle parts of it. The reason assigned was, that he had not an officer to whom he could trust so important a charge. He himself had good reason for thinking so, as he had obtained the presidentship by rebelling while in charge of this same fortress. After we left South America, he paid the penalty in the usual manner, by being conquered, taken prisoner, and shot.

# "A Wretched State"

Darwin was not a whole lot more impressed by Lima than he had been by its seaport.

Lima stands on a plain in a valley, formed during the gradual retreat of the sea. ...Steep barren hills rise like islands from the plain, which is divided, by straight mud-walls, into large green fields. In these scarcely a tree grows excepting a few willows, and an occasional clump of bananas and of oranges. The city of Lima is now in a wretched state of decay: the streets are nearly unpaved; and heaps of filth are piled up in all directions, where the black gallinazos, tame as poultry, pick up bits of carrion. The houses have generally an upper story, built on account of the earthquakes, of plastered woodwork but some of the old ones, which are now used by several families, are immensely large, and would rival in suites of apartments the most magnificent in any place. Lima, the City of the Kings, must formerly have been a splendid town. The extraordinary number of churches gives it, even at the present day, a peculiar and striking character.

One day I went out with some merchants to hunt in the immediate vicinity of the city. I had an opportunity of seeing the ruins of one of the ancient Indian villages, with its mound like a natural hill in the centre. The remains of houses, enclosures, irrigating streams, and burial mounds, scattered over this plain, cannot fail to give one a high idea of the condition and number of the ancient population. When their earthenware, woollen clothes, utensils of elegant forms cut out of the hardest rocks, tools of copper, ornaments of precious stones, palaces, and hydraulic works, are considered, it is impossible not to respect the considerable advance made by them in the arts of civilization. The burial mounds, called *Huacas*, are really stupendous; although in some places they appear to be natural hills incased and modelled.

## City of the Kings

Lima has acquired a reputation as the archetypal third-world metropolis, its population swollen beyond measure or management by the influx of immigrants from an impoverished hinterland. At its antique heart, however, can still be seen traces of the colonial grandeur of the center established by Pizarro and his conquistadors in 1535 as *Ciudad de los Reyes*, the "City of the Kings." The capital of Peru since the country gained its independence in 1826, it was sacked by Chilean forces during the War of the Pacific (1879–83).

*Right: An illustration of a mummy from a huaca in Pisco, near Lima.*
*Below: An 1870s photograph of Lima.*

# Enchanted
# Galápagos

*"The day was glowing hot, and the scrambling over the rough surface and through the intricate thickets was very fatiguing; but I was well repaid by the strange Cyclopean scene. ...I met two large tortoises, ...[one] stared at me and slowly walked away; the other gave a deep hiss, and drew in its head."*

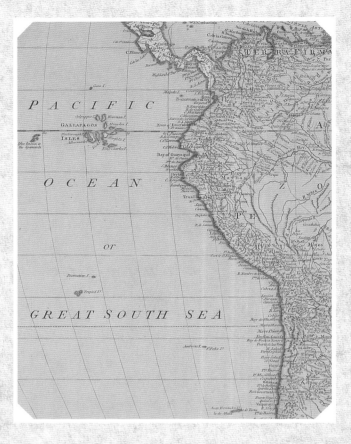

cal questions arising out of Lyell's account of the creation of the earth that he sometimes seemed less interested in living flora and fauna than in fossils.

In going to the Galápagos, Darwin had hoped to find fossils of newer provenance than any he had encountered previously on his travels. The volcanic nature of the islands was well attested. In forcing their way up from the seabed they would surely have brought to light sedimentary layers of relatively recent formation: he looked forward to studying these with Lyell's theories in mind. As it turned out, there was no sign of sediment at all: the islands seemed solid masses of lava—just about the least likely source of fossil evidence there could be.

So, a geological let-down, then, but in every other respect, surely, from the naturalist's point of view this must have been the experience of a lifetime? Well, yes and no…. Yes, in the sense that this visit was indeed ultimately to change Darwin's life (not to mention modern science); no, in the sense that Darwin was completely unaware of this at the time. Hence his impatience with the islands' "sterile" rocks and "stunted" brushwood, his complaints that even the bushes "smelt unpleasantly." Though obviously amused by the islands' famous giant tortoises, he

D arwin's visit to the Galápagos Islands is far and away the most celebrated section of his voyage: many people are unaware that the *Beagle* actually took him anywhere else. Today, tourists flock to see one of the world's great wildlife sanctuaries—and rightly so: there are giant tortoises, marine iguanas, sea-lion colonies, and more than eighty bird species in the islands, including several not seen anywhere else. They come too as pilgrims to honor one of modern science's secular saints, Charles Darwin, and the theory of evolution, which was crucially catalyzed here.

That being the case, it is odd to come to this part of Darwin's record of his travels and find how muted, for the most part, his initial reaction was. If anything, he was disappointed to arrive at the archipelago and find it so unrelentingly drab in its appearance, so unrelievedly volcanic in its mineralogical makeup. For the Darwin who did disembark here on September 17, 1805, we must keep reminding ourselves, was not the "Father of Evolution" we think we know. Though a naturalist of wide-ranging interests, for a year or so now he had been so preoccupied with those geologi-

*Above: Pinnacle Point stands out from the shore of Bartholomé Island.* ***Below:*** *Resplendent in rust and black, a marine iguana basks on a rock on Hood Island.*

We feel the more astonished at the number of their aboriginal beings, and at their confined range. Seeing every height crowned with its crater, and the boundaries of most of the lava-streams still distinct, we are led to believe that within a period geologically recent the unbroken ocean was here spread out. Hence, both in space and time, we seem to be brought somewhat near to that great fact——that mystery of mysteries—— the first appearance of new beings on this earth.

remained resistant to the charm of their "hideous-looking ...stupid, and sluggish" marine iguanas, though he did observe aspects of their behavior with apparent interest.

In reading Darwin's account with the benefit of a century and a half's hindsight, we face what amounts to a twofold challenge. First, if we are to appreciate the full distance to be covered by Darwin's intellectual voyage in the years to come, we have to try hard to see the Galápagos from an "evolution-free" perspective. Yet at the same time, if we are to see the true significance of Darwin's visit to the islands we have to recognize the ways in which, as Darwin himself had come to realize a few years later, the archipelago amounted to "a little world within itself," and hence a compelling paradigm for creation as a whole. "Considering the small size of the islands," Darwin said then:

# A Fateful Encounter

On September 7 the *Beagle* set sail from Callao, and eight days later, Darwin was within sight of the Galápagos Islands—little guessing how fateful an encounter this was eventually to prove.

This archipelago consists of ten principal islands, of which five much exceed the others in size. They are situated under the equatorial line, and between five and six hundred miles to the westward of the coast of America. The constitution of the whole is volcanic. With the exception of some ejected fragments of granite, which have been most curiously glazed and altered by the heat, every part consists of lava, or of sandstone resulting from the attrition of such materials. The higher islands (which attain an elevation of 3,000, and even 4,000 feet) generally have one or more principal craters towards their centre, and on their flanks smaller orifices. I have no exact data from which to calculate, but I do not hesitate to affirm, that there must be, in all the islands of the archipelago, at least two thousand craters....

Considering that these islands are placed directly under the equator, the climate is far from being excessively hot; this seems chiefly caused by the singularly low temperature of the surrounding water, brought here by the great southern Polar current. Excepting during one short season, very little rain falls, and even then it is irregular; but the clouds generally hang low.

Hence, whilst the lower parts of the islands are very sterile, the upper parts, at a height of a thousand feet and upwards, possess a damp climate and a tolerably luxuriant vegetation. This is especially the case on the windward sides of the islands, which first receive and condense the moisture from the atmosphere.

An unprepossessing, even unpleasant scene greeted Darwin when he first made landfall on the Galápagos:

In the morning (17th) we landed on Chatham Island, which, like the others, rises with a tame and rounded outline, broken here and there by scattered hillocks, the remains of former craters. Nothing could be less inviting than the first appearance. A broken field of black basaltic lava, thrown into the most rugged waves, and crossed by great fissures, is everywhere covered by stunted, sun-burnt brush-

*Below, left: A giant tortoise patrols the rim of the Alcedo volcano, Isabela Island.*

## The Enchanted Isles

The Galápagos Islands were discovered by accident in 1535, when Tomás de Berlanga, Bishop of Panama, was becalmed off the coast of Ecuador and dragged off course by a current. He and his crew only narrowly escaped death, and the whole experience was so overwhelmingly negative that he dismissed the islands as "worthless" and didn't even bother to claim them for the Spanish crown. They received their modern name from the saddle-shaped shells their tortoises had: the word *galápago* meant "saddle" in the Spanish of the time.

Though they became known to seafarers as *Las Encantadas*, the "Enchanted Isles," this was an ironic title referring to the way they seemed to come and go, swallowed up in the mists which frequently surrounded them.

## A Base for Buccaneers

The remoteness of the Galápagos appealed to English buccaneers, who used it as a base from which to attack Spanish shipping in the Pacific. Men like William Dampier and Ambrose Cowley may have been pirates but they were also patriots, a fact reflected in the names they gave the islands. Obeisance was thus done to the Stuart kings James and Charles, their noble counselors the Duke of Albemarle and Count Chatham, and even to a British ship, HMS *Indefatigable*. These names stuck through the eighteenth century when the islands became a stopping-off point for whalers.

At that point, however, they had officially been renamed just three years previously, following the islands' annexation by the newly-formed Republic of Ecuador. Given his British loyalties—and, of course, the *Beagle*'s old Admiralty charts—Darwin used the earlier English names.

**Above:** *As its name suggests, the lava cactus is quite at home in arid lava fields, as here on Fernandina Island.*

Soon, though, this volcanic landscape began to grow on the young Englishman, the semi-infernal scene taking an imaginative hold over him.

wood, which shows little signs of life. The dry and parched surface, being heated by the noon-day sun, gave to the air a close and sultry feeling, like that from a stove: we fancied even that the bushes smelt unpleasantly. Although I diligently tried to collect as many plants as possible, I succeeded in getting very few; and such wretched-looking little weeds would have better become an arctic than an equatorial *flora*. The brushwood appears, from a short distance, as leafless as our trees during winter; and it was some time before I discovered that not only almost every plant was now in full leaf, but that the greater number were in flower. The commonest bush is one of the *Euphorbiaceae*: an acacia and a great odd-looking cactus are the only trees which afford any shade. After the season of heavy rains, the islands are said to appear for a short time partially green....

One night I slept on shore on a part of the island, where black truncated cones were extraordinarily numerous: from one small eminence I counted sixty of them, all surmounted by craters more or less perfect. The greater number consisted merely of a ring of red scoriae or slags, cemented together: and their height above the plain of lava was not more than from fifty to a hundred feet; none had been very lately active. The entire surface of this part of the island seems to have been permeated, like a sieve, by the subterranean vapours: here and there the lava, whilst soft, has been blown into great bubbles; and in other parts, the tops of caverns similarly formed have fallen in, leaving circular pits with steep sides.

His first sight of the famous tortoises, on September 21, had Darwin reaching into ancient Greek mythology for his description of a "Cyclopean" scene—and to the Biblical Book of Genesis.

# Charles Island

*Right:* Few species have caught the imagination more than the giant tortoises of the Galápagos, though their real nature remains obstinately unfathomable.

The day was glowing hot, and the scrambling over the rough surface and through the intricate thickets, was very fatiguing; but I was well repaid by the strange Cyclopean scene. As I was walking along I met two large tortoises, each of which must have weighed at least two hundred pounds: one was eating a piece of cactus, and as I approached, it stared at me and slowly walked away; the other gave a deep hiss, and drew in its head. These huge reptiles, surrounded by the black lava, the leafless shrubs, and large cacti, seemed to my fancy like some antediluvian animals. The few dull-coloured birds cared no more for me than they did for the great tortoises.

On September 23, noted Darwin, "the *Beagle* proceeded to Charles Island."

This archipelago has long been frequented, first by the bucaniers, and latterly by whalers, but it is only within the last six years, that a small colony has been established here. The inhabitants are between two and three hundred in number; they are nearly all people of colour, who have been banished for political crimes from the Republic of the Equator, of which Quito is the capital. The settlement is placed about four and a half miles inland, and at a height probably of a thousand feet. In the first part of the road we passed through leafless thickets, as in Chatham Island. Higher up, the woods gradually became greener; and as soon as we crossed the ridge of the island, we were cooled by a fine southerly

## A Mischievous Remark?

Was there a note of mischief—perhaps unconscious—in that remark about the "antediluvian" appearance of the giant tortoises, given the controversy by this time surrounding the whole question of Noah's Flood? The "Uniformitarianism" of Darwin's mentor, Charles Lyell, was clear in its rejection of the Biblical chronology for creation. It was dismissive too of the claim by some "catastrophists" that a single great inundation might account for all the world's sedimentary rocks, and the fossils embedded in them—supposedly the relics of that earlier, condemned creation described in Genesis.

*Above: Almost indistinguishable from the black lava upon which it clambers, a marine iguana is seen on Fernandina Island. Opposite, below: Flamingos make their stately way across the waters of a salt lagoon on Floreana (Charles Island).*

## Place of Peace

The Isla Floreana, as Charles Island had officially been known since the Galápagos' annexation by the newly formed Republic of Ecuador, was, as Darwin noted, the site of a penal colony. Like many of his generation of Latin American revolutionaries, its founder, General José de Villamil, was an idealist, and he had dreamt of building a utopia here. At this *Asilo de Paz* ("Refuge of Peace"), as he called his colony, enemies of the Republic would come to see the folly of their ways, and hardened criminals be reformed through communitarian sharing and hard work. Not for the first time or the last, high ideals foundered on the hard rock of human nature. A disillusioned Villamil quit his colony just two years after Darwin's visit.

breeze, and our sight refreshed by a green and thriving vegetation…. The houses are irregularly scattered over a flat space of ground, which is cultivated with sweet potatoes and bananas. It will not easily be imagined how pleasant the sight of black mud was to us, after having been so long, accustomed to the parched soil of Peru and northern Chile. The inhabitants, although complaining of poverty, obtain, without much trouble, the means of subsistence. In the woods there are many wild pigs and goats; but the staple article of animal food is supplied by the tortoises.

# Of Lava, Lizards and Tortoises

**September 29th.**—We doubled the south-west extremity of Albemarle Island, and the next day were nearly becalmed between it and Narborough Island. Both are covered with immense deluges of black naked lava, which have flowed either over the rims of the great caldrons, like pitch over the rim of a pot in which it has been boiled, or have burst forth from smaller orifices on the flanks; in their descent they have spread over miles of the sea coast. On both of these islands, eruptions are known to have taken place; and in Albemarle, we saw a small jet of smoke curling from the summit of one of the great craters. In the evening we anchored in Bank's Cove, in Albemarle Island. The next morning I went out walking. To the south of the broken tuff-crater in which the *Beagle* was anchored ['tuff' is stone formed from solidified volcanic ash], there was another beautifully symmetrical one of an elliptic form; its longer axis was a little less than a mile, and its depth about 500 feet. At its bottom there was a shallow lake, in the middle of which a tiny crater formed an islet. The day was overpoweringly hot, and the lake looked clear and blue: I hurried down the cindery slope, and, choked with dust, eagerly tasted the water—but, to my sorrow, I found it salt as brine.

The rocks on the coast abounded with great black lizards, between three and four feet long; and on the hills, an ugly yellowish-brown species was equally common. We saw many of this latter kind, some clumsily running out of the way, and others shuffling into their burrows. I shall presently describe in more detail the habits of both these reptiles. The whole of this northern part of Albemarle Island is miserably sterile.

**October 8th.**—We arrived at James Island: this island, as well as Charles Island, were long since thus named after our kings of the Stuart line. Mr Bynoe, myself, and our servants were left here for a week, with provisions and a tent, whilst the *Beagle* went for water. We found here a party of Spaniards, who had

*Above: The crews of visiting ships (including the Beagle) butchered the giant tortoises on so large a scale that their survival was eventually threatened. This photograph was taken in 1903. Below: The sun sets slowly over Albemarle Island.*

*"The breast-plate roasted …with the flesh on it, is very good; and the young tortoises make excellent soup."*

been sent from Charles Island to dry fish, and to salt tortoise-meat. About six miles inland, and at the height of nearly 2,000 feet, a hovel had been built in which two men lived, who were employed in catching tortoises, whilst the others were fishing on the coast. I paid this party two visits, and slept there one night…. While staying in this upper region, we lived entirely upon tortoise-meat: the breast-plate roasted (as the Gauchos do *carne con cuero* ["meat with the skin"]), with the flesh on it, is very good; and the young tortoises make excellent soup; but otherwise the meat to my taste is indifferent.

I will first describe the habits of the tortoise (*Testudo nigra*, formerly called *Indica*), which has been so frequently alluded to. These animals are found, I believe, on all the islands of the archipelago; certainly on the greater number. They frequent in preference the high damp parts, but they likewise live in the lower and arid districts. I have already shown, from the numbers which have been caught in a single day, how very numerous they must be. Some grow to an immense size: Mr. Lawson, an Englishman, and vice-governor of the colony, told us that he had seen several so large, that it required six or eight men to lift them from the ground; and that

## A "World Within Itself"

Some sense of the significance of this trip was beginning to sink in by the time Darwin prepared the second edition of *The Voyage of the Beagle* in 1845 and added this thought to his earlier account:

The natural history of these islands is eminently curious, and well deserves attention. Most of the organic productions are aboriginal creations, found nowhere else; there is even a difference between the inhabitants of the different islands; yet all show a marked relationship with those of America, though separated from that continent by an open space of ocean, between 500 and 600 miles in width. The archipelago is a little world within itself, or rather a satellite attached to America, whence it has derived a few stray colonists, and has received the general character of its indigenous productions. Considering the small size of the islands, we feel the more astonished at the number of their aboriginal beings, and at their confined range. Seeing every height crowned with its crater, and the boundaries of most of the lava-streams still distinct, we are led to believe that within a period geologically recent the unbroken ocean was here spread out. Hence, both in space and time, we seem to be brought somewhat near to that great fact—that mystery of mysteries—the first appearance of new beings on this earth.

*Above:* Giant tortoises and domestic cattle graze side by side on Santa Cruz.

cactus. Those which frequent the higher and damp regions, eat the leaves of various trees, a kind of berry (called guayavita) which is acid and austere, and likewise a pale green filamentous lichen (*Usnera plicata*), that hangs from the boughs of the trees.

The tortoise is very fond of water, drinking large quantities, and wallowing in the mud. The larger islands alone possess springs, and these are always situated towards the central parts, and at a considerable height. The tortoises, therefore, which frequent the lower districts, when thirsty, are obliged to travel from a long distance. Hence broad and well-beaten paths branch off in every direction from the wells down to the sea-coast; and the Spaniards by following them up, first discovered the watering-places. When I landed at Chatham Island, I could not imagine what animal travelled so methodically along well-chosen tracks. Near the springs it was a curious spectacle to behold many of these huge creatures, one set eagerly travelling onwards with outstretched necks, and another set returning, after having drunk their fill. When the tortoise arrives at the spring, quite regardless of any spectator, he buries his head in the water above his eyes, and greedily swallows great mouthfuls, at the rate of about ten in a minute. The inhabitants say each animal stays three or four days in the neighbourhood of the water, and then returns to the lower country; but they differed respecting the frequency of these visits. The animal probably regulates them

some had afforded as much as two hundred pounds of meat. The old males are the largest, the females rarely growing to so great a size: the male can readily be distinguished from the female by the greater length of its tail. The tortoises which live on those islands where there is no water, or in the lower and arid parts of the others, feed chiefly on the succulent

# Boring Birds

Darwin found no less than twenty-six distinct species of land birds on his visit to the Galápagos Islands, the overwhelming majority being, he was subsequently advised, "undescribed kinds, which inhabit this archipelago, and no other part of the world." But if they were rare, they didn't otherwise come up to the Englishman's exacting standards. "The general character of the plumage of these birds is extremely plain" and with "little beauty," he remarked critically; adding, "None of the birds are brilliantly coloured, as might have been expected in an equitorial district."

There is something in what he says, perhaps, when it comes to the Galápagos dove (*Zenaida galapagoensis*), its appeal definitely subtle rather than striking. Something of the same might be said of the Galápagos mockingbird (*Nesomimus parvulus*). But as for the buzzard—what is now known as the Galápagos hawk (*Buteo galapagoensis*)—just how colorful did he want a buzzard to be? His comments seem completely unfair as far as the Galápagos heron (*Butorides sundevalli*) is concerned, or the Galápagos rail (*Laterallis spilonotus*). Described by Darwin simply as "a water-rail which lives near the summits of the mountains," this is, by any standards, a handsome bird. Just how attractive some of the Galápagos' bird species are can be seen in the portraits below.

| | | | | |
|---|---|---|---|---|
| *Red-billed tropic bird* | *Red-footed booby* | *Short-eared owl* | *Great blue heron* | *Lava heron* |
| *Mockingbird* | *Frigate bird* | *Swallow-tailed gull* | *Flightless cormorants* | *Vermilion flycatcher* |
| *Galápagos hawk* | *Waved albatross* | *Blue-footed booby* | *Oystercatcher* | *Masked booby* |

## Finch Phenomenon

If the Galápagos Islands initially underwhelmed Darwin—no luxuriant tropical paradise with swaying palms and gorgeous parakeets, but a scattering of rocks with only the scrubbiest of vegetation—the famous finches that would one day prove his springboard to scientific breakthrough also seemed to him irredeemably drab. In fact, he had so little idea of their significance that they have only the briefest cameo role in his original journal: he merely mentioned that "doves and finches swarmed" around the edge of a little pool. It was only after John Gould, an avian expert back in London, had systematically ordered Darwin's collection of specimens in 1837 that their potential importance even began to dawn upon him.

The point, put very simply, was that thirteen different species were identified, all strikingly similar apart from the form and function of their beaks. These ranged from being thick and stubby, ideal for crushing buds and for cracking open seeds, to long and slender, best suited to hunting out insects from tiny crevices. The different species were distributed across the archipelago, each apparently equipped to thrive under the particular conditions of the island on which it lived. This opened up the possibility that, separated out across the far-flung island group, populations of what had once been a single species had gone their separate evolutionary ways. Over time, it seemed, they had developed in response to the demands made by their different habitats, growing apart by a process of what would later be called "adaptive radiation."

## The One that Got Away

Darwin might have liked the Galápagos a little better if he had met the islands' resident penguin population, but this delight appears to have been denied him. Numbers of Galápagos penguins have never been large: their range is localized even within the archipelago, where they favor the remotest coasts; today, indeed, this is an endangered species.

A lively and engaging creature, the Galápagos penguin has the distinction of being the only penguin species to be found in the northern hemisphere. Its presence here seems to be explained by the powerful northward sweep of the coldwater Peru current, bringing with it rich fish stocks—and apparently, at some point in the distant past, a group of penguins. It has had to adapt to its new environment, for while it is spared the bitter cold of the Antarctic, it must instead contend with the searing equatorial sun. Characteristically, Galápagos penguins are seen standing hunched forward to shade the bare-skinned webs of their feet from the punishing rays; they pant to rid their bodies of excess heat.

according to the nature of the food on which it has lived. It is, however, certain, that tortoises can subsist even on these islands where there is no other water than what falls during a few rainy days in the year.

The tortoises, when purposely moving towards any point, travel by night and day, and arrive at their journey's end much sooner than would be expected. The inhabitants, from observing marked individuals, consider that they travel a distance of about eight miles in two or three days. One large tortoise, which I watched, walked at the rate of sixty yards in ten minutes, that is 360 yards in the hour, or four miles a day—allowing a little time for it to eat on the road. …They were at this time (October) laying their eggs. The female, where the soil is sandy, deposits them together, and covers them up with sand; but where the ground is rocky she drops them indiscriminately in any hole: Mr Bynoe found seven placed in a fissure. The egg is white and spherical; one which I measured was seven inches and three-eighths in circumference, and therefore larger than a hen's egg. The young tortoises, as soon as they are hatched, fall a prey in great numbers to the carrion-feeding buzzard. The old ones seem generally to die from accidents, as from falling down precipices: at least, several of the inhabitants told me, that they never found one dead without some evident cause.

The inhabitants believe that these animals are absolutely deaf; certainly they do not overhear a person walking close behind them. I was always amused when overtaking one of these great monsters, as it was quietly pacing along, to see how suddenly, the instant I passed, it would draw in its head and legs, and uttering a deep hiss fall to the ground with a heavy sound, as if struck dead. I frequently got on

their backs, and then giving a few raps on the hinder part of their shells, they would rise up and walk away—but I found it very difficult to keep my balance. …

There can be little doubt that this tortoise is an aboriginal inhabitant of the Galapagos; for it is found on all, or nearly all, the islands, even on some of the smaller ones where there is no water; had it been an imported species, this would hardly have been the case in a group which has been so little frequented.

*Above: A baby tortoise hatches from its egg, as recorded in an early illustration. **Opposite**: A sea lion sprawls in the sunshine, ashore on Seymore Island.*

## A Walking Water Supply

"I believe it is well ascertained," wrote Darwin:

That the bladder of the frog acts as a reservoir for the moisture necessary to its existence: such seems to be the case with the tortoise. For some time after a visit to the springs, their urinary bladders are distended with fluid, which is said gradually to decrease in volume, and to become less pure. The inhabitants, when walking in the lower district, and overcome with thirst, often take advantage of this circumstance, and drink the contents of the bladder if full: in one I saw killed, the fluid was quite limpid, and had only a very slightly bitter taste.

Darwin has been borne out in his conjecture. So large does the giant tortoise's bladder become, indeed, that many nineteenth-century naturalists assumed it was a separate, specially designated sac for storing water. Modern research confirms, however, that in arid conditions urine is retained for long periods after drinking for reabsorption by the body, to be finally released when rain allows the supply to be refreshed.

## An Opportunity Missed?

The man running the prison on Charles Island at the time of the *Beagle*'s visit was, as Darwin reported, an Englishman working for the Ecuadorian government. Nicholas Lawson appears to have been friendly and very helpful and Darwin clearly talked with him at some length. He paid less heed than he might have done, however, to one chance remark of the vice-governor's, that he could tell which island an individual tortoise came from by the shape of its shell. Did Darwin dismiss this claim as an empty brag, or as unscientific island myth, or did he simply have his mind on other matters (we have to keep reminding ourselves that evolution really wasn't much in Darwin's thoughts at this stage of his career)? There is no way of knowing now, though had he but seen it, Lawson was offering him a crucial insight on a plate: British micropaleontologist Paul Chambers points to this as a "eureka moment" missed. In time, however, his finches would lead him to the same conclusions by another route, and then Lawson's remark would come back to him, and confirm him in his conviction.

# The Marine Iguana

Darwin next turned his attention to the islands' other distinguished reptiles, its land and marine iguanas: he would find these a good deal less engaging. "The two species agree pretty closely in general appearance," as he explains, "but one is aquatic and the other terrestrial in its habits…"

First for the aquatic kind (*Amblyrhyncus cristatus*). This lizard is extremely common on all the islands throughout the achipelago. It lives exclusively on the rocky sea-beaches, and is never found—at least

## "Imps of Darkness"

Today the marine iguanas of the Galápagos are a much-loved tourist attraction, but early visitors were unanimous on their repulsiveness. The "officers and gentlemen" who ten years previously had come this way with Captain Lord Byron on the HMS *Blonde* during a voyage to the Sandwich Islands were agreed that these were quite "the ugliest living creatures we ever beheld."

They are like the alligator, but with a more hideous head, and of a soot-black colour, and sat on the black lava rocks like so many imps of darkness.

It was long assumed that Captain Byron, as cousin and successor of the famous British Romantic poet, was the obvious author for the account of the expedition from which this quote comes. The textual evidence suggests otherwise, though—and in any case, even if it were, it would reflect a sad falling-off in the family's poetic fortunes. Neatly expressed as it is, the image betrays a crashingly conventional view of an outcast, ill-begotten animal with whom the author of *Manfred* and *Cain* would surely have found himself in impassioned sympathy.

*Above:* "Implike" indeed, marine iguanas soak up the sun crowded together on the rocks of San Fernandina.

I never saw one—even ten yards inshore. It is a hideous-looking creature, of a dirty black colour, stupid, and sluggish in its movements. The usual length of a full-grown one is about a yard, but there are some even four feet long; I have seen a large one which weighed twenty pounds. On the island of Albemarle they seem to grow to a greater size than on any other. …When in the water this lizard swims with perfect ease and quickness, by a serpentine movement of its body and flattened tail—the legs, during this time, being motionless and closely collapsed on its sides. A seaman on board sank one, with a heavy weight attached to it, thinking thus to kill it directly; but when, an hour afterwards, he drew up the line, the lizard was quite active. Their limbs and strong claws are admirably adapted for crawling over the rugged and fissured masses of lava, which everywhere form the coast. In such situations, a group of six or seven of these hideous reptiles may oftentimes be seen on the black rocks, a few feet above the surf, basking in the sun with outstretched legs.

*"It is a hideous-looking creature, of a dirty black colour, stupid, and sluggish in its movements."*

I opened the stomachs of several, and found them largely distended with minced sea-weed, of that kind which grows in thin foliaceous expansions of a bright green or a dull red colour. I do not recollect having observed this sea-weed in any quantity on the tidal rocks; and I have reason to believe it grows at the bottom of the sea, at some little distance from the coast.

The nature of this lizard's food, as well as the structure of its tail, and the certain fact of its having been seen voluntarily swimming out at sea, absolutely prove its aquatic habits; yet there is in this respect one strange anomaly, namely, that when frightened it will not enter the water. Hence it is easy to drive these lizards down to any little point overhanging the sea, where they will sooner allow a person to catch hold of their tails than jump into the water. They do not seem to have any notion of biting; but when much frightened they squirt a drop of fluid from each nostril. One day I carried one to a deep pool left by the retiring tide, and threw it in several times as far as I was able. It invariably returned in a direct line to the spot where I stood. It swam near the bottom, with a very graceful and rapid movement, and occasionally aided itself over the uneven ground with its feet. As soon as it arrived near the edge, but still being under water, it tried to conceal itself in the tufts of sea-weed, or it entered some crevice. As soon as it thought the danger was past, it crawled out on the dry rocks, and shuffled away as quickly as it could. I several times caught this same lizard, by driving it down to a point, and though possessed of such perfect powers of diving and swimming, nothing would induce it to enter the water; and so often as I threw it in, it returned in the manner above described. Perhaps this singular piece of apparent stupidity may be accounted for by the circumstance, that this reptile has no enemy whatever on shore, whereas at sea it must often fall a prey to the numerous sharks. Hence, probably, urged by a fixed and hereditary instinct that the shore is its place of safety, whatever the emergency may be, it there takes refuge…

*"…this reptile has no enemy whatever on shore, whereas at sea it must often fall a prey to the numerous sharks."*

The "drop of fluid" that spurts from each "nostril" is actually the salt removed from seawater swallowed in the course of feeding and then secreted from special glands situated between the eyes. It is indeed ejected abruptly in times of stress, and often collects to form a white cap atop the iguana's black head, underlining its unprepossessing image in the eyes of many beholders.

*Below: "When not frightened, they slowly crawl along with their tails and bellies dragging on the ground." A land iguana on Santa Cruz Island.*

# The Iguana Ashore

"We will now turn to the terrestrial species," Darwin continued, giving it the Latin name *Amblyrhyncus subcristatus*, though later biologists would call it *Conolophus subcristatus*. This is marked out from its marine cousin in part by its possession of a rounded tail, rather than a flattened one for swimming. This feature was at first missed, though, as Darwin explains, because the specimen first sent home was "badly stuffed."

This species, differently from the last, is confined to the central part of the archipelago…. It would appear as if it had been created in the centre of the archipelago, and thence had been dispersed only to a certain distance.

In the central islands they inhabit both the higher and damp, as well as the lower and sterile, parts; but in the latter they are much the most numerous. I cannot give a more forcible proof of their numbers, than by stating that when we were left at James Island, we could not for some time find a spot free from their burrows on which to pitch our tent. These lizards, like their brothers the sea-kind, are ugly animals; and from their low facial angle have a singularly stupid appearance. In size perhaps they are a little inferior to the latter, but several of them weighed between ten and fifteen pounds each. In their movements they are lazy and half torpid. When not frightened, they slowly crawl along with their tails and bellies dragging on the ground. They often stop, and doze for a minute with closed eyes, and hind legs spread out on the parched soil.

They inhabit burrows, which they sometimes excavate between fragments of lava, but more generally on level patches of the soft volcanic sandstone. The holes do not appear to be very deep, and they enter the ground at a small angle; so that when walking over these lizard-warrens, the soil is constantly giving way, much to the annoyance of the tired walker. This animal, when making its burrow,

*Above: "They consume much of the succulent cactus." A land iguana eats* Opuntia, *South Plaza Island.*

alternately works the opposite sides of its body. One front leg for a short time scratches up the soil, and throws it towards the hind foot, which is well placed so as to heave it beyond the mouth of the hole. This side of the body being tired, the other takes up the task, and so on alternately. I watched one for a long time, till half its body was buried; I then walked up and pulled it by the tail, at this it was greatly astonished, and soon shuffled up to see what was the matter; and then stared me in the face, as much as to say, "What made you pull my tail?"

They feed by day, and do not wander far from their burrows; if frightened, they rush to them with a most awkward gait. Except when running down hill, they cannot move very fast, apparently from the lateral position of their legs. They are not at all timorous: when attentively watching any one, they curl their tails, and raising themselves on their front legs, nod their heads vertically, with a quick movement, and try to look very fierce; but in reality they are not at all so: if one just stamps on the ground, down go their tails, and off

*"If two are placed on the ground and held together, they will fight, and bite each other till blood is drawn"*

they shuffle as quickly as they can. I have frequently observed small fly-eating lizards, when watching anything, nod their heads in precisely the same manner; but I do not at all know for what purpose. If this *Amblyrhynchus* is held and plagued with a stick, it will bite it very severely; but I caught many by the tail, and they never tried to bite me. If two are placed on the ground and held together, they will fight, and bite each other till blood is drawn.

The individuals (and they are the greater number) which inhabit the lower country, can scarcely taste a drop of water throughout the year; but they consume much of the succulent cactus, the branches of which are occasionally broken off by the wind. I several times threw a piece to two or three of them when together; and it was amusing enough to see them trying to seize and carry it away in their mouths, like so many hungry dogs with a bone. They eat very deliberately, but do not chew their food. The little birds are aware how harmless these creatures are: I have seen one of the thick-billed finches picking at one end of a piece of cactus (which is in request among all the animals of the lower region), whilst a lizard was eating at the other end; and afterwards the little bird with the utmost indifference hopped on the back of the reptile.

# A State of Innocence

Any fantasies the naturalist might have been nurturing that the Galápagos constituted some sort of earthly paradise had been promptly banished by the sight of the islands' "dry and parched surface" and "wretched-looking little weeds." In one respect, though, the archipelago was Edenlike: its birds in particular seemed to inhabit a state of innocence, in which they had not yet learned to fear human beings. The fact intrigued Darwin, as well it might—after all, as he himself observed, it was not as though he and his companions were the first visitors to the islands.

So, "I will conclude my description of the natural history of these islands by giving an account of the extreme tameness of the birds."

This disposition is common to all the terrestrial species; namely, to the mocking-thrushes, the finches, wrens, tyrant-flycatchers, the dove, and carrion-buzzard. All of them are often approached sufficiently near to be killed with a switch, and sometimes, as I myself tried, with a cap or hat. A gun is here almost superfluous; for with the muzzle I pushed a hawk off the branch of a tree. One day, whilst lying down, a mocking-thrush alighted on the edge of a pitcher, made of the shell of a tortoise, which I held in my hand, and began very quietly to sip the water; it allowed me to lift it from the ground whilst seated on the vessel: I often tried, and very nearly succeeded, in catching these birds by their legs. Formerly the birds appear to have been even tamer than at present. ...It is surprising that they have not become wilder; for these islands during the last hundred and fifty years have been frequently visited by bucaniers and whalers; and the sailors, wandering through the wood in search of tortoises, always take cruel delight in knocking down the little birds. These birds, although now still more persecuted, do not readily become wild. In Charles Island, which had then been colonized about six years, I saw a boy sitting by a well with a switch in his hand, with which he killed the doves and finches as they came to drink. He had already procured a little heap of them for his dinner, and he said that he had constantly been in the habit of waiting by this well for the same purpose. It would appear that the birds of this archipelago, not having as yet learnt that man is a more dangerous animal than the tortoise or the *Amblyrhynchus*, disregard him, in the same manner as in England shy birds, such as magpies, disregard the cows and horses grazing in our fields.

*Left:* "The upper parts...possess a damp climate and a tolerably luxuriant vegetation." "Tolerable" trees clothe a hillside on Floreana Island. *Above:* A Blue-footed booby scratches its head on Hood Island. *Opposite:* Another day approaches its end on Bartholomé Island.

# Oceania

*"The Tahitians, with their naked, tattooed bodies, their heads ornamented with flowers, …seen in the dark shade of these groves, would have formed a fine picture of man inhabiting some primeval land."*

The *Beagle* now steered a course across the deep Pacific into that region known as the South Seas, whose tiny islands loomed so large in the Western imagination. The discoveries of French navigator Louis Antoine Bougainville, who in the late 1760s explored Samoa, the Solomon Islands and the New Hebrides, were still fresh in the European mind; those of Captain James Cook were even more so for an Englishman like Darwin. Cook had made three epic expeditions from 1768 onward, his voyages taking him as far afield as the Southern Ocean and Alaska, but it was his travels in the tropics that had inspired an age.

Through his reports English-speaking readers had learned of places like Tahiti, Tonga and the New Hebrides that seemed not so much geographical locations as answers to a prayer. That there might be a serpent in this paradise became clear with tidings of cannibalism among its native tribes, and Captain Cook's own death in a skirmish in 1780. That the white man

*Previous pages: Coconut palms sway above a coral beach lapped by the gentle waves of an azure ocean: the archetypal tropical paradise, as exemplified by Napuka, in the Tuamotu group.* **Above:** *This antique map is centered on the South Sea Islands.*

himself could be corrupted became evident in 1789, when the crew of HMS *Bounty* mutinied near the Tonga Islands. It was an ugly affair: their captain and loyal shipmates only survived by great good fortune, and by the remarkable feat of seamanship that saw them sailing their open boat more than 3,600 miles to safety.

But the instinct that had motivated the mutineers to stay in Polynesia was readily understood—such a paradise once found should not be surrendered. That feeling struck a chord with the growing number who felt themselves marooned in their European homeland, out of place amid the discontents of their own society. There were many who, in the words of the great romantic poet and rebel Lord Byron (1829), "...languished for some sunny isle/Where summer years and summer women smile." They yearned not only for year-round sunshine and sexual liberation (though that certainly sounded good) but a utopia underwritten by a bounteous nature:

*The gushing fruits that nature gave untilled;*
*The wood without a path—but where they willed;*
*The field o'er which promiscuous Plenty poured*
*Her horn; the equal land without a lord;...*
*Where Nature owns a nation as her child,*
*Exulting in the enjoyment of the wild;*
*Their shells, their fruits, the only wealth they know,*
*Their unexploring navy, the canoe...*

Even now, almost two centuries later, it is a vision to stir the soul, though obviously a romantic idealization. That it could so easily be projected on to the South Seas just demonstrates how remote the region continued to be; how unreal its inhabitants still were for Westerners.

For these were actual islands, not some poetic fantasy; these "savages" had societies, histories and traditions of their own. Much as it may have pleased Byron to think of a people at peace with itself and content not to strive for greater things or greener pastures, the Polynesians' canoes had been anything but "unexploring." Long before Bougainville and Cook, around

*Above: All the delicate beauty of the tropics is to be found embodied in these exotic frangipani blossoms. Below: Boats bob just offshore in this drawing of Tahiti, 1911.*

1500 B.C., their Lapita forebears had set out from a homeland somewhere on the Southeast Asian coast. Taking a series of gigantic leaps into a geographic unknown, they had made their way south and eastward from island to island over many generations. Eventually they had made it all the way across the Pacific to New Zealand, where the ancestors of the Maoris had arrived around A.D. 1000.

So the South Sea Islanders had come a long way before they were "discovered" by the outside world. Their apparent "innocence" made that hard for Westerners to understand. Armed as they were with so many preconceptions, Europeans found it hard to see Pacific realities clearly: Darwin was no exception, though he did try.

# Tahiti

"The survey of the Galapagos Archipelago being concluded," wrote Darwin in his journal for October 20, "we steered towards Tahiti and commenced our long passage of 3,200 miles." Just under a month later, on November 15, they reached Tahiti.

At daylight, Tahiti, an island which must for ever remain classical to the voyager in the South Sea, was in view. At a distance the appearance was not attractive. The luxuriant vegetation of the lower part could not yet be seen, and as the clouds rolled past, the wildest and most precipitous peaks showed themselves towards the centre of the island. As soon as we anchored in Matavai Bay, we were surrounded by canoes. This was our Sunday, but the Monday of Tahiti: if the case had been reversed, we should not have received a single visit; for the injunction not to launch a canoe on the sabbath is rigidly obeyed. After dinner we landed to enjoy all the delights produced by the first impressions of a new country, and that country the charming Tahiti. A crowd of men, women, and children, was collected on the memorable Point Venus, ready to receive us with laughing, merry faces.

The land capable of cultivation, is scarcely in any part more than a fringe of low alluvial soil, accumulated round the base of the mountains, and protected from the waves of the sea by a coral reef, which encircles the entire line of coast. Within the reef there is an expanse of smooth water, like that of a lake, where the canoes of the natives can ply with safety and where ships anchor. The low land which comes down to the beach of coral-sand, is covered by the most beautiful productions of the intertropical regions. In the midst of bananas, orange, cocoa-nut, and bread-fruit trees, spots are cleared where yams, sweet potatoes, and sugar-cane, and pine-apples are cultivated. Even the brush-wood is an imported fruit-tree, namely, the guava, which from its abundance has become as noxious as a weed. In Brazil I have often admired the varied beauty of the bananas, palms, and orange-trees contrasted together; and here we also

## A Dangerous Archipelago

More than seventy scattered atolls make up what is now called the Tuamotu Archipelago, since 1996 an autonomous territory of French Polynesia. It was long referred to as the Dangerous Archipelago for the obvious reason that its low-lying coral reefs and islets were a major hazard for seafarers across several hundred square miles of the South Pacific. The first European navigator to come this way was Magellan, who in 1521 discovered the atoll of Puka Puka; the chart was only completed by Captain FitzRoy on this very voyage. His addition of Kauehi and Taiaro brought the total number of islands to seventy-eight. Despite visits by successive European expeditions through the eighteenth century and the presence of competing Catholic and Protestant missionaries from France and Britain through the nineteenth, the islands' remoteness have remained their defining characteristic. The Tahitian name "Tuamotu" means "distant islands," and it was that same sense of a place out of sight and out of mind that prompted France to use the archipelago for a series of nuclear tests in the 1960s.

**Above:** *The sun sets over Mangareva, an island of the "Dangerous Archipelago," or Tuamotu group.*
**Right:** *Tahitian men sport crowns of foliage in this nineteenth-century engraving.*

have the bread-fruit, conspicuous from its large, glossy, and deeply digitated leaf.

I was pleased with nothing so much as with the inhabitants. There is a mildness in the expression of their countenances which at once banishes the idea of a savage; and intelligence which shows that they are advancing in civilization. Most of the men are tattooed, and the ornaments follow the curvature of the body so gracefully, that they have a very elegant effect. One common pattern…is somewhat like the crown of a palm-tree. It springs from the central line of the back, and gracefully curls round both sides. The simile may be a fanciful one, but I thought the body of a man thus ornamented was like the trunk of a noble tree embraced by a delicate creeper. …

## Breadfruit

Nothing better illustrates the luxurious ease of island life in the South Seas better than the fact that bread grows on trees—or at least that breadfruit (*Artocarpus altilis*) does, the next best thing. Within a tough, melonlike rind are contained seeds surrounded by a generous mass of starchy, fibrous flesh, the texture of bread. In the heat and moisture of its native tropics, the tree grows quickly and produces in abundance: a large fruit may be a foot across and weigh as much as ten pounds in all.

*Below: An orange twilight tinges the sky above Moorea, a close neighbor to Tahiti.* **Opposite:** *Palms crowd to the shoreline all around Tahiti.*

The women are tattooed in the same manner as the men, and very commonly on their fingers. One unbecoming fashion is now almost universal: namely, shaving the hair from the upper part of the head, in a circular form, so as to leave only an outer ring. The missionaries have tried to persuade the people to change this habit; but it is the fashion, and that is a sufficient answer at Tahiti, as well as at Paris.

# A Tropical Paradise

"On the morning of the 17th," wrote Darwin,

I went on shore, and ascended the nearest slope to a height of between two and three thousand feet. The outer mountains are smooth and conical, but steep; and the old volcanic rocks, of which they are formed, have been cut through by many profound ravines, diverging from the central broken parts of the island to the coast. Having crossed the narrow low girt of inhabited and fertile land, I followed a smooth steep ridge between two of the deep ravines. The vegetation was singular, consisting almost exclusively of small dwarf ferns, mingled higher up, with coarse grass; it was not very dissimilar from that on some of the Welsh hills, and this so close above the orchard of tropical plants on the coast was very surprising. At the highest point, which I reached, trees again appeared. When in the evening I descended from the mountain,

a man, whom I had pleased with a trifling gift, met me, bringing with him hot roasted bananas, a pine-apple, and cocoa-nuts. After walking under a burning sun, I do not know anything more delicious than the milk of a young cocoa-nut. Pine-apples are here so abundant that the people eat them in the same waste-ful manner as we might turnips. They are of an excel-lent flavour—perhaps even better than those cultivated in England; and this I believe is the highest compliment which can be paid to any fruit.

**November 18th.**—In the morning I came on shore early, bringing with me some provisions in a bag, and two blankets for myself and servant. These were lashed to each end of a long pole, which was alter-nately carried by my Tahitian companions on their shoulders. These men are accustomed thus to carry, for a whole day, as much as fifty pounds at each end of their poles. I told my guides to provide themselves with food and clothing; but they said that there was plenty of food in the mountains, and for clothing, that their skins were sufficient. Our line of march was the valley of Tiaauru, down which a river flows into

## Lapita Legacy

"Charming…laughing, merry faces…cheerful…mildness": the Tahitians had, for Darwin, the grace of unspoiled children. The Edenlike ease and beauty of their envi-ronment may indeed have suggested the human race in its ingenuous infancy, yet these men and women were heirs to a long and adventurous history.

We know little of their story in detail, but its baldest outlines have been uncovered by archeologists investigating the dispersal of the Lapita Culture through Oceania. The name "Lapita" comes from a site in New Caledonia at which some distinctively decorated pottery was unearthed in the 1950s. With their intricately geometric, swirling patterns pricked out in the wet clay as though tattooed—and often with faces and figures worked into the overall design—these were works of great imagination and accomplishment.

Subsequent excavations have shown that Lapita was just one point on a progressive eastward expan-sion believed to have begun in the vicinity of Southeast Asia around 1500 B.C. Spreading slowly but surely through Melanesia and Micronesia, the migration had reached Tonga and Samoa by 1000 B.C., and con-tinued east into Polynesia (and ultimately Hawaii) and south to New Zealand. Each leg of this great migra-tion was a voyage of discovery in itself, often over hundreds of miles of open sea.

a mountain gorge far more magnificent than anything which I had ever before beheld. Until the midday sun stood vertically over the ravine, the air felt cool and damp, but now it became very sultry. Shaded by a ledge of rock, beneath a facade of columnar lava, we ate our dinner. My guides had already procured a dish of small fish and fresh-water prawns.

Darwin's guides then led the way up a steep rock face, which they climbed "by the aid of ropes," to a ledge above. Tahiti had already, as Darwin has mentioned, attained "classical" status as island paradise, a wonderful South Sea idyll of ease and plenty. His experience that night, though, as his companions pitched camp and then prepared a sumptuous feast from nature's freely yielded bounty, was like some vision of a primeval "golden age."

In the evening we reached a flat little spot on the banks of the same stream, which we had continued to follow, and which descends in a chain of water-falls: here we bivouacked for the night. On each side of the ravine there were great beds of the mountain-banana, covered with ripe fruit. Many of these plants were from twenty to twenty-five feet high, and from three to four in circumference. By the aid of strips of bark for rope, the stems of bamboos for rafters, and the large leaf of the banana for a thatch, the Tahitians in a few minutes built us an excellent house; and with withered leaves made a soft bed.

They then proceeded to make a fire, and cook our evening meal. A light was procured, by rubbing a blunt pointed stick in a groove made in another, as if with intention of deepening it, until by the friction the dust became ignited. A peculiarly white and very light wood (the *Hibiscus tiliareus*) is alone used for

the sea by Point Venus. This is one of the principal streams in the island, and its source lies at the base of the loftiest central pinnacles, which rise to a height of about 7,000 feet. The whole island is so mountainous that the only way to penetrate into the interior is to follow up the valleys. Our road, at first, lay through woods which bordered each side of the river; and the glimpses of the lofty central peaks, seen as through an avenue, with here and there a waving cocoa-nut tree on one side, were extremely picturesque. The valley soon began to narrow, and the sides to grow lofty and more precipitous. After having walked between three and four hours, we found the width of the ravine scarcely exceeded that of the bed of the stream. On each hand the walls were nearly vertical, yet from the soft nature of the volcanic strata, trees and a rank vegetation sprung from every projecting ledge. These precipices must have been some thousand feet high; and the whole formed

*Left:* A Tahitian man spreads vanilla pods out to dry in the tropical sun.
*Above, left:* Water cascades down a luxuriantly forested valley in this typical scene from the Tahitian interior.

this purpose: it is the same which serves for poles to carry any burden, and for the floating out-riggers to steady their canoes. ...The Tahitians having made a small fire of sticks, placed a score of stones, of about the size of cricket-balls, on the burning wood. In about ten minutes the sticks were consumed, and the stones hot. They had previously folded up in small parcels of leaves, pieces of beef, fish, ripe and unripe bananas, and the tops of the wild arum. These green parcels were laid in a layer between two layers of the hot stones, and the whole then covered up with earth, so that no smoke or steam could escape. In about a quarter of an hour, the whole was most deliciously cooked. The choice green parcels were now laid on a cloth of banana leaves, and with a cocoa-nut shell we drank the cool water of the running stream; and thus we enjoyed our rustic meal.

I could not look on the surrounding plants without admiration. On every side were forests of banana; the fruit of which, though serving for food in various ways, lay in heaps decaying on the ground. In front of us there was an extensive brake of wild sugar-cane. ...There were, moreover, several other wild fruits, and useful vegetables. The little stream, besides its cool water, produced eels, and cray-fish. I did indeed admire this scene, when I compared it with an uncultivated one in the temperate zones. I felt the force of the remark, that man, at least savage man, with his reasoning powers only partly developed, is the child of the tropics.

**November 20th.**—In the morning we started early, and reached Matavai at noon. On the road we met a large party of noble athletic men, going for wild bananas. I found that the ship, on account of the difficulty in watering,

## An Outstanding Achievement

The invention of the outrigger was a stroke of prehistoric genius: this low-tech addition coaxed high performance out of what were essentially Stone Age craft. The main hull of the Polynesian canoe, though often ornately carved and—at up to 80 feet—longer than those created by most other early cultures, was nevertheless a dugout, intrinsically cumbersome and unwieldy. A sail could not realistically be fitted to such a vessel since it would fatally destabilize it, the first significant buffet of crosswind turning it over. The use of the outrigger made all the difference: now the canoe could scud across the waves swept along by the wind, making its way over hundreds of miles of open ocean.

*Right:* Sugar cane was native to Southeast Asia but carried south and eastward through the Pacific by successive waves of emigrants; by Darwin's time it was growing wild in Tahiti.

had moved to the harbour of Papawa, to which place I immediately walked. This is a very pretty spot. The cove is surrounded by reefs, and the water as smooth as in a lake. The cultivated ground, with its beautiful productions, interspersed with cottages, comes close down to the water's edge.

Finally, on November 26, came a fond farewell.

In the evening, with a gentle land-breeze, a course was steered for New Zealand; and as the sun set, we had a farewell view of the mountains of Tahiti—the island to which every voyager has offered up his tribute of admiration.

## Island Intoxicant

Prior to the arrival of Europeans in the eighteenth century, the inhabitants of the South Seas had no alcohol. They did, however, have *ava*, or *kava*, as it is also known. This root could be chewed (Darwin tried it but did not like its strong flavor); most often though, this was just the preliminary to a protracted steeping in cold water. Taken as a drink, *ava* had powerful intoxicating effects. Unlike alcohol, however, the drink did not induce physical torpor or emotional changes. The missionaries saw *ava* as analogous to alcohol, but it was never really such a demon drink.

*Left: Even by Tahiti's exotic standards, the torch lily (Tritoma Kniphofia uvaria) is striking.*

## A Royal Visit

On November 25, the officers of the *Beagle* made a great show of formality for to welcome Pomare Vahine III, Queen of Tahiti, on board. Darwin was far less impressed by her than he had been by her subjects: "The queen is a large awkward woman, without any beauty, grace or dignity," he records. "She has only one royal attribute," he continues: "a perfect immovability of expression under all circumstances, and that rather a sullen one." Was it the idea of a Tahitian woman in a position of regal authority, rather than of submissive cheerfulness, that so irked Darwin—or a certain discomfort, never quite acknowledged, at being complicit in a cynical burlesque of power and pomp?

Queen Pomare's insignificance was only underlined by her imperious airs; the carriage she was sent by Queen Victoria would only make her pretensions seem more absurd. The population of Tahiti fell by 25 per cent during the ten years of her reign from 1827, her subjects carried off by tuberculosis, smallpox, dysentery and sexually transmitted diseases. She was as powerless to protect them from such threats as she was to resist the exploitation and abuse of western seafarers who sold them alcohol, and treated Tahiti as one great brothel. All the flotsam of the West was washing up here: deserting sailors and convicts escaped from the Australian penal colonies set themselves up as little lords in the villages and outlying islands. There were much worse oppressors here than any missionaries.

## The Savage Soul

Darwin was anxious, on meeting the Tahitians, "to form, from my own observation, a judgment of their moral state," he says—"although such judgment would necessarily be very imperfect," he concedes. Ever since the first Europeans came to the South Seas in the 1760s—explorers like Louis Antoine de Bougainville and Captain Cook—the debate had raged over whether the island should be seen as heaven on earth or seductive hell. Some found confir-

mation in the island idyll of the views of French *philosophe* Jean Jacques Rousseau that man was born in natural innocence and corrupted only by civilization. His notion of the "noble savage" had caught the imagination of the Enlightenment—now it seemed this paragon was alive, and living in Tahiti. Christian missionaries took a very different view. Pointing to a real—though much-exaggerated—tradition of can-nibalism in the islands, they argued that the natives needed to be saved from their moral squalor.

It wasn't just such obvious abuses that they objected to: island life offended them in just about every way. Nature was simply so bounteous here it was a reproach to the Christian work ethic—no one had to earn their breadfruit here by the sweat of their brow. And the islanders' free and easy sexual attitudes—much exploited by early European visitors—outraged the missionaries' moral code.

American novelist Herman Melville, who spent time in Tahiti after jumping ship here in 1842, charged the missionaries with destroying a naturally joyful way of life. Darwin upheld the missionaries' point of view, but saw enought of the beauty and bounty of Tahiti to appreciate the idyll the islanders' might have lost.

# New Zealand, New Horizon

In the evening of December 19, noted Darwin,

We saw in the distance New Zealand. We may now consider that we have nearly crossed the Pacific. It is necessary to sail over this great ocean to comprehend its immensity. Moving quickly onwards for weeks together, we meet with nothing but the same blue, profoundly deep, ocean. Even within the archipelagoes, the islands are mere specks, and far distant one from the other. Accustomed to look at maps drawn on a small scale, where dots, shading, and names are crowded together, we do not rightly judge how infinitely small the proportion of dry land is to water of this vast expanse. The meridian of the Antipodes has likewise been passed; and now every league, it made us happy to think, was one league nearer to England. ...A gale of wind lasting for some days, has lately given us full leisure to measure the future stages in our homeward voyage, and to wish most earnestly for its termination.

December 21st.—Early in the morning we entered the Bay of Islands [near the northernmost tip of the North Island], and being becalmed for some hours near the mouth, we did not reach the anchorage till the middle of the day. The country is hilly, with a smooth outline, and is

*"Moving quickly onwards for weeks together, we meet with nothing but the same blue, profoundly deep, ocean. ...the islands are mere specks."*

Perhaps feeling nostalgic for home, Darwin liked the cottage gardens of the English settlers but found the North Island's subtropical lushness, and its native peoples, alienating. "In the morning I went out walking," he noted in his journal for December 22,

But I soon found that the country was very impracticable. All the hills are thickly covered with tall fern, together with a low bush which grows like a cypress; and very little ground has been cleared or cultivated. I then tried the sea-beach; but proceeding towards either hand, my walk was soon stopped by salt-water creeks and deep brooks. The communication between the inhabitants of the different parts of the bay, is (as in Chiloe) almost entirely kept up by boats. I was surprised to find that almost every hill which I ascended, had been at some former time more or less fortified. . . .

I should think a more warlike race of inhabitants could not be found in any part of the world than the New Zealanders. Their conduct on first seeing a ship, as described by Captain Cook, strongly illustrates this: the act of throwing volleys of stones at so great and novel an object, and their defiance of "Come on shore and we will kill and eat you all," shows uncommon boldness. This warlike spirit is evident in many of their customs, and even in their smallest actions.

deeply intersected by numerous arms of the sea extending from the bay. The surface appears from a distance as if clothed with coarse pasture, but this in truth is nothing but fern. On the more distant hills, as well as in parts of the valleys, there is a good deal of woodland. The general tint of the landscape is not a bright green; and it resembles the country a short distance to the south of Concepcion in Chile. In several parts of the bay, little villages of square tidy looking houses are scattered close down to the water's edge. Three whaling-ships were lying at anchor, and a canoe every now and then crossed from shore to shore; with these exceptions, an air of extreme quietness reigned over the whole district. Only a single canoe came alongside. This, and the aspect of the whole scene, afforded a remarkable, and not very pleasing contrast, with our joyful and boisterous welcome at Tahiti.

## "Nothing but Fern"

New Zealand is believed to have more than 200 species of fern—now one of the most widely recognized national emblems. Ferns are fascinating plants, far older than more superficially attractive flowering plants: they are now known to have entered the fossil record in the Lower Devonian period, some 200 million years ago. By about 300 million years ago, they had inherited the earth. From tiny dwarves to giant tree-ferns, they were the dominant flora.

The mild, moist conditions of New Zealand's North Island suit the fern to perfection: its complicated reproductive processes depend on the presence of water. Rather than producing female seeds for fertilization by male pollen, the fern typically produces spores which, separating from the parent plant, grow independently as *gametophytes*: these cross-fertilize each other more conventionally to produce a new generation of ferns. Where dry conditions mean that there is not enough moisture for sperm to swim, the individual *gametophyte* or *prothallus* may simply grow of its own accord. The result, though a viable fern, is the sole product of its parent plant, so can neither advance nor avail itself of genetic diversity.

## The Body Inscribed

The word "tattaw" was originally Polynesian, and it was with the islands that the practice of tattooing was most strongly associated— and, of course, with the Maoris of New Zealand. For them, as for the Scythians of the western steppe 2,700 years ago, it was a mark of tribal identity and rank—the higher-born the person, the more ornate the patterning. That being tattooed was painful was also crucial to the appeal of what was regarded as a mark of maturity and courage.

"No doubt the extraordinary manner in which tattooing is here practised, gives a disagreeable expression to their countenances," wrote Darwin. "The complicated but symmetrical figures covering the whole face, puzzle and mislead an unaccustomed eye: it is moreover probable, that the deep incisions, by destroying the play of the superficial muscles, give an air of rigid inflexibility."

Next day Darwin took himself off on another long walk, to Waimate, where he had been told he would find a little English colony. First, however, he had to make his way across vast acreages of thick, green fern, and make a stop with his guides at another Maori village.

On coming near one of the huts I was much amused by seeing in due form the ceremony of rubbing, or, as it ought to be called, pressing noses. The women, on our first approach, began uttering something in a most dolorous voice; they then squatted themselves down and held up their faces; my companion standing over them, one after another, placed the bridge of his nose at right angles to theirs, and commenced

*Above:* An explosion of lush greenery in New Zealand. Darwin found the country *"very impractible. ...very little ground has been cleared or cultivated."*

pressing. This lasted rather longer than a cordial shake of the hand with us, and as we vary the force of the grasp of the hand in shaking, so do they in pressing. During the process they uttered comfortable little grunts....

The ceremony of pressing noses having been duly completed with all present, we seated ourselves in a circle in the front of one of the-hovels, and rested there half-an-hour. All the hovels have nearly the same form and dimensions, and all agree in being filthily dirty. They resemble a cow-shed with one end open, but having a partition a little way within, with a square hole in it, making a small gloomy chamber. ...

At length we reached Waimate. After having passed over so many miles of an uninhabited useless country, the sudden appearance of an English farm-house, and its well-dressed fields, placed there as if by an enchanter's wand, was exceedingly pleasant.

...Several young men, redeemed by the missionaries from slavery, were employed on the farm. They were dressed in a shirt, jacket, and trousers, and had a respectable appearance...These young men and boys appeared very merry and good-humoured. In the evening I saw a party of them at cricket: when I thought of the austerity of which the missionaries have been accused, I was amused by observing one of their own sons taking an active part in the game. ...Late in the evening I went to Mr Williams's house, where I passed the night. I found there a large party of children, collected together for Christmas Day, and all sitting round a table at tea. I never saw a nicer or more merry group; and to think that this was in the centre of the land of cannibalism, murder, and all atrocious crimes!

## Kupe's Country

The true discoverer of New Zealand, according to the Maori oral tradition, was named Kupe, leader of an expedition that made the long voyage south from Hawaiki, Polynesia. Two *waka* or canoes were involved, the second captained by Kupe's friend Ngahue. They sailed steadily southward for many days. At last, the story goes, Kupe's wife spotted a long white cloud on the far horizon—a sure sign to these early navigators that here was land. In honor of this moment, they named the new country *Aotearoa*, "Land of the Long White Cloud."

Myth it may be, but the Maori account rings true in all essentials. The Polynesians planted seeds here that they had brought from home, tradition has it: several died, but the *kumara* survived and saw them through the year. That would place their landfall in the far north of the North Island, whose subtropical climate alone would have sustained this sweet potato. The immigrants had been fortunate, first in not sailing slightly to the east and ending up amid the frigid expanse of the Antarctic Ocean, and second in finding the only part of New Zealand that would support their staple crop.

By tradition, Kupe's party returned home to Hawaiki and told their friends and neighbors what they had found. A second expedition was organized with the aim of establishing a permanent settlement. No historical document can possibly confirm this old tradition, but recent research has found DNA evidence to support it.

*Above: This settler's homestead in New Zealand was photographed in 1906. Below, right: Darwin put his faith in small churches like this for the redemption of New Zealand's native people.*

## A Warlike Race?

Like many another culture, the Maoris were governed by a warrior ethic and by the tradition of ritualized warfare that went with it. Yet there were no apparent precedents for the sort of intertribal slaughter that had come with the "Musket Wars," or the smoldering resentment that had come to characterize relations with white whalers and settlers in the country. In the decades leading up to Darwin's visit, Maoris had carried out massacres of Europeans—but they had themselves been victims of equally appalling atrocities. Racially identical though they were, the Maoris did differ in culture and experience from the Tahitians, but the distinction Darwin drew seems largely a matter of positive and negative stereotyping. To him, the Tahitians represented the appealing exoticism of a romantically imagined tropical *dolce vita*, the Maoris a barbaric "Other."

## Trench Warfare

The Maoris had been building defensive ditch-and-stockade systems around hilltops for centuries before the arrival of Europeans in New Zealand. At their simplest, these resembled the hill forts of Iron Age Europe, but these *pas* grew in sophistication as the circumstances changed. The introduction of firearms, bought from foreign traders, destabilized Maori society, especially in the South Island, sparking off what were called the "Musket Wars" (1818–33)

between rival tribes. Dugouts and firing pits were constructed, the Maoris anticipating in their *pas* designs and tactics that would figure in later conflicts in the West, such as the American Civil War and the First World War.

## Mission Accomplished

New Zealand's second oldest house (1832), the "English farm-house" at Waimate, was built from kauri wood by local Maoris converted to Christianity. For a time in the 1840s, this was the center of Christianity in New Zealand: it was home to Bishop Selwyn, first leader of the colony's Anglican Church. Today Waimate is no more than a backwater, a village outside the small provincial town of Kerikeri, but the remaining mission house has been preserved as a historic monument.

# Wildlife in the Wars

Darwin was struck by the apparent paucity of wildlife in New Zealand. "In the woods I saw very few birds," he noted.

With regard to animals, it is a most remarkable fact, that so large an island, extending over more than 700 miles in latitude, and in many parts ninety broad, with varied stations, a fine climate, and land of all heights, from 14,000 feet downwards, with the exception of a small rat, did not possess one indigenous animal. The several species of that gigantic genus of birds, the Deinornis seem here to have replaced mammiferous quadrupeds, in the same manner as the reptiles still do at the Galapagos archipelago. It is said that the common Norway rat, in the short space of two years, annihilated in this northern end of the island, the New Zealand species.

Christmas Day found Darwin first in reflective mood.

In a few more days the fourth year of our absence from England will be completed. Our first Christmas Day was spent at Plymouth, the second at St. Martin's Cove, near Cape Horn; the third at Port Desire, in Patagonia; the fourth at anchor in a wild harbour in the peninsula of Tres Montes, this fifth here, and the next, I trust in Providence, will be in England. We attended divine service in the chapel of Pahia; part of the service being read in English, and part in the native language. Whilst at New Zealand we did not hear of any recent acts of cannibalism; but Mr. Stokes found burnt human bones strewed round a fire-place on a small island near the anchorage; but these remains of a comfortable banquet might have been lying there for several years. It is probable that the moral state of the people will rapidly improve.

## "The Famous Kauri Pine"

Darwin was unimpressed by the sight of a forest of kauri pine: "I measured one of the noble trees, and found it thirty-one feet in circumference above the roots. There was another close by, which I did not see, thirty-three feet; and [another] no less than forty feet," he noted. A noble tree indeed, the kauri was used by the Maoris for building their great canoes and for the construction of dwellings, but was felled in vast numbers in lumber and land-clearing programs in the late nineteenth century. Today only pockets of the North Island's native forest survive, but these are now rigorously protected by the New Zealand government.

*Right:* It did not occur to Darwin for a moment that the Maoris might have a culture worth keeping. They felt differently, as this early-twentieth-century photograph shows.
*Opposite:* Lumberjacks work to fell a kauri pine in the depths of the New Zealand forest.

## Mourning the Moa

When he called the dinornithiformes a "gigantic genus," Darwin was referring to the physical stature of its members, but this family of flightless birds had been extensive enough as well with some twenty species. In size these had ranged from a respectable 40 inches tall to a truly "gigantic" 13 feet in the case of *Dinornis maximus*, the giant moa. Sadly, all had been hunted to virtual extinction before the first European settlers had arrived—the last survivors are thought to have been killed by about 1800.

The Latin name *Dinornis* means "terrible bird" (just as *Dinosaur* meant "terrible lizard") but in fact these birds were harmless herbivores. Strange they certainly were: not only were the dinornithiformes flightless but they did not have even the basic forms of wings.

They were not closely related to New Zealand's most famous flightless bird, the kiwi, of which Darwin, as it happens, made no mention. But since the islands were free not only of humans but of animal predators until comparatively recently, it is hardly surprising that flightless birds should have evolved in numbers here.

Out walking with his missionary friends the next day, Darwin was brought face to face with the old Maori ways once more when, arriving in a village, he found it in mourning.

The daughter of a chief, who was still a heathen, had died there five days before. The hovel in which she had expired had been burnt to the ground: her body being enclosed between two small canoes, was placed upright on the ground, and protected by an enclosure bearing wooden images of their gods, and the whole was painted bright red, so as to be conspicuous from afar. Her gown was fastened to the coffin, and her hair being cut off was cast at its foot. The relatives of the family had torn the flesh of their arms, bodies, and faces, so that they were covered with clotted blood; and the old women looked most filthy, disgusting objects. On the following day some of the officers visited this place, and found the women still howling and cutting themselves.

**December 30th.**—In the afternoon we stood out of the Bay of Islands, on our course to Sydney. I believe we were all glad to leave New Zealand. It is not a pleasant place. Amongst the natives there is absent that charming simplicity which is found in Tahiti; and the greater part of the English are the very refuse of society. Neither is the country itself attractive. I look back but to one bright spot, and that is Waimate, with its Christian inhabitants.

# On the Southern Continent

*"Farewell, Australia! You are a rising child, and doubtless
some day will reign a great princess in the South."*

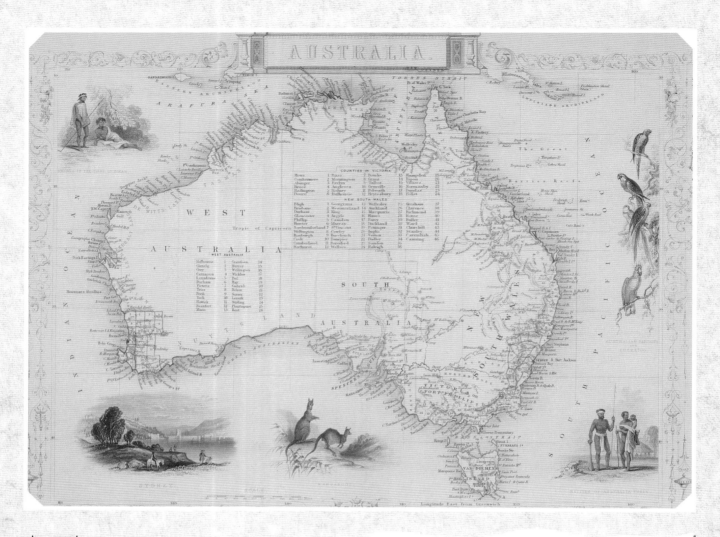

*Previous pages: Pelicans preen their feathers on the Australian coast.* **Above:** *Exotic images surround the map of a continent-country whose interior remained a blank well into modern times.* **Below:** *Aborigines dance, with boomerangs raised, in this nineteenth-century engraving.*

"That great America on the other side of the sphere," Herman Melville called Australia. The comparison holds good in many ways. One, unfortunately, is with regard to the fate of its indigenous inhabitants, as Darwin himself was only too well aware. "Wherever the European has trod," he remarked, "death seems to pursue the aboriginal." It would be nice to be able to report that Darwin summarily denounced the treatment of Australia's Aborigines in ringing terms. Nice, but untrue. It would have been a little anachronistic if he had—Darwin was an Englishman of his own class and time—yet his hesitancy may also have been rooted in the fact that, grave as it was, this issue alone could not account for his more general feelings of discomfort in the country.

One respect in which Australia differs from America is in its pre-existence as geographical hypothesis long before its finding for real by European navigators.

America took Columbus completely by surprise (indeed, it's believed that in 1506 he went to his grave still firmly convinced that his famous voyages had taken him to the East Indies). But the existence of a Southern Continent had been discussed since medieval times, sizes and shapes postulated to "balance" out the forms of the known, northerly world. This fundamentally Australian gap between imagination and reality, between expectation and experience, is re-enacted for Darwin's reader almost comically in the succession of famous animal-freaks that (the platypus apart) he fails to see. But it troubled him more profoundly, just as it troubled Australia's settlers, making its mark both on the country's history and its modern psyche.

The Australian author of *Schindler's List*, Thomas Keneally addresses his own country's genocidal inheritance in the novel *Bettany's Book* (2000). It describes a country constructed largely in this very space between theoretical forms and actual existence. Forged letters from home free "bereaved" transportees to re-marry.

*Left: Sacred to the Aborigines for millennia, Uluru is a vast natural monolith in the Australian desert.*
*Bottom: A very different divine order is represented by these early settlers, off to church in New South Wales.*

A man's dying testimony, being given in Irish, is not recorded and simply ceases to exist with him; absconding convicts, lost to the law, roam the back country as nonpeople. There is no list for exterminated Aborigines: unacknowledged by the official figures, they may be killed as animal pests—and so they are, by otherwise decent settlers. These assumptions have their counterparts among the Aborigines. In spite of strict rules governing sexual contact, their women freely trade sexual favours with the new white settlers. No taboo is broken, Keneally's narrator is told, since the whites aren't real people, only spirits.

Another modern Australian author, the Lebanese-descended David Malouf, sees his country as an Eden inhabited in frustration and rage. One of his short stories, "Blacksoil Country" (2000) sums up this paradox perfectly. An enraged settler shoots and kills an Aboriginal trespasser, a depressing, and so far banal, tale, which, however, ends with an ironic twist when we see that, his own young son having been murdered in reprisal, he is now tied to his land by the same bonds of blood that have always rooted the natives. Unhappy and embittered he may be, yet for the first time he is at home in this most alien of lands. All the shopping malls and office blocks in the world, it is implied, cannot concrete over a wilderness that resides in Australians' own souls and originates in the historical oppression not only of Australia's natives but of large sections of its incoming white "elite."

Darwin himself seems to have picked up on some of this: the Australian wilderness genuinely disturbed him more than it delighted him, and he was more repelled than invigorated by his sense of the country coming into existence all around him. A young nation it may have been, but it clearly struck him as a juvenile delinquent: the reaction of a staid and snobbish Englishman? Perhaps, but only partly.

# First Impressions

Through the first days of 1836, the *Beagle* made steady progress toward the eastern coast of Australia, and on January 12 the expedition at last made landfall.

Early in the morning a light air carried us towards the entrance of Port Jackson. Instead of beholding a verdant country, interspersed with fine houses, a straight line of yellowish cliff brought to our minds the coast of Patagonia. A solitary lighthouse, built of white stone, alone told us that we were near a great and populous city. Having entered the harbour, it appears fine and spacious, with cliff-formed shores of horizontally stratified sandstone. The nearly level country is covered with thin scrubby trees, bespeaking the curse of sterility. Proceeding further inland, the country improves: beautiful villas and nice cottages are here and there scattered along the beach. In the distance stone houses, two and three stories high, and windmills standing on the edge of a bank, pointed out to us the neighbourhood of the capital of Australia.

At last we anchored within Sydney Cove. We found the little basin occupied by many large ships, and surrounded by warehouses. In the evening I walked through the town, and returned full of admiration at the whole scene. It is a most magnificent testimony to the power of the British nation. Here, in a less promising country, scores of years have done many more times more than an equal

*"My first feeling was to congratulate myself that I was born an Englishman."*

number of centuries have effected in South America. My first feeling was to congratulate myself that I was born an Englishman.

Darwin wasted no time before hiring horses and a guide to take him "to Bathurst, a village about one hundred and twenty miles in the interior, and the centre of a great pastoral district."

On the morning of the 16th (January) I set out on my excursion. The first stage took us to Paramatta, a small country town, next to Sydney in importance ... In all respects there was a close resemblance to England: perhaps the alehouses here were more numerous. The iron gangs, or parties of convicts who have committed here some offense, appeared the least like England: they were working in chains, under the charge of sentries with loaded arms.

The power which the government possesses, by means of forced labour, of at once opening good roads throughout the country, has been, I believe, one

*Left: North Head, near Sydney: the greenness of this coast was to prove deceptive. **Above:** By the end of the nineteenth century, Sydney was a prosperous and forward-looking city.*

## "The Loveliest Harbor in the World"

Now known internationally as Sydney Harbor, Port Jackson's claim to be "the loveliest harbor in the world" is inevitably disputed, but no one questions that it's a clear contender. It's ironic, then, to recall just how unhappy its first European inhabitants were to be there when the first penal settlement was established in 1788. There were about 800 prisoners, some with families, with troops of marines to guard them, as well as some 400 sailors who had crewed the eleven ships of the "First Fleet" for their 15,000-mile voyage.

Things began badly and got worse. The fleet's intended destination just down the coast at Botany Bay turned out to be too bleak and arid a site for settlement. Port Jackson seemed more promising, but only marginally. Fresh water was hard to come by; the hunting in the hinterland was meager; the timber to be cleared, thick and impossibly resilient. Though the party had brought a few horses, cattle, sheep, goats and poultry, the grazing was inadequate and there wasn't enough manure to make the sun-scorched land agriculturally productive. Before they could even think about that, though, they had to break up the virgin land for cultivation, a task for which they were completely unequipped. With no limestone in the vicinity, they could not make mortar for construction. In short, it became increasingly evident to the officers in charge as dreary days went by and the only real achievement was the steady diminution of the party's provisions that no one back in England had thought the whole thing through.

And there wasn't the sense of kinship or collective purpose that had come to the rescue of America's Pilgrim Fathers. Despite what was becoming a desperate situation, and much against some of the officers' better judgment, the "us" and "them" distinctions between guards and convicts was strictly maintained. And the convicts weren't natural colonists: it was in part their antisocial attitude and general fecklessness that had got them into trouble in the first place—they weren't the stuff of which pioneers are generally made. Those with initiative tried to escape, making for China, which, with the unquestioning acceptance of the utterly uneducated, they believed lay just over the hills, a hundred miles to northward. Those who survived sunstroke, starvation, dehydration or Aboriginal attack by and large dragged themselves home, desperate to be readmitted to their prison.

Time passed, and by trial and error they finally managed to make the settlement work. Through the nineteenth century it went from strength to strength. To the natural beauties of the haven were added such manmade features as a fine suspension bridge and stunning opera house. Today Sydney is one of the world's great cities.

*Right: Governor Arthur Phillips inspects the Port Jackson penal colony in 1788.*

main cause of the early prosperity of this colony. I slept at night at a very comfortable inn at Emu ferry, thirty-five miles from Sydney, and near the ascent of the Blue Mountains. This line of road is the most frequented, and has been the longest inhabited of any in the colony. The whole land is enclosed with high railings, for the farmers have not succeeded in rearing hedges. There are many substantial houses and good cottages scattered about; but although considerable pieces of land are under cultivation, the greater part yet remains as when first discovered.

The extreme uniformity of the vegetation is the most remarkable feature in the landscape of the greater part of New South Wales. Everywhere we have an open woodland, the ground being partially covered with a very thin pasture, with little appearance of verdure. The trees nearly all belong to one family, and mostly have their leaves placed in a vertical, instead of as in Europe, in a nearly horizontal

position: the foliage is scanty, and of a peculiar pale green tint, without any gloss. Hence the woods appear light and shadowless: this, although a loss of comfort to the traveller under the scorching rays of summer, is of importance to the farmer, as it allows grass to grow where it otherwise would not. The leaves are not shed periodically: this character appears common to the entire southern hemisphere, namely, South America, Australia, and the Cape of Good Hope. The inhabitants of this hemisphere, and of the intertropical regions, thus lose perhaps one of the most glorious, though to our eyes common, spectacles in the world—the first bursting into full foliage of the leafless tree. They may, however, say that we pay dearly for this by having the land covered with mere naked skeletons for so many months. . . .

At sunset, a party of a score of the black aborigines passed by, each carrying, in their accustomed manner, a bundle of spears and other weapons. By giving a leading young man a shilling, they were easily detained, and threw their spears for my amusement. They were all partly clothed, and several could speak a little English: their countenances were good-humoured and pleasant, and they appeared far from being such utterly degraded beings as they have usually been represented. In their own arts they are

## A Convict Culture

The sighting of some cabins occupied by "squatters" prompts Darwin, in his daily journal for January 20, to provide a handy at-a-glance guide to some of Australia's social types.

A "Squatter" is a freed or "ticket of leave" [freed on probation] man, who builds a hut with bark in unoccupied ground, buys or steals a few animals, sells spirits without a license, receives stolen goods and so at last becomes rich and turns farmer. He is the horror of all his honest neighbours. A "Crawler" is an assigned convict, who runs away and lives how he can by labor or petty theft. The "Bush Ranger" is an open villain, who subsists by highway robbery and plunder; generally he is desperate and will sooner be killed than taken alive. In the country it is necessary to understand these three names, for they are in perpetual use.

admirable. A cap being fixed at thirty yards distance, they transfixed it with a spear, delivered by the throwing-stick with the rapidity of an arrow from the bow of a practised archer. In tracking animals or men they show most wonderful sagacity; and I heard of several of their remarks which manifested considerable acuteness. They will not, however, cultivate the ground, or build houses and remain stationary, or even take the trouble of tending a flock of sheep when given to them. On the whole they appear to me to stand some few degrees higher in the scale of civilization than the Fuegians.

## The Incredible Atlatl

Darwin's use of the phrase "throwing stick" is confusing, because the Australian did frequently employ hurled wooden sticks in hunting; sometimes these were aerodynamically carved so as to fly farther and with greater force—boomerangs. From the context, though, it is clear that Darwin was referring to the device known to archeologists as the *atlatl*, a native American term for a technology in use by paleolithic hunters all over the world.

A wooden rod some two feet long, with weights and a hook at one end to catch the base of the spear shaft, the *atlatl* allows a spear to be thrown with far greater speed and force. Prior to its invention, the spear had only been effective when used for thrusting at a cornered animal at close-quarters—a potentially dangerous situation for the hunter. The introduction of the *atlatl*, however, relaunched the spear as a powerful projectile: this deceptively simple implement represented a technological revolution.

## The First Australians

Australia's Aborigines appear to have reached the continent around 50,000 years ago. It is assumed that they came from somewhere in Southeast Asia, very likely via the islands of Melanesia: from New Guinea there would have been a comparatively short crossing over the Torres Strait. Some sort of sea voyage by dugout canoe or similar craft would certainly have been necessary.

Dispersing throughout the continent in small hunter-gatherer groups, the Aborigines diverged culturally as well: by the time the Europeans came some 200 distinct languages were spoken. They had no writing, and the basic rhythms of their lives changed little over millennia, so their culture offers few meaningful points of comparison with those of the Western world. Darwin's contemporaries dismissed them as savages, and in many cases hunted them down as so many animal pests. A series of massacres took place in the decades after Darwin came this way—though the numbers involved are disputed to this day. They have indeed become a matter of deep soul-searching and bitter controversy in an age for which the Aboriginal achievement has been assessed anew. Today Australians—and the world—can marvel at minds that could make the whole landscape resonate through special spatio-historical "songlines" and celebrate an ancestral "Dreamtime" in an oral tradition as rich and energetic as any literary one.

*Opposite: Darwin attributed the "light and shadowless" appearance of the New South Wales woods to the scanty foliage of their eucalyptus trees.*

# Culture Shock

Darwin was struck by the easy way in which Stone Age and nineteenth century coexisted at this moment in Australian history, but seemed unsure whether to be more delighted or dismayed.

It is very curious thus to see in the midst of a civilized people, a set of harmless savages wandering about without knowing where they shall sleep at night, and gaining their livelihood by hunting in the woods. As the white man has travelled onwards, he has spread over the country belonging to several tribes. ...The number of aborigines is rapidly decreasing. In my whole ride, with the exception of some boys brought up by Englishmen, I saw only one other party. This decrease, no doubt, must be partly owing to the introduction of spirits, to European diseases (even the milder ones of which, such as the measles, prove very destructive), and to the gradual extinction of the wild animals. ...Besides the several evident causes of destruction, there appears to be some more mysterious agency generally at work. Wherever the European has trod, death seems to pursue the aboriginal. We may look to the wide extent of the Americas, Polynesia, the Cape of Good Hope, and Australia, and we find the same result. ...The varieties of man seem to act on each other in the same way as different species of animals—the stronger always extirpating the weaker. It was melancholy at New Zealand to hear

*"Wherever the European has trod, death seems to pursue the aboriginal."*

the fine energetic natives saying that they knew the land was doomed to pass from their children. ...

The Rev. J. Williams, in his interesting work, says, that the first intercourse between natives and Europeans, "is invariably attended with the introduction of fever, dysentery, or some other disease, which carries off numbers of the people."

## Epidemic Invasion

The Aboriginal population fell by an estimated 90 per cent over the nineteenth and early twentieth centuries. Casual murder by white farmers was a factor; some historians suggest a deliberate policy of genocide on the part of the authorities, but, as in the Americas, the main problem was one of unwitting biological warfare. Along with modern civilization, incoming Europeans brought bacilli and viruses to which they themselves had inherited immunity from generations of ancestors, but against which the Aborigines had no defense. Centuries of travel, trade and war between the communities of Africa and Eurasia had meant a promiscuous sharing of germs, while large-scale intermarriage had meant an extension of the gene pool. Having dwelt apart for thousands of years, the natives of Australia had developed no immunity, even against apparently trivial illnesses. Smallpox cut a swathe through this population, but so too did diseases regarded as relatively trivial in the West: venereal diseases, flu, chicken pox and measles.

*Left: Long before 1925 when this drawing was made, Australia's Aborigines had been a people brought low by epidemic: like America's native peoples, they had no immunity to common Old World ailments.*

Again he affirms, "It is certainly a fact, which cannot be controverted, that most of the diseases which have raged in the islands during my residence there, have been introduced by ships; and what renders this fact remarkable is, that there might be no appearance of disease among the crew of the ship which conveyed this destructive importation." ...From these facts it would almost appear as if the effluvium of one set of men shut up for some time together was poisonous when inhaled by others.

By the morning of January 19, Darwin and his party were approaching the Blue Mountains.

From so grand a title as Blue Mountains, and from their absolute altitude, I expected to have seen a bold chain of mountains crossing the country; but instead of this, a sloping plain presents merely an inconsiderable front to the low land near the coast. ...But when once on the sandstone platform, the scenery becomes exceedingly monotonous. ...

*Above:* Dwarfed by the trees and rocks among which they walk, nineteenth-century settlers make their way along a gully in the Blue Mountains.

## Miasma Attack

Darwin's assumption that the "effluvium" of men confined together could account for the spread of sickness reminds us of how very different the scientific world he lived in was from ours. It comes tantalizingly close to being true: such close proximity would indeed have been unhealthy—but not for the reasons he suggested. But that was the way with "miasmatism" —one of early modern science's great near misses; and not to be displaced by modern "germ theory" for another generation yet. In Darwin's day, doctors subscribed to the theory that diseases were caused by "miasmas"—toxic gases produced by rotten matter and spread by bad smells. Scientifically baseless though it may have been, miasmatism did inspire efforts to end insanitary conditions in urban slums and sewage systems, so it certainly had some positive results.

Soon after leaving the Blackheath, we descended from the sandstone platform by the pass of Mount Victoria ...We now entered upon a country less elevated by nearly a thousand feet, and consisting of granite. With the change of rock, the vegetation improved, the trees were both finer and stood farther apart; and the pasture between them was a little greener and more plentiful. At Hassan's Walls, I left the high road, and made a short detour to a farm called Walerawang, to the superintendent of which I had a letter of introduction from the owner in Sydney. Mr Browne had the kindness to ask me to stay the ensuing day, which I had much pleasure in doing. This place offers an example of one of the large farming, or rather sheep-grazing establishments of the colony. Cattle and horses are, however, in this case rather more numerous than usual, owing to some of the valleys being swampy and producing a coarser pasture. Two or three flat pieces of ground near the house were cleared and cultivated with corn, which the harvestmen were now reaping. ...Although the farm was well stocked with every necessary, there was an apparent absence of comfort; and not one single woman resided here. The sunset of a fine day will generally cast an air of happy contentment on any scene; but here, at this retired farm-house, the brightest tints on the surrounding woods could not make me forget that forty hardened, profligate men were ceasing from their daily labours, like the slaves from Africa, yet without their holy claim for compassion.

Early on the next morning, Mr. Archer, the joint superintendent, had the kindness to take me out kangaroo-hunting. We continued riding the greater part of the day, but had very bad sport, not seeing a kangaroo, or even a wild dog. ...A few years since this country abounded with wild animals; but now the emu is banished to a long distance, and the kangaroo is become scarce. It may be long before these animals are altogether exterminated, but their doom is fixed.

## The Paradoxical Platypus

The name "platypus" comes from the Greek words *platy* ("broad") and *pus* ("foot")—but this animal's wide, webbed feet are the least of its peculiarities. The most striking of these is its leathery duck-bill, but it has a good many others, from its lack of any discernible neck or external ears (despite acute hearing) to the venom-secreting spurs on the insides of the male's hind legs. But pride of place in its collection of eccentricities must surely be taken by the fact that this is a mammal that lays eggs like a bird or reptile. The young are suckled like any other infant mammals.

## The Missing Marsupials

Of Australia's famously distinctive (and diverse) fauna, Darwin seems to have seen little. He was aware of the exoticism of Australia's wildlife species, though, and later scientists, inspired by Darwin's writings, would find themselves fascinated by the extent to which this isolated continent seemed to have gone its own separate evolutionary way.

Nowhere is this more apparent than it is in the example of the marsupials—possums apart, a group confined to Australasia. These mammals differ from their relatives in many ways—most obviously in their way of carrying their young in pouches—though they differ from one another almost as much. Marsupials of many different kinds occupy a wide range of evolutionary "niches," not just the kangaroo and wallaby but the burrowing wombat, the tree-dwelling phalanger, the cuddly koala and the lively bandicoot.

*Below, left: A koala does what it does best: sleeps. Below, right: Darwin first noted seeing large flocks of cockatoos while out hunting with Mr. Archer.*

## Meditations on an Ant-lion

The ant-lion is also known as the "doodlebug." It lives in dry and fine-grained sand, digging itself a steep-sided, conical hole and lurking in the bottom. When an insect strays into this trap, it tries to scramble out but cannot keep its footing—especially under fire from a jet of sand grains sprayed up at it by the ant-lion. Hence the hapless victim generally ends up falling into the ant-lion's waiting jaws.

The ant-lion has been a longstanding subject of discussion among biologists interested in how not just physical form but complex behaviors might evolve. As Darwin records in his daily diary for January 19, 1836, he was just reflecting on how different the flora and fauna of Australia were from the rest of the world—and musing on the thought that "two distinct Creators" might have been at work, when, "Whilst thus thinking, I observed the conical pitfall of a Lion-Ant [sic]. A fly fell in and immediately disappeared; then came a large but unwary Ant; his struggles to escape being very violent, the little jets of sand…were promptly directed against him…. His fate however was better than that of the poor fly's." What struck Darwin is the improbability that these two creatures could have been brought into existence independently of one another. "What would the Disbeliever say to this?" he asked. "Would any two workmen ever hit on so beautiful, so simple and yet so artificial a contrivance? It cannot be thought so. The one hand has surely worked throughout the universe."

It is intriguing, and perhaps revealing, that Darwin toned down his language slightly for the *Voyage of the Beagle* as published in 1839, and omitted his more theological reflections altogether from the 1845 edition.

*Above: More than anything else, the merino sheep would provide the basis for Australia's early prosperity*

On January 20, Darwin completed a "long day's ride to Bathurst."

Before joining the highroad we followed a mere path through the forest; and the country, with the exception of a few squatters' huts, was very solitary. We experienced this day the sirocco-like wind of Australia, which comes from the parched deserts of the interior. Clouds of dust were travelling in every direction; and the wind felt as if it had passed over a fire. I afterwards heard that the thermometer out of doors had stood at 119 degrees, and in a closed room at 96 degrees. In the afternoon we came in view of the downs of Bathurst. These undulating but nearly smooth plains are very remarkable in this country, from being absolutely destitute of trees. They support only a thin brown pasture. We rode some miles over this country, and then reached the township of Bathurst, seated in the middle of what may be called either a very broad valley, or narrow plain. …The secret of the rapidly growing prosperity of Bathurst is that the brown pasture, which appears to the stranger's eye so wretched, is excellent for sheep-grazing.

On the whole, from what I heard, more than from what I saw, I was disappointed in the state of society…. The whole population, poor and rich, are bent on acquiring wealth: amongst the higher orders, wool and sheep-grazing form the constant subject of conversation. There are many serious drawbacks to the

## Into the Interior

The first permanent settlement to be established inland, Bathurst was the direct result of an 1814 expedition into the New South Wales interior, commissioned by the governor. Evans named the river it stood upon the "Macquarie" in honor of the governor since 1809. Born on the Isle of Ulva, off Mull, in the Scottish Hebrides, Lachlan Macquarie (1762–1824) was a decent and enlightened man, if a little inclined to arrogance. His achievements in New South Wales have earned him the title of "Father of Australia," but his liberal-mindedness was not appreciated at the time. The colony's "free settlers" considered him far too solicitous of their convict neighbors, and far too ready to regard them as "real" Australians. It was typical of him, for example, that he gave Evans's convict companions their freedom as a gesture of thanks: he was replaced as governor in 1821.

comforts of a family, the chief of which, perhaps, is being surrounded by convict servants. How thoroughly odious to every feeling, to be waited on by a man who the day before, perhaps, was flogged, from your representation, for some trifling misdemeanor. ...I am not aware that the tone of society has assumed any peculiar character; but with such habits, and without intellectual pursuits, it can hardly fail to deteriorate. My opinion is such, that nothing but rather sharp necessity should compel me to emigrate.

The convicts were a bad influence not only on the sons of the law-abiding but on each other: in such degraded company, how could anyone reform?

*Above: Tasmanian Aborigines are grouped before their huts in this riverside settlement. Below: The city of Hobart sprawls along the shores of its 'snug cove' in this early photograph.*

# Van Diemen's Land

On January 30, reported Darwin, the *Beagle* "sailed for Hobart Town in Van Diemen's Land": Tasmania, as it is known today.

On the 5th of February, after a six days' passage, of which the first part was fine, and the latter very cold and squally, we entered the mouth of Storm Bay: the weather justified this awful name. The bay should rather be called an estuary, for it receives at its head the waters of the Derwent. Near the mouth, there are some extensive basaltic platforms; but higher up the land becomes mountainous, and is covered by a light wood. The lower parts of the hills which skirt the bay are cleared; and the bright yellow fields of corn, and dark green ones of potatoes, appear very luxuriant. Late in the evening we anchored in the snug cove, on the shores of which stands the capital of Tasmania. The first aspect of the place was very inferior to that of Sydney; the latter might be called a city, this is only a town. It stands at the base of Mount Wellington, a mountain 3,100 feet high, but of little picturesque beauty; from this source, however, it receives a good supply of water. Round the cove there [is] a small fort. Coming from the Spanish settle-

## The Cruel Shore

*"Maggie, Maggie May,/They have taken her away/To walk upon Van Diemen's cruel shore..."* So begins the chorus of the traditional Liverpool folksong, first sung at a time when hundreds of hardened criminals like Maggie (a prostitute who "rolled," or stole, from her clients) were being forced to make the long voyage into antipodean exile every year. Lying to the southeast of the Australian mainland, the great island we know as Tasmania had been discovered by Dutch navigator Abel Tasman in 1642. He, however, had deferentially named it after his countryman Anthony van Diemen, then the governor general of the East Indies.

Britain, taking possession in the 1780s, opened its second important penal settlement there in 1803. As New South Wales began to tempt increasing numbers of immigrants, the authorities in London decided to make Van Diemen's Land its penal sink: the worst of England's criminals were sent here, and "free settlers" were actively discouraged. From 1840, transportations to Port Jackson–Sydney ceased, and all prisoners sent into exile ended up here. But the pressure from law-abiding emigrants mounted, and the authorities found themselves in the uncomfortable position of appearing to give convicted criminals a form of preferential treatment. Free emigration was allowed; the last prisoners were shipped out in 1853, and in 1856 the policy of transportation was officially abandoned. Van Diemen's land was given a new and more respectable identity under the name of Tasmania, and from that moment it has never looked back.

ments, where such magnificent care has generally been paid to the fortifications, the means of defence in these colonies appeared very contemptible.

Once again, Darwin finds his sympathies divided and his conscience troubled over the treatment of indigenous populations.

All the aborigines have been removed to an island in Bass's Straits, so that Van Diemen's Land enjoys the great advantage of being free from a native population. This most cruel step seems to have been quite unavoidable, as the only means of stopping a fearful succession of robberies, burnings, and murders, committed by the blacks; and which sooner or later would have ended in their utter destruction. I fear there is no doubt, that this train of evil and its consequences, originated in the infamous conduct of some of our countrymen. Thirty years is a short period, in which to have banished the last aboriginal from his native island—and that island nearly as large as Ireland. The correspondence on this subject, which took place between the government at home and that of Van Diemen's Land, is very interesting. Although numbers of natives were shot and taken prisoners in the skirmishing, which was going on at intervals for several years; nothing seems fully to have impressed them with the idea of our overwhelming power, until the whole island, in 1830, was put under martial law, and by proclamation the whole population commanded to assist in one great attempt to secure the entire race.

From 5,000 at the start of the century, Tasmania's Aboriginal population had fallen to a couple of hundred in Darwin's day. By 1876, there would be none. Darwin was genuinely disturbed by the injustice, but ultimately accepted it. He was able to make "several pleasant little excursions" during the *Beagle*'s stay in Hobart,

Chiefly with the object of examining the geological structure of the immediate neighbourhood. The main points of interest consist, first in some highly fossiliferous strata, belonging to the Devonian or Carboniferous period; secondly, in proofs of a late

## Wild Spirits

Two Tasmanian species Darwin managed to miss were extraordinary even by Australasian standards: the Tasmanian wolf (or thylacine, *Thylacinus cynocephalus, see* illustration below, at right) and the Tasmanian devil (*Sarcophilus harrisii, see* photograph at left). The former is no more a wolf than the latter is a devil: both are marsupials, so related to the kangaroo and wombat.

Sadly, the Tasmanian wolf was hunted to extinction in the first half of the twentieth century, persecuted, with government backing, for stealing sheep. But the smaller Tasmanian devil, (adults weigh around 12 pounds), which preys on everything from frogs to birds and the wallabies, is still surprisingly common, though as a nocturnal hunter, comparatively seldom seen. Its diabolical reputation comes from the strangeness of its appearance in European eyes, from its boldness when cornered and from the scary way its pale ears turn red when it is angry. But Tasmanians swear that, treated right, it can be tamed—can indeed become positively angelic: an affectionate companion and devoted pet.

small rise of the land; and lastly, in a solitary and superficial patch of yellowish limestone or travertin, which contains numerous impressions of leaves of trees, together with land-shells, not now existing. It is not improbable that this one small quarry includes the only remaining record of the vegetation of Van Diemen's Land during one former epoch.

The climate here is damper than in New South Wales, and hence the land is more fertile. Agriculture flourishes; the cultivated fields look well, and the gardens abound with thriving vegetables and fruit-trees. …In many parts the Eucalypti grew to a great size, and composed a noble forest. In some of the dampest ravines, tree-ferns flourished in an extraordinary manner; I saw one which must have been at least twenty feet high to the base of the fronds, and was in girth exactly six feet. The fronds forming the most elegant parasols, produced a gloomy shade, like that of the first hour of the night.

*Left: A koala sits in a Eucalyptus tree.*

## City of Darwin

Darwin's account of his time in Australia can strike the reader as a long series of expected sights unseen: the kangaroo, the koala, the Great Barrier Reef, for instance. One of the most strikings of these omissions is any mention of the city that now bears his name, of which he was never to come within a thousand miles. The modern capital of the Northern Territories, moreover, stands on the shores of what is called the Beagle Gulf—so it definitely seems to be our Darwin for which it's named.

In fact, the *Beagle* did come here on a subsequent voyage three years later, in 1839. And it was captained by John Lort Stokes, a Lieutenant on the 1831–36 voyage who had got to know the young naturalist well. He named the gulf after his vessel and the nearby harbor Port Darwin for his friend, though the larger town that grew up just inland was named Palmerston. The city was renamed "Darwin" in 1912.

# "Dull and Uninteresting"

On February 7, said Darwin, "the *Beagle* sailed from Tasmania, and on the 6th of the ensuing month, reached King George's Sound, situated close to the S. W. corner of Australia. We stayed there eight days; and we did not during our voyage pass a more dull and uninteresting time." Thankfully, there was one event to relieve the monotony of the *Beagle*'s stay.

A large tribe of natives, called the White Cockatoo men happened to pay the settlement a visit while we were there. These men, as well as those of the tribe belonging to King George's Sound, being tempted by the offer of some tubs of rice and sugar, were persuaded to hold a "corrobery," or great dancing-party. As soon as it grew dark, small fires were lighted, and the men commenced their toilet, which consisted in painting themselves white in spots and lines. As soon as all was ready, large fires were kept blazing, round which the women and children were collected as spectators; the Cockatoo and King George's men formed two distinct parties, and generally danced in answer to each other. The dancing consisted in their running either sideways or in Indian file into an open space, and stamping the ground with great force as they marched together. Their heavy footsteps were accompanied by a kind of grunt, by beating their clubs and spears together, and by various other gesticulations, such as extending their arms and wriggling their bodies. It was a most rude, barbarous scene, and, to our ideas, without any sort of meaning; but we observed that the black women and children watched it with the greatest pleasure. Perhaps these dances originally represented actions, such as wars and victories. ...Every one appeared in high spirits, and the group of nearly naked figures, viewed by the light of the blazing fires, all moving in hideous harmony, formed a perfect display of a festival amongst the lowest barbarians.

Darwin's description is of interest, not only in its vividness and broad sympathy, but in its revelation that the participants in this "party" were effectively paid performers, persuaded by the "offer of some tubs of rice and sugar." The heritage industry had apparently already been born.

It was with mixed feelings that Darwin departed from Australia.

After several tedious delays from clouded weather, on the 14th of March, we gladly stood out of King George's Sound on our course to Keeling Island. Farewell, Australia! you are a rising child, and doubtless some day will reign a great princess in the South: but you are too great and ambitious for affection, yet not great enough for respect. I leave your shores without sorrow or regret.

*Above: Natural pinnacles of limestone are a feature of southwestern Australia's Nambung National Park. Left: Aborigines celebrate a wedding in this old engraving.*

# Homeward Bound

*"We feel surprise when travellers tell us of the vast dimensions of the Pyramids and other great ruins, but how utterly insignificant are the greatest of these, when compared to these mountains of stone accumulated by the agency of various minute and tender animals!"*

It would be wrong to dismiss the final leg of Darwin's voyage as merely a tying up of loose ends, a closing chapter—partly because "closure" was the last thing that it brought. The true significance of this expedition—for Darwin and for science—would only start to shake down when he got home and, over months and even years, worked through the implications of his various findings.

It would be wrong, too, because Darwin made some of his most prized discoveries on this homeward stretch: he assumed it would be his work on coral atolls, conceived on the Keeling Islands, that were to secure him his footnote in scientific history. For us that work, though ingenious, has been almost totally eclipsed by the evolutionary thinking. And yet, things change, ideas develop—so, when all's said and done, who knows?

Who, for example, could have guessed that the work of Jean Baptiste Fourier (1768–1830) would be so radically reappraised almost two centuries after his death? He was long forgotten outside specialized circles, but in terms of enduring significance, he might yet give his younger contemporary a run for his money. An educated young man, Darwin had certainly heard of this great French mathematician, but not of his work on the heat-retaining properties of gases (1827). Fourier

*Previous pages:* "The whole island…was adorned with an air of perfect elegance." Darwin was enchanted by the beauty of Mauritius. **Above:** The homeward leg would take the Beagle across both Indian and Atlantic Oceans.

was, essentially, the man who first proposed the idea of the "greenhouse effect": in the twenty-first century, his legacy haunts us all.

This process is a perfectly natural one by which carbon dioxide and water vapor in the earth's atmosphere trap heat from the sun that might otherwise be reflected away. In moderation it is benign: without it the Ice Age would have continued indefinitely. The problem is that, thanks to pollution from industry, aircraft and motor vehicles, the last century has seen an unprecedented accumulation of greenhouse gases—not just carbon dioxide (of which the average car produces several tons each year), but carbon monoxide and CFCs (chlorofluorocarbons, used in aerosols). The net result, say many scientists, has been measurable global warming, with the expectation of higher mean temperatures to come. Since water expands as it gets warmer, and because of the melting of the polar ice sheets, sea levels will inevitably rise.

By how much is not clear: estimates for the rise by the end of the century range from as little as 3 to as much as 35 inches. But even a slight rise could have grave consequences for coral islands like the Keelings, which are nowhere more than a few feet above sea level. The problem is not so much that entire islands would be covered in water as that the normal storm surges and high tides would do more damage to cultivable land and water supplies.

Darwin was fascinated by the struggle between raging waves and slowly accreting coral in the Keeling Islands, but has the balance between them now been fatally disrupted? Darwin's own countrymen—his own relations, indeed—had been in the very vanguard of the Industrial Revolution. The benefits of that revolution over 200 years have been obvious and incalculable: living standards in the developed world have been transformed. The costs have been less evident, accumulating gradually in invisible carbon emissions whose possible implications are only now being recognized.

Could Darwin's precious reefs themselves be killed by climbing water temperatures? That would be a tragic irony indeed. Reports in the 1980s and early '90s showed reefs being ravaged in this way worldwide, including the Keelings. Sober ecologists predicted the complete extinction of the functioning coral reef. Yet today, just a few years later, the situation seems a little less bleak. There are clear indications now that many reefs are being rebuilt by different corals, species marginalized before but now free to thrive and spread. However, conservationists warn against premature assumptions: we cannot know how diverse or durable these renewed reefs will prove; nor how well future generations will adapt to continued warming. Yet there could hardly be a more striking illustration of the continuing (not to say the evolving) significance of Darwin's theories as we feel our way into an uncertain future.

*Below:* *Evolution is very much in action on the world's gradually warming coral reefs.*

# The Keeling Islands

On April 1, wrote Darwin, "We arrived in view of the Keeling or Cocos Islands, situated in the Indian Ocean, and about 600 miles distant from the coast of Sumatra."

This is one of the lagoon-islands (or atolls) of coral formation, similar to those in the Low Archipelago which we passed near.... The ring-formed reef of the lagoon-island is surmounted in the greater part of its length by linear islets. On the northern or leeward side, there is an opening through which vessels can pass to the anchorage within. On entering, the scene was very curious and rather pretty; its beauty, however, entirely depended on the brilliancy of the surrounding colours. The shallow, clear, and still water of the lagoon, resting in its greater part on white sand, is, when illumined by a vertical sun, of the most vivid green. This brilliant expanse, several miles in width, is on all sides divided, either by a line of snow-white breakers from the dark heaving waters of the ocean, or from the blue vault of heaven by the strips of land, crowned by the level tops of the cocoa-nut trees. As a white cloud here and there affords a pleasing contrast with the azure sky, so in the lagoon, bands of living coral darken the emerald green water.

The next morning after anchoring, I went on shore on Direction Island. The strip of dry land is only a few hundred yards in width; on the lagoon side there

*"A beach of glittering white sand formed a border to these fairy spots."*

is a white calcareous beach, the radiation from which under this sultry climate was very oppressive; and on the outer coast, a solid broad flat of coral-rock served to break the violence of the open sea. Excepting near the lagoon, where there is some sand, the land is entirely composed of rounded fragments of coral. In such a loose, dry, stony soil, the climate of the intertropical regions alone could produce a vigorous vegetation. On some of the smaller islets, nothing could be more elegant than the manner in which the young and full-grown cocoa-nut trees, without destroying each other's symmetry, were mingled into one wood. A beach of glittering white sand formed a border to these fairy spots.

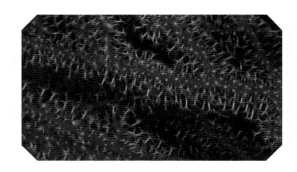

## Coral Construction

A riot of kaleidoscopic color, the coral reef looks like an underwater flowerbed, but those gorgeous blooms are produced by tiny animal polyps, not by plants. Stranger still is the skeletal base of calcium carbonate that each polyp secretes to anchor itself in place while its waving tentacles catch microscopic plankton drifting by. About one-tenth of an inch across, the coral grows in collective colonies in a wide range of shapes and sizes according to the species: what we might loosely call "a coral" could be a mass of many thousands. When the polyp dies, the mineral deposit remains and another polyp establishes itself on top of it: so, over years, centuries and millennia, are mighty reefs formed.

The flora and fauna of the islands were limited, but to Darwin intriguing by virtue of the fact that everything had to be here by chance, having wandered or drifted to this distant spot from somewhere else.

I will now give a sketch of the natural history of these islands, which, from its very paucity, possesses a peculiar interest. The cocoa-nut tree, at first glance, seems to compose the whole wood; there are however, five or six other trees. One of these grows to

*Left: The banana blossom and its fruit have the look of an overgrown orchid. Opposite, below: Sun, sea and sand: the tropical paradise.*

a very large size, but from the extremes of softness of its wood, is useless; another sort affords excellent timber for ship-building. Besides the trees, the number of plants is exceedingly limited, and consists of insignificant weeds. In my collection, which includes, I believe, nearly the perfect Flora, there are twenty species, without reckoning a moss, lichen, and fungus. To this number two trees must be added; one of which was not in flower, and the other I only heard of.... I do not include in the above list the sugar-cane, banana, some other vegetables, fruit-trees, and imported grasses. As the islands consist entirely of coral, and at one time must have existed as mere water-washed reefs, all their terrestrial productions must have been transported here by the waves of the sea. In accordance with this, the Florula has quite the character of a refuge for the destitute: Professor Henslow informs me that of the twenty species nineteen belong to different genera, and these again to no less than sixteen families!

The list of land animals is even poorer than that of the plants. Some of the islets are inhabited by rats, which were brought in a ship from the Mauritius, wrecked here.... There are no true land-birds, for a snipe and a rail (*Gallirallus phillippensis*), though living entirely in the dry herbage, belong to the order of Waders. Birds of this order are said to occur on several of the small low islands in the Pacific.... Of reptiles I saw only one small lizard. Of insects I took pains to collect every kind. Exclusive of spiders, which were numerous, there were thirteen species. ...Although the productions of the land are thus scanty, if we look to the waters of the surrounding sea, the number of organic beings is indeed infinite.

## Environment Under Threat

As well as boasting the unique Cocos buff-banded rail, the Keeling Islands have the largest colony of red-footed boobies in the Indian Ocean. There are also turtles galore: maturing green turtles and hawksbills come in their thousands each year to gorge themselves on the sponges and seaweeds that flourish just offshore.

Since 1995 the most northerly of the Keeling Islands has been a designated wildlife sanctuary, the Pulu Keeling National Park, but it remains very much an environment under threat. The atoll ecosystem is as precarious as the islands are exotic, and a range of measures have had to be taken to protect it. The soles of visitors' shoes and boots have to be cleaned, for instance, to prevent the transfer of harmful bacteria, while their clothes are checked for seeds, to make sure new plant species are not unwittingly imported to overwhelm existing flora.

# Land or Sea?

*Above:* Its house on its back, a hermit crab scuttles along the shoreline. *Below:* Regional varieties of the gannet are distributed around the world.

The long strips of land, forming the linear islets, have been raised only to that height to which the surf can throw fragments of coral, and the wind heap up calcareous sand. The solid flat of coral rock on the outside, by its breadth, breaks the first violence of the waves, which otherwise, in a day, would sweep away these islets and all their productions. The ocean and the land seem here struggling for mastery: although terra firma has obtained a footing, the denizens of the water think their claim at least equally good. In every part one meets hermit crabs of more than one species, carrying on their backs the shells which they have stolen from the neighbouring beach. Overhead, numerous gannets, frigate-birds, and terns, rest on the trees; and the wood, from the many nests and from the smell of the atmosphere, might be called a sea-rookery. The gannets, sitting on their rude nests, gaze at one with a stupid yet angry air. The noddies, as their name expresses, are silly little creatures. But there is one charming bird: it is a small, snow-white tern, which smoothly hovers at the distance of a few feet above one's head, its large black eye scanning, with quiet curiosity, your expression....

It is excusable to grow enthusiastic over the infinite numbers of organic beings with which the sea of the tropics, so prodigal of life, teems; yet I must confess I think those naturalists who have described, in well-known words, the submarine grottoes decked with a thousand beauties, have indulged in rather exuberant language.

On April 6, Darwin rcorded his amazed reaction at the sight of so many microorganisms holding their own in everlasting contest with the mighty ocean.

It is impossible to behold these waves without feeling a conviction that an island, though built of the hardest rock, let it be porphyry, granite, or quartz, would ultimately yield and be demolished by such an irresistible power. Yet these low, insignificant coral-islets stand and are victorious: for here another power, as an antagonist, takes part in the contest. The organic forces separate the atoms of carbonate of lime, one

by one, from the foaming breakers, and unite them into a symmetrical structure. Let the hurricane tear up its thousand huge fragments; yet what will that tell against the accumulated labour of myriads of architects at work night and day, month after month? Thus do we see the soft and gelatinous body of a polypus, through the agency of the vital laws, conquering the great mechanical power of the waves of an ocean which neither the art of man nor the inanimate works of nature could successfully resist.

And on a less epic scale, Darwin was also impressed by the robber crab:

It is very common on all parts of the dry land, and grows to a monstrous size. ...The front pair of legs terminate in very strong and heavy pincers, and the last pair are fitted with others weaker and much narrower. It would at first be thought quite impossible for a crab to open a strong cocoa-nut covered with the husk. ...The crab begins by tearing the husk, fibre by fibre, and always from that end under which the three eye-holes are situated; when this is completed, the crab commences hammering with its heavy claws on one of the eye-holes till an opening is made. Then turning round its body, by the aid of its posterior and narrow pair of pincers, it extracts the white albuminous substance. I think this is as curious a case of instinct as ever I heard of, and likewise of adaptation in structure between two objects apparently so remote from each other in the scheme of nature, as a crab and a cocoa-nut tree.

## Birgus Latro

The robber crab, as its Latin name has it, or coconut crab, is indeed a remarkable creature. Technically it is a hermit crab, one that protects its soft and vulnerable hindquarters by making a portable home for itself in an abandoned seashell. As the crab matures it develops its own hard external plating, necessary because, as Darwin says, it grows to a "monstrous" size. Its giant claws have been known to lift weights of more than 60 pounds. Talking later with another explorer of the region, Darwin heard that:

[He] confined one in a strong tin-box, which had held biscuits, the lid being secured with wire; but the crab turned down the edges and escaped. In turning down the edges, it actually punched many small holes quite through the tin!

*Left: Coconut palms sway against an azure sky.*

One of the most miraculous features of the Keeling Islands only became evident as the *Beagle* left the atoll, on the morning of April 12:

We stood out of the lagoon on our passage to the Isle of France. I am glad we have visited these islands: such formations surely rank high amongst the wonderful objects of this world. Captain Fitz

Roy found no bottom with a line 7,200 feet in length, at the distance of only 2,200 yards from the shore; hence this island forms a lofty submarine mountain, with sides steeper even than those of the most abrupt volcanic cone. The saucer-shaped summit is nearly ten miles across; and every single atom, from the least particle to the largest fragment of rock, in this great pile, which however is small compared with very many other lagoon-islands, bears the stamp of having been subjected to organic arrangement. We feel surprise when travellers tell us of the vast dimensions of the Pyramids and other great ruins, but how utterly insignificant are the greatest of these, when compared to these mountains of stone accumulated by the agency of various minute and tender animals! This is a wonder which does not at first strike the eye of the body, but, after reflection, the eye of reason.

*"This is a wonder which does not at first strike the eye of the body, but, after reflection, the eye of reason."*

# Pretty as a Picture

Mauritius, Darwin decided, when it came into sight on April 29, was so strikingly picturesque it might have been laid out for their delight:

In the morning we passed round the northern end of Mauritius, or the Isle of France. From this point of view the aspect of the island equalled the expectations raised by the many well-known descriptions of its beautiful scenery. The sloping plain of the Pamplemousses [grapefruit], interspersed with houses, and coloured by the large fields of sugar-cane of a bright green, composed the foreground. The brilliancy of the green was the more remarkable because it is a colour which generally is conspicuous only from a very short distance. Towards the centre of the island

## Extolling the Atoll

Darwin offered a theory on the formation of coral atolls that has been largely borne out by subsequent research. He believed that the story began with a volcanic eruption, and the creation of a mountain pushing up through the ocean floor, rising high enough to break the surface. This produced a roughly circular, conical island, around which an encircling reef then formed—for coral can grow only between certain depths. It must be covered at low water on the one hand, because it is quickly killed by the rays of the sun; too deep, though, and it lacks the light to live. It thus naturally creates a ring around the island, with breaks in indented areas where the sea floor falls away more quickly; a quiet lagoon is enclosed within the surrounding reef.

Through subsequent seismic activity, the volcanic cone that constitutes the island starts to subside gradually. Only the lowest levels die; above, polyps pile up slowly and steadily, the reef rising up toward the light. In time, what was once a towering peak may have sunk altogether from sight, but its imprint endures in

the coral atoll. As waves pound the top layers of the reef, a form of sandy soil results; in time it may support trees and wildlife, like the Keeling Islands. "The reef-constructing corals have indeed reared and preserved wonderful memorials of the subterranean oscillations of level; we see in each barrier-reef a proof that the land has there subsided, and in each atoll a monument over an island now lost," mused Darwin.

## Paul et Virginie

Conspicuous by its absence from Darwin's account of his time in Mauritius is any mention of Paul and Virginia who, their fictionality apart, might claim to be the most famous islanders of all time. Jacques-Henri Bernardin de Saint-Pierre (1737–1814), a disciple of Rousseau, had put Mauritius on the map of romantic Europe with his novel about two children who fall in love before being forced apart by the conventions of European society.

A Paul and Virginia industry erupted in Europe; there were umpteen editions of the novel, but it didn't stop there: there were engravings, wallpaper, terra-cotta figures, candelabra and commemorative kitsch of every kind. Tourists beat a path to Mauritius to muse, and shed a sensitive tear—and so an obliging entrepreneur even put up headstones to mark their nonexistent "graves."

That Darwin did not mention the characters' existence in his notes must have been a deliberate show of fastidiousness from a skeptical young scientific blade.

*Above:* Clear waters lap in wavelets against the coral sand of a Mauritius beach. *Below:* "Pretty well cultivated": Darwin loved to see a landscape set to work, as here in Mauritius.

groups of wooded mountains rose out of this highly cultivated plain; their summits, as so commonly happens with ancient volcanic rocks, being jagged into the sharpest points. Masses of white clouds were collected around these pinnacles, as if for the sake of pleasing the stranger's eye. The whole island, with its sloping border and central mountains, was adorned with an air of perfect elegance: the scenery, if I may use such an expression, appeared to the sight harmonious. . . .

**May 1st.**—Sunday. I took a quiet walk along the seacoast to the north of the town. The plain in this part is quite uncultivated; it consists of a field of black lava, smoothed over with coarse grass and bushes, the latter being chiefly Mimosas. The scenery may be described as intermediate in character between that of the Galapagos and of Tahiti; but this will convey a definite idea to very few persons. It is a very pleasant country, but it has not the charms of Tahiti, or the grandeur of Brazil. . . .

From our elevated position we enjoyed an excellent view over the island. The country on this side appears pretty well cultivated, being divided into fields and studded with farm-houses. I was, however, assured that, of the whole land, not more than half is yet in a productive state. If such be the case, considering the present large export of sugar, this island, at some future period when thickly peopled, will be of great value. Since England has taken possession of it, a period of only twenty-five years, the export of sugar is said to have increased seventy-five fold. One great cause of its prosperity is the excellent state of the roads. In the neighbouring Isle of Bourbon, which remains under the French government, the roads are still in the same miserable state as they were here only a few years ago. Although the French residents must have largely profited by the increased prosperity of their island, yet the English government is far from popular.

*Above: As its name suggests, the Madagascar fody was introduced to Mauritius. **Below:** Mauritius is dominated by dramatic peaks.*

# St. Helena

Next day, the *Beagle* put to see again, and Darwin found nothing else worthy of notice until, having rounded the Cape of Good Hope into the Atlantic, they arrived off St. Helena on July 8.

This island, the forbidding aspect of which has been so often described, rises abruptly like a huge black castle from the ocean. Near the town, as if to complete nature's defence, small forts and guns fill up every gap in the rugged rocks. The town runs up a flat and narrow valley; the houses look respectable, and are interspersed with a very few green trees. When approaching the anchorage there was one striking view: an irregular castle perched on the summit of a lofty hill, and surrounded by a few scattered fir-trees, boldly projected against the sky.

*"The island…rises abruptly like a huge black castle from the ocean."*

The next day I obtained lodgings within a stone's throw of Napoleon's tomb; it was a capital central situation, whence I could make excursions in every direction. During the four days I stayed here, I wandered over the island from morning to night, and examined its geological history. My lodgings were situated at a height of about 2,000 feet; here the weather was cold and boisterous, with constant showers of rain; and every now and then the whole scene was veiled in thick clouds.

Like the Keeling Islands, St Helena had a strikingly foreign flora. Its plants had not stowed away on ocean currents though, but been brought deliberately. Thanks to the cold waters of the Benguela Current, the island's climate and rainfall levels resemble those of Darwin's native land rather than those of a tropical island.

Near the coast the rough lava is quite bare: in the central and higher parts, feldspathic rocks by their decomposition have produced a clayey soil, which, where not covered by vegetation, is stained in broad

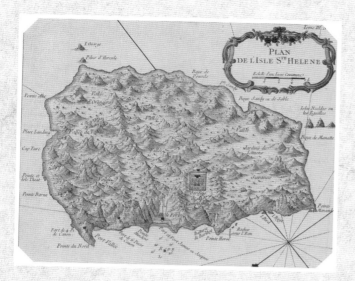

*Above:* St. Helena was a vital waystation and strategic stronghold in the days of sail. *Below, right:* Many of the island's trees were imported, like this weeping willow.

## Jailhouse Rock?

St. Helena's most famous resident, then as now, was Napoleon Bonaparte, the great French general and later Emperor Napoleon I. He had been sent here as a prisoner after his final defeat at Waterloo in 1815, and would remain a captive till his death of stomach cancer in 1821. After him, however, St. Helena saw few prisoners for quite some time: a jail was built in 1827 but had two inmates. It wasn't until the end of the century that the island was to become a place of incarceration on a significant scale. During the Second Boer War (1899–1902), when Afrikaner farmers in South Africa rose up against British rule, the island saw service once again. Lord Kitchener sent some 6,000 Boer prisoners-of-war to St. Helena.

bands of many bright colours. At this season, the land moistened by constant showers, produces a singularly bright green pasture, which lower and lower down, gradually fades away and at last disappears. In latitude 16 degrees, and at the trifling elevation of 1,500 feet, it is surprising to behold a vegetation possessing a character decidedly British. The hills are crowned with irregular plantations of Scotch firs; and the sloping banks are thickly scattered over with thickets of gorse, covered with its bright yellow flowers. Weeping-willows are common on the banks of the rivulets, and the hedges are made of the blackberry, producing its well-known fruit. When we consider that the number of plants now found on the island is 746, and that out of these fifty-two alone are indigenous species, the rest having been imported, and most of them from England, we see the reason of the British character of the vegetation. Many of these English plants appear to flourish better than in their native country; some also from the opposite quarter of Australia succeed remarkably well. The many imported species must have destroyed some of the native kinds; and it is only on the highest and steepest ridges that the indigenous Flora is now predominant. ...There is so little level or useful land, that it seems surprising how so many people, about 5,000, can subsist here. The lower orders, or the emancipated slaves, are I believe extremely poor: they complain of the want of work.

From the reduction in the number of public servants owing to the island having been given up by the East Indian Company, and the consequent emigration of many of the richer people, the poverty probably will increase. …

I so much enjoyed my rambles among the rocks and mountains of St. Helena, that I felt almost sorry on the morning of the 14th to descend to the town. Before noon I was on board, and the Beagle made sail.

## The Struggle for St. Helena

"It is quite extraordinary," noted Darwin in a journal entry of July 13, "the scrupulous degree to which the coast must formerly have been guarded. There are alarm houses, alarm guns and alarm stations on every peak." There had been good reason for such precautions: possession of the island had long been bitterly contested.

St. Helena had been discovered in 1502 by Portugal's Joāno de Nova, but the first settlement was established by the Dutch in 1645. They forsook St. Helena for South Africa around 1650, and the British East India Company were quick to snap up a possession whose value as a waystation for shipping between Europe and the East was by now becoming clear. The Dutch recovered the island for a few months in 1673. But despite a French raid in 1706, St. Helena remained in British hands thereafter, the East India Company handing administration over to the Crown in 1834.

# Ascension Island

"On the 19th of July we reached Ascension," announced Darwin. "Those who have beheld a volcanic island, situated under an arid climate, will at once be able to picture to themselves [its] appearance." For those who haven't, fortunately, he offered a little coaching:

They will imagine smooth conical hills of a bright red colour, with their summits generally truncated, rising separately out of a level surface of black rugged lava. A principal mound in the centre of the island, seems the father of the lesser cones. It is called Green Hill, its name being taken from the faintest tinge of that colour, which at this time of the year is barely perceptible from the anchorage. To complete the desolate scene, the black rocks on the coast are lashed by a wild and turbulent sea.

The settlement is near the beach; it consists of several houses and barracks placed irregularly, but well built of white freestone. The only inhabitants are marines, and some negroes liberated from slaveships, who are paid and victualled by government. There is not a private person on the island. Many of the marines appeared well contented with their situation; they think it better to serve their one-and-twenty years on shore, let it be what it may, than in a ship; in this choice, if I were a marine, I should most heartily agree. …

One of my excursions took me towards the southwest extremity of the island. The day was clear and hot, and I saw the island, not smiling with beauty, but staring with naked hideousness. The lava streams are covered with hummocks, and are rugged to a degree which, geologically speaking, is not of easy explanation. The intervening spaces are concealed with layers of pumice, ashes and volcanic tuff.

*Opposite: Seabirds by the thousand throng the foreground in this early photograph of Ascension Island. Opposite, top: The coast of Bahia, Brazil, as revealed in a colorized photograph.*

## A Cinder in the Sea

Darwin quoted with both amusement and approbation the observation apparently made by the wits of St. Helena: "We know we live on a rock, but the poor people at Ascension live on a cinder." Mineralogically speaking, there is something in what they say, though in truth both islands are volcanic in formation. Ascension is smaller and more rugged, though, with a great deal less fertile soil: it was first occupied in 1815 by the British, who saw it as a base from which to intercept any attempt to "spring" Napoleon from his place of exile. It remains a British territory, though in the last century it has more often been used by the U.S. military, for whom it was a vital base for mid-Atlantic refueling stops during World War II. From the late 1950s it became a vital hub for missile tracking and communications surveillance in the Cold War.

NATO service personnel apart, the island's most important inhabitants are its seabirds, especially the sooty terns or "wideawakes," for which this remains one of the world's most important breeding centers.

# Back to Brazil

"On leaving Ascension," Darwin continued, "we sailed for Bahia, on the coast of Brazil, in order to complete the chronometrical measurement of the world. We arrived there on August 1st, and," he said:

Stayed four days, during which I took several long walks. I was glad to find my enjoyment in tropical scenery had not decreased from the want of novelty, even in the slightest degree. The elements of the scenery are so simple, that they are worth mentioning, as a proof on what trifling circumstances exquisite natural beauty depends.

The country may be described as a level plain of about three hundred feet in elevation, which in all parts has been worn into flat-bottomed valleys. This structure is remarkable in a granitic land, but is nearly universal in all those softer formations of which plains are usually composed. The whole surface is covered by various kinds of stately trees, interspersed with patches of cultivated ground, out of which houses, convents, and chapels arise. It must be remembered that within the tropics, the wild luxuriance of nature is not lost even in the vicinity of large cities: for the natural vegetation of the hedges and hill-sides overpowers in picturesque effect the artificial labour of man. Hence, there are only a few spots where the bright red soil affords a strong contrast with the universal clothing of green. From the edges of the plain there are distant views either of the ocean, or of the great Bay with its low-wooded shores, and on which numerous boats and canoes show their white sails. Excepting from these points, the scene is extremely limited; following the level pathways, on each hand, only glimpses into the wooded valleys below can be obtained. The houses I may add, and especially the sacred edifices, are built in a peculiar and rather fantastic style of architecture. They are all whitewashed; so that when illumined by the brilliant sun of midday, and as seen against the pale blue sky of the horizon, they stand out more like shadows than real buildings.

Such are the elements of the scenery, but it is a hopeless attempt to paint the general effect. ...Who from seeing choice plants in a hothouse, can magnify some into the dimensions of forest trees, and crowd others into an entangled jungle? Who when examining in the cabinet of the entomologist the gay exotic butterflies, and singular cicadas, will associate with these lifeless objects, the ceaseless harsh music of the latter, and the lazy flight of the former—the sure accompaniments of the still, glowing noonday of the tropics? It is when the sun has attained its greatest height, that such scenes should be viewed: then the dense splendid foliage of the mango hides the ground with its darkest shade, whilst the upper branches are rendered from the profusion of light of the most brilliant green.

*Left:* The "gay exotic butterflies" were just one element in the kaleidoscope of color that was the tropical forest. *Below:* "The dense splendid foliage of the mango."

permission to pass through their gardens to an uncultivated hill, for the purpose of viewing the country. I feel glad that this happened in the land of the Brazilians, for I bear them no good will—a land also of slavery, and therefore of moral debasement.

Darwin's last days in Pernambuco seem to have prompted further reflections on the institution of slavery, an issue on which he had always felt strongly. "On the 19th of August we finally left the shores of Brazil," he wrote.

I thank God, I shall never again visit a slave-country. To this day, if I hear a distant scream, it recalls with painful vividness my feelings, when passing a house near Pernambuco, I heard the most pitiable moans, and could not but suspect that some poor slave was being tortured, yet knew that I was as powerless as a child even to remonstrate. I suspected that these moans were from a tortured slave, for I was told that

"In the afternoon we stood out to sea," recorded Darwin on August 6,

With the intention of making a direct course to the Cape de Verd Islands. Unfavourable winds, however, delayed us, and on the 12th we ran into Pernambuco, a large city on the coast of Brazil, in latitude 8 degrees south. We anchored outside the reef; but in a short time a pilot came on board and took us into the inner harbour, where we lay close to the town. ...

I must here commemorate what happened for the first time during our nearly five years' wandering, namely, having met with a want of politeness. I was refused in a sullen manner at two different houses, and obtained with difficulty from a third,

## The City on the Reef

Darwin may not have been impressed by Pernambuco, but other visitors have been more susceptible to the charms of what has in recent years emerged as a lively tourist center known as "the Venice of Brazil." Today, it is more often known as "Recife," a name it takes from the long, straight reef that runs along the shore just off the coast. Olinda, the provincial capital, until it was overtaken by Recife in the eighteenth century, has now received recognition as a UNESCO world heritage city.

this was the case in another instance. Near Rio de Janeiro I lived opposite to an old lady, who kept screws to crush the fingers of her female slaves. I have stayed in a house where a young household mulatto, daily and hourly, was reviled, beaten, and persecuted enough to break the spirit of the lowest animal. I have seen a little boy, six or seven years old, struck thrice with a horse-whip (before I could interfere) on his naked head, for having handed me a glass of water not quite clean; I saw his father tremble at a mere glance from his master's eye. These latter cruelties were witnessed by me in a Spanish colony, in which it has always been said, that slaves are better treated than by the Portuguese, English, or other European nations. I have seen at Rio de Janeiro a powerful negro afraid to ward off a blow directed, as he thought, at his face. I was present when a kind-hearted man was on the point of separating forever the men, women, and little children of a large number of families who had long lived together. I will not even allude to the many heart-sickening atrocities which I authentically heard of—nor would I have mentioned the above revolting details, had I not met with several people, so blinded by the constitutional gaiety of the negro as to speak of slavery as a tolerable evil. Such people have generally visited at the houses of the upper classes, where the domestic slaves are usually well treated, and they have not, like myself,

*"We steered, thanks to God, a direct course for England."*

lived amongst the lower classes. Such inquirers will ask slaves about their condition; they forget that the slave must indeed be dull, who does not calculate on the chance of his answer reaching his master's ears.

…Those who look tenderly at the slave owner, and with a cold heart at the slave, never seem to put themselves into the position of the latter; what a cheerless prospect, with not even a hope of change! picture to yourself the chance, ever hanging over you, of your wife and your little children—those objects which nature urges even the slave to call his own—being torn from you and sold like beasts to the first bidder! And these deeds are done and palliated by men, who profess to love their neighbours as themselves, who believe in God, and pray that his Will be done on earth!…

"I suffer very much from sea-sickness," Darwin admitted in his diary for that day, though taking comfort from the fact that he was at least "on the road to England." His mood soon lifted though: by August 31 he was able to record the expedition's arrival, "after a most excellent passage," at Porto Praya, four-and-a-half years after his previous visit to the Cape Verde Islands. A few days later in the Canary Islands, he was excited to meet "some old English friends amongst the insects, and of birds, the starling, water wagtail, chaffinch and blackbird." A short stop off the coast of St Michael's (São Miguel) in the Azores to pick up any letters for England and then, the *Beagle* "getting a good offing from the land, we steered, thanks to God, a direct course for England."

*Above: Brazilian slaves depicted in a romanticized nineteenth-century engraving. Right: Porto Praya can clearly be seen in this French map of the Cape Verde Islands (1746).*

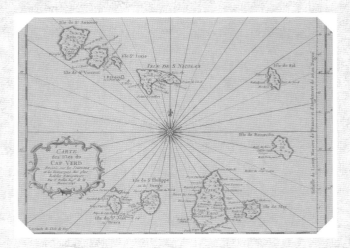

# Epilogue

*"The wide world does not contain so happy a prospect as the rich cultivated land of England."*

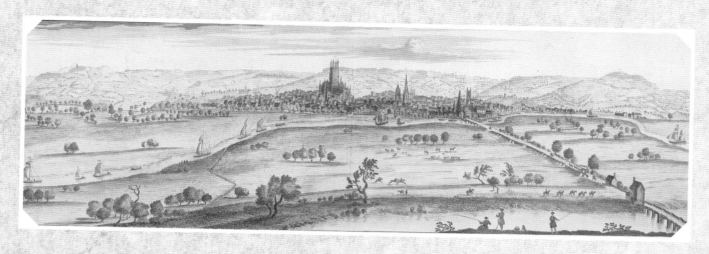

No great fanfare awaited Darwin when the *Beagle* returned to England: there was no indication as yet of just how far-reaching his findings were to prove; he himself had as yet to appreciate their full significance. His most powerful impression on landing, in fact, was one of relief to be ashore, for his old enemy seasickness had kept him in its grip for the last few days. After that, he thought of his family, promptly heading back to Shrewsbury on the mail coach to be reunited with his parents and sisters—and the English countryside. "I arrived here yesterday morning at breakfast time," he told FitzRoy in a letter,

& thank God, found all my dear good sisters & father quite well. My father appears more cheerful and very little older than when I left. My sisters assure me I do not look the least different, & I am able to return the compliment. Indeed all England appears changed, excepting the good old town of Shrewsbury & its inhabitants—which for all I can see to the contrary may go on as they now are to Doomsday.... The first day in the mail tired me, but as I drew nearer to Shrewsbury everything now looked more beautiful & cheerful. In passing Gloucestershire & Worcestershire I wished much for you to admire the fields, woods & orchards. The stupid people on the coach did not seem to think the fields one bit greener than usual, but I am sure we should have thoroughly agreed that the wide world does not contain so happy a prospect as the rich cultivated land of England.

There were shades of the Prodigal Son's return: "I am a very great man at home," Darwin told FitzRoy: he had clearly grown even in his father's skeptical estimation.

There would be some scientific response, too, in the months that followed his homecoming: Charles Lyell greeted him enthusiastically, for one—it was already clear that Darwin's observations did his geological theories no harm at all. Anything in the way of an evolutionary theory was still some way off for Darwin, though the door to such thinking had been opened by the conclusions he had been coming to about the world's great age. It was through Lyell that Darwin met Richard Owen, a brilliant young anatomist, who helped him make some sort of order out of the collection of

*Left: The* Beagle *anchored in Falmouth, England, on October 2, 1836.* **Above:** *Pastoral Gloucestershire, in a 1734 painting.* **Opposite:** *England's rural scenes gladdened Darwin's travel-weary heart.*

bones he had brought back from the Argentinean pampas. Owen would become a bitter critic of Darwin's theories, but his assistance at this stage helped establish the immense diversity—and in many cases, size—of South America's extinct species. (Owen was sufficiently a scientist himself to appreciate that successions of species had replaced one another over enormous stretches of time, but he accounted for this by a process of "continuous creation," authored by a divine intelligence.) Perhaps the most crucial single pointer, though, would come from ornithologist James Gould. It was to him that Darwin had handed all the finchlike birds he had collected in the Galápagos Islands without a second thought; and it was he who now revealed that they were not merely finchlike but actually finches (see "Finch Phenomenon," page 141). Darwin was fascinated by this apparent anomaly, but it was still to be some years before he was able to formulate his account of how it had come about.

Meanwhile, he continued to live and work quietly, though settled now in London rather than in Shrewsbury. Despite periodic trips away in pursuit of his work, he was happy for the most part to remain at home. In 1839 he married his cousin Emma Wedgwood, and they moved to a house in rural Kent, to the southeast of London. Theirs was to be a close and loving family, though Emma never ceased worrying about the irreligious direction in which she felt her husband's researches were taking him. And they were not without their share of tragedies: in particular in 1851, when their beloved daughter Annie died of tuberculosis. His bitter grief at this bereavement, Randal Keynes has suggested in a brilliant recent study, was important in pushing Darwin toward agnosticism and his ultimate view of a relentlessly amoral evolutionary order. If this is so, then it is not a case of Darwin's scientific findings forcing out religion, as Emma feared, but of spiritual disenchantment driving a move to scientific rationalism.

Only gradually over several years, though, did Darwin put together his theory of evolution through natural selection, and even then he only published it, in 1858, when his hand was forced. Another naturalist, Alfred Russel Wallace, had reached conclusions strikingly similar to his own. Darwin had corresponded with Wallace for some time, and encouraged his interest in evolution, but Wallace had developed his own theory unassisted. Scrupulously, Darwin published Wallace's work at the same time as he did his own. But it was Darwin's case, as argued fully in his book *On the Origin of Species by Natural Selection* (1859), that would ultimately carry the day.

## The Nearly Man

Born in Monmouthshire (now Gwent), Wales, in 1823, Alfred Russel Wallace was the third of nine children: his father was an impoverished country lawyer. Growing up with a passion for zoology, he was inspired (in part by Darwin's *Voyage of the Beagle*) to travel the world: he funded his explorations by collecting animal specimens. He got himself on the natural history map in the form of a line drawn between the islands of Borneo and Celebes. This line, Wallace observed, in an expedition to the Malayan Archipelago in the 1850s, marked the boundary between the different faunas of Oceania and Asia.

A worthy accomplishment, to be sure, but comparatively negligible when one reflects how close Wallace came to claiming Darwin's title as the father of evolutionary thought. Ultimately, Darwin's theory was the more sophisticated, taking into account not just environmental factors but competition within species, but there is no doubt that Wallace was within an ace of stealing Darwin's thunder.

It would not do so immediately, by any means. As Alfred Russel Wallace was to write, "Truth is born into this world only with pangs and tribulations, and every fresh truth is received unwillingly." Darwin's earlier reluctance to publish had been based on his understanding that any theory of the type he was proposing to advance would prompt the rage and derision of his scientific opponents, and the deep sadness and anxiety of many of his friends. So it was to prove: the *Origin of Species* was greeted by a critical furore; it was denounced as an "abuse of science" by Richard Owen. The critical demolitions were long on outrage, strikingly short on specific objections, but this didn't matter when the specter of the ape-man could be evoked.

This—entirely imaginary—being was most most famously summoned up at a public debate held in Oxford in 1860, when the conservative Bishop Wilberforce ("Soapy Sam") disputed with Thomas

*Left: Thomas Henry Huxley, Darwin's greatest champion. Below: From primitive fish to human beings: the very notion of evolution was bound to shock the nineteenth-century world profoundly.*

Henry Huxley, the self-styled "Darwin's Bulldog." Wilberforce concluded his presentation by asking, sneeringly, whether it was through his grandfather or grandmother's side that his opponent had been descended from an ape. A lapse in good manners in any age, this was unpardonable rudeness in Victorian England, and Huxley was well able to turn it to his advantage. "If then," he said majestically, "the question is put to me would I rather have a miserable ape for a grandfather or a man highly endowed by nature and possessed of great means and influence and yet who employs these faculties and that influence for the mere purpose of introducing ridicule into a grave scientific discussion I unhesitatingly affirm my preference for the ape."

Darwin never really suggested for a moment that men and women were descended from apes, of course: that apes and humans had common *ancestors* is now generally acknowledged. In the nineteenth century, though, the idea that any connection whatsoever might exist was for most people quite unthinkable, and Bishop Wilberforce was not the only person to regard it with ridicule. It was treated that way in part because it genuinely seemed too laughable to be true; in part because deep down people must have wondered if there weren't something in it. However great the differences may be, the similarities between humans and the higher apes are patently obvious: what if we weren't quite as unique as we'd always assumed? At stake were not simply self-esteem, but the values held most sacred over centuries; the sense that men and women stood apart from the animal kingdom as rulers of creation; the confident assumption that they had immortal souls.

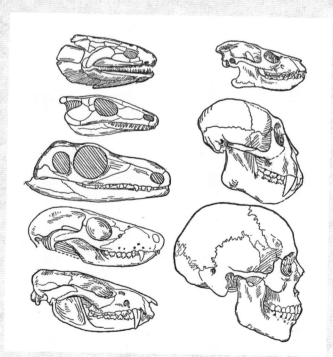

# A Controversial Legacy

The debates that raged around evolutionary theory often generated a great deal more heat than light: Darwin's ideas were widely misunderstood—and not just by his detractors. The application of biological concepts to economics or politics may offer vivid analogies, but can do no more: yet opinion formers rushed in where true scientists feared to tread. At the beginning of the 1880s, dismissing humanitarian concerns about the plight of the poor in London's East End during an economic downturn, London's *Times* newspaper was unapologetic in its refusal to be moved. "There is no one to blame for this," it said flatly: "It is the result of Nature's simplest laws!" *Laissez-faire* capitalism was only one ideology that found comfort in a crass misreading of evolutionary theory; imperialism too invoked a debased Darwinism in its support. Some nations, it was said, were "superior" to others: they would "naturally" achieve ascendancy over the rest. Darwin's countrymen were in the late-nineteenth century building an empire in India and Africa: it was nice to believe that this dominance arose from an inevitable destiny.

Racism of one sort or another may have been an age-old problem, but now it could wear a cloak of pseudo-science. By 1899, Houston Stewart Chamberlain was seriously advancing the view that the "Aryan" stock of the German and Anglo-Saxon races was inherently superior to any other. His ideas would be taken up with

## "The Survival of the Fittest"

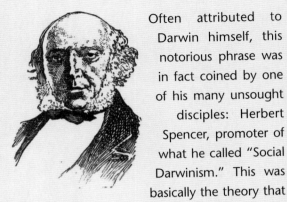

Often attributed to Darwin himself, this notorious phrase was in fact coined by one of his many unsought disciples: Herbert Spencer, promoter of what he called "Social Darwinism." This was basically the theory that in the red-blooded struggle for economic survival, the strongest would thrive, while the weakest would fall by the wayside. Wealth was the mark of success, which was in turn an indication of an individual's "fitness"; this would be transmitted to their descendants and consolidated down the generations. Poverty, on the other hand, was the mark of unfitness and of failure. The weak should be allowed to perish, rather than drag down the population as a whole.

Not surprisingly, such thinking found favor with the wealthiest in late-nineteenth-century British and American society and with that caste of writers and journalists who catered to their tastes. Social Darwinism did not simply confer a "scientific" authority on the status quo, licensing inequalities of fortune and status; it took want and even starvation in its stride. Spencer had all the bland ruthlessness of the mechanistic thinker, even giving the Irish famine the thumbs up: the weak and "unfit" had been weeded out, and evolutionary progress made, he argued approvingly.

*Left: London's "naturally" poor inhabitants? (Harper's Weekly, 1859).* **Opposite, top:** *James Island seen from Bartholomé Island, in the Galápagos.* **Opposite, center:** *Darwin as an old man.*

murderous enthusiasm by Adolf Hitler and eventually end up at Auschwitz. But to focus too much on the "Final Solution" is to risk ignoring the remarkable extent to which similar sorts of thinking permeated more "respectable" society. Everything from U.S. immigration policy to the treatment of the mentally handicapped was influenced by an often explicitly stated concern to "improve" the "stock." None of this had anything to do with Darwin, of course, but the ideas of natural selection and Darwinian struggle had caught the imagination.

Not all would be swayed: some drew back from the harsh inhumanity of the various sub–Darwinisms; others rejected the theory of evolution on religious grounds. The Bible was the Word of God, they insisted: it was not for mortal men or women to choose to read it anything but literally. At Dayton, Tennessee, in 1925, John Scopes, a substitute biology teacher who had discussed evolutionary theory with his students was arraigned at what was immediately named the "Monkey Trial" in the nation's press. The controversy continues—has even deepened in recent decades, with a resurgent religious right calling for Creationism to be taught in schools. Evolution is just a theory, it is said—sometimes implying it were merely roughed out on the back of an envelope—and scientists claim far too much on its behalf. On the contrary, perhaps only the scrupulous diffidence of the scientific community has caused it to stop short of insisting on evolution as a proven fact: the evidence in its favor is overwhelming.

The controversy seems set to rumble on: the voyage of the *Beagle* may long since have ended but the intellectual exploration Darwin embarked upon still continues. Whether we accept its implications or not, there is no question of the significance of a scientific question that has loomed larger than any other over the modern age.

## The Beagle Comes to Rest

Early in 2004, researchers in southeast England's Essex marshes made a remarkable discovery when they came upon the ruined hull of HMS *Beagle* sunk in shallow water. After its historic round-the-world voyage, Darwin's ship had been handed over to the Customs department and used to patrol the myriad inlets of this complicated coast. In the 1860s, the aging vessel had been anchored permanently in the estuary of the River Roach and used as a floating lookout post. In 1870 she had been sold for scrap, and her superstructure stripped, but the remains of the hull appeared to be there—and, it is hoped, recoverable.

# Bibliographic Afterword: The Evolution of a Book

In 1839, the London publisher Henry Colburn issued a set of volumes under the imposing, if uncatchy, title *Narrative of the Surveying Voyages of His Majesty's Ships Adventure and Beagle, between the years 1826 and 1836*, describing their examination of the southern shores of South America, and the *Beagle's* circumnavigation of the globe. Volume I consisted of the formal report of Captain P. Parker King, commander of an earlier expedition that, though related to the *Beagle's*, had not involved Charles Darwin; Volume II was that of Darwin's captain (and, eventually, friend), Robert FitzRoy. Darwin's own *Journal and Remarks* appeared as Volume III, but, though presented rather as an afterthought, it was soon far outstripping the others in terms of sales.

The modern reader cannot escape a consciousness of the *Journal's* monumental status in the history of science, so its sheer readability, its personality, and good humor, as well as its excitement, come as a surprise. To begin with, though, nobody had any sense of quite how important Darwin's findings were eventually going to be, so the success of his account was just about entirely due to the vividness of his writing. A second impression, renamed *Journal of Researches*, appeared later in 1839 and was several times reprinted; a much-revised edition appeared (under the same title) in 1845. These were the works that were to become known as *The Voyage of the Beagle*. Each text has its recommendations: this book draws on both, as well as making occasional (and clearly signposted) reference to the journal Darwin kept aboard the *Beagle*.

The intention of this book is to give the freshest and most stimulating possible sense of Darwin's account in its historical and scientific context. It makes no claims to completeness, nor does it explore in any depth the differences of detail and emphasis between Darwin's two editions, interesting as these may be. A complete edition of Darwin's works has been undertaken by Paul Barrett and R.B. Freeman (New York University Press, 1987–90);

1845 edition. As for the *Voyage of the Beagle* in particular, a complete text of the 1845 edition is available from The Online Literature Library. The 1839 text is harder to get hold of, though Janet Browne and Michael Neve's Penguin Classics edition (1989) offers an abridged version. *Charles Darwin's Beagle Diary* (ed. R.D. Keynes, Cambridge University Press, 1988) provides Darwin's impressions of his voyage in their most direct form. Much of these notes were incorporated directly into the account written up subsequently in the *Voyage of the Beagle*. Faithful as it is, however, this later account has a narrative drive and structure completely lacking in the initial notes, which is why it has been preferred over the "original" as the basis for this book.

As might be expected given the significance of the subject, background reading abounds: Darwin is still very much at the center of debates in both science and morality. There is no way a brief bibliography can hope to do justice to the scale and diversity of discussion the *Beagle* voyage has prompted: the list below makes just a very few suggestions on works of the most general interest and immediate relevance.

Browne, E. Janet, *Charles Darwin: Voyaging* (Princeton, NJ: Princeton University Press, 1995).

—*Charles Darwin: The Power of Place* (New York: Knopf, 2002).

Darwin, Charles (ed. Nora Barlow), *The Autobiography of Charles Darwin, 1809–1882* (London: Collins, 1958; repr. New York: W.W. Norton & Company, 1993).

Keynes, R.D., *Fossils, Finches, and Fuegians: Darwin's Adventures and Discoveries on the Beagle* (New York: Oxford University Press, 2003).

Zimmer, Carl, *Evolution: The Triumph of an Idea* (New York: HarperCollins, 2001).

Many of Darwin's letters to fellow scientists and other figures are also available from the online database of the Darwin Correspondence Project, University Library, Cambridge, CB3 9DR, United Kingdom.

# Acknowledgments

The publisher would like to thank Wolfgang Kaehler and Jennifer June for their help in the preparation of this book. All photographs in this book are © **Wolfgang Kaehler** unless otherwise listed here. Grateful acknowledgment is made to the following individuals and institutions for permission to reproduce illustrations and photographs:

© **2005 JupiterImages Corporation:** 7(b), 8(t,c), 11, 14, 16, 17(c), 23(b), 26, 27(b), 29, 30(l), 31, 32, 36(t), 37, 40, 41, 42, 43, 45, 46(b), 47(b), 48, 49, 51, 52, 53, 56, 57(b), 58, 59(t), 60(b), 61(t), 62, 63, 64(b), 65(b), 70, 72, 74, 82, 86(t), 87, 88, 91(b), 92, 94, 96, 97(c), 100, 103, 104(t), 105(b), 107(t), 109(b), 110, 116, 118(b), 119, 120, 121, 122(t&b,l), 124(b), 125, 126, 128, 129(c), 132(t), 135(c), 143, 152, 153(b), 155(b), 157(b), 158(b), 161, 162(t), 163(t&r), 164, 165, 166, 167(b), 170, 171, 172(t), 173, 175, 176(t), 177, 178(b,l), 179, 180, 181, 182, 183, 186, 187, 188(r), 193(t,l), 195, 196, 197(t&b), 198(t), 199, 201(t), 202, 203, 204, 205(c); **Library of Congress, Prints and Photographs Division:** 7(t), 8(b), 9, 10, 15(b), 21, 28, 30(r), 44(t), 57(c), 86(b), 89, 112, 118(t), 124(t), 127, 129(t&b), 138(t), 167(t).

# Index

Illustrations are shown in *italic* type.

Allende, Salvador 88
alpacas 45, 60
altitude sickness 119, 120
Andes, the *see* Cordillera, the
anteaters 63
Argentina 24–83, 86, 87, 96, 117, 120–23: Aconcagua 88, 89, *89*, 109, 118, 123; Bahia Blanca 36, 37, 64; Beagle Channel *73, 77, 83*; Buenos Aires 26, 35, 37, *37*, 42, 44, 45, 49; great drought, the 45; Lake District *33*; Mendoza 42, 89, 117, 119, 120, 121–22; pampas 24–53, 65, 117, 121, 202; Patagonia 26, 33–36, 54–67, 93; Port Desire 58, *59*, 66; Port Famine 80–82; Puerto San Julian 57, 61, 62, 63; Punta Arenas 57, Río Negro 33–34, 50, 66; Santa Fe 40, 42, 43, 45, 48; Uspallata Pass 121, *121*, 123, 127 *see also* Falkland Islands; gauchos; indigenous peoples; Río de la Plata; Tierra del Fuego
armadillos 36, 63, 64, *64*
Ascension Island 196–97
Atlantic Ocean, the 6, 14–18, 102–03, 119, 123, 195–99
Australia 168–83, 195: Darwin 182; Sydney (Port Jackson) 172–74, *172*, 182; Uluru *171*
Balmaceda, José Manuel 88
Bay of Biscay 16
*Beagle*, HMS *14*: preparations for the voyage 15; fate of the 205
Belgrano, Gen. Manuel 41

birds *4*, 47, *47*, 48, 59, *59*, 68–69, *71*, 79, 97, 104, 107, 109, *109*, 132, 137, 140–41, *140*, *141*, 148, 166–67, 189, 194, 196, 197 *see also* boobies; condors; finches; flamingos; frigate birds; hummingbirds; macaws; pelicans; penguins; petrels; swans; toucans
Bolivia 121
boobies *140*, *148*, 189
butterflies 19, 198
Brazil 12–23, 35, 65, 154, 193, 197–99: Bahia 17, 18; Corcovado, the 19, *19*, 22, *22*, *23*; rainforests *12–13*, *15*, 17, 19, *19*, 23, *23*, 192; Rio de Janeiro *15*,18, 19, 21, 22, *23*, 28, 199
Britain, colonial 79, 81, 87, 196
cacti 94, *94*, 135, *135*, 136, 139, 147
camels 45, 60, 63
Canary Islands, the 16–17, *16*, 199: Grand Canary Island 16; Tenerife 16, *16*
Cape of Good Hope, the 194
Cape Verde Islands, the 16–17, 61, 199, 199: Santiago (St. Jago) 16–17, 61
capybaras 32, 37, 63, 64, 107
cattle 26, 29, 37, 46, *46*, 50, 92, *139*, *see also* gauchos; guasos
cephalopods 17
Chile 34, 66, 84–113, 119, 123–29, 162: Atacama Desert, the 117, *117*, 126–27, *126*, *127*; Beagle Channel *73, 77, 83*, ; Cape Horn 75, *76*, 88, 107, 108; Cauquenes 95, 96; Concepcion 111, *112*, 162; Chonos Archipelago 98–113; Iquique 127, 128; Osorno 102, 109, *109*; Quillota Valley 90–92,

93; Santiago 87, 91, 94–95, *95*, 118; Uspallata Pass 121, *121*, 123, 127; Valparaiso 86, *86*, 88, *88*, 89, 91, 93, 97, *97*, 102, 117, 121 *see also* Tierra del Fuego
cicadae 23, 59, 198
Cocos (Keeling) Islands, the 183, 186–87, *187*, 188–92
colonial powers *see individual countries*
condors 66, *66*
Cook, Capt. James 73, 152, 153
coral reefs 154, 186–87, *187*, 188–92, *188*, *192*
Cordillera, the 27, *54–55*, 62–63, 65, 66, *66*, 67, *67*, 88, *90*, 91, 93, 95, *97*, 100–01, 109, 113, 116–27
cougars *see* pumas
cowboys *see* gauchos, guasos
crabs 190–91, *190*, *191*
Creationism 9, 62–63, 136, 203–05
crickets 23
Darwin, Charles 7, *205*: attitudes toward indigenous peoples 14–15, 22, 26, 43, 48, 70–71, 73, 76–77, 92, 109, 113, 155–57, 161, 163–64, 170, 176; early life 7; education 7–9; evolution, observations leading to theory 7, 10, 36–37, 62–64, 71, 100–01, 117, 121, 132–33, 139, 144, 178, 186–87, 201–05; health 16, 87, 97, 119, 199, 120, 122; marriage 202; *On the Theory of Natural Selection* (1859) 202; seasickness 16, 199
Darwin, Erasmus 8, *8*, 21
Darwinism (Social) 71, 77, 204–05
deserts 58, 117, *117*, 126–27, *126*, *127*, 128
Drake, Sir Francis 61

Dutch (colonial power) 196
earthquakes 110–11, 112, 113
Ecuador 34, 95, 127, 130–49: Galápagos Islands, the 2, 34, 130–49, 193, 202, 205; Quito 136
Edentata 63, 64 see also sloths
England 7, 8, 14–15, 195, 199, 200–05 see also Britain, colonial
evolution, theory of 7, 10, 36–37, 62–64, 71, 100–01, 117, 121, 132–33, 139, 144, 178, 186–87, 201-05
extinct species 36, 44, 63, 79, 167: mastodons 44, 45; toxodons 36, 44, 45, 63, 64
Falkland Islands 68–69, 71, 78, 78, 79
ferns 162, 163, 163
finches 141, 141, 148, 202
FitzRoy, Capt. Robert 11, 64, 73, 81, 82, 100, 104, 106, 111, 113, 154, 191–92, 201–02: death of 11
flamingos 34, 34, 137
fossils 36, 36, 44, 44, 45, 61, 63, 119, 124, 132: ammonites 62 see also extinct species; shells
Fourier, Jean Baptiste 186
foxes 57, 79, 105
France, French colonies 78, 79, 154, 192, 194–95, 196
frigate birds 3, 140
frogs 23
Galápagos Islands, the see Ecuador
gauchos 29–32, 30, 31, 32, 35, 49–50, 51, 52–53, 52, 53, 79, 92, 138 see also Argentina
geology 9–10, 44, 59, 61–63, 67, 89–90, 93, 94, 105, 106, 113, 118–19, 121, 123, 126, 132, 134–35, 201
giant animals 36, 60, 63, 167 see also extinct species
glaciers 67, 83, 83, 100, 101, 120
global warming 186–87
goats 61
Gould, James 202
grasshoppers 59
greenhouse effect 186–87
guanacos 45, 59, 60–61, 60, 61, 63, 64, 93, 120
guasos 92, 92
health 43, 87, 97, 176, 177 see also Darwin, Charles: health
horses 44, 45, 49–50, 65
hummingbirds 91
Huxley, Thomas Henry 203, 203
Ice Age, the 45
iguanas 2, 130–31, 132, 133, 133, 137, 144–47, 144, 145, 146, 147
Incas 95, 116, 116, 117, 124, 127
Indian Ocean, the 186, 188–92
indigenous peoples 26, 27, 34, 43, 43, 77, 120, 120, 127: Aboriginal Australians 78, 170–71, 170, 171, 174–83, 175; Araucanians 87, 95, 96, 96, 103, 110, 110, 111, 113, 125; cannibalism 49, 164; Darwin's attitudes toward 14–15, 22, 26, 43, 48, 70–71, 73, 76–77, 92, 109, 113, 155–57, 161, 163–64, 170, 176; depopulation and genocide 43, 57, 171, 176,

181; Fuegians 11, 70–71, 72–74, 72, 74, 76–77, 80, 82, 175; languages 73, 74, 110; Lapíta peoples 153, 157, 157; Maori 77, 153, 162–67, 162, 165, 167; Tahitians 153, 155–56, 155, 157, 158–59, 158, 160; Tehuelche 56, 57, 57, 59, 60, 60, 63, 65, 65
insects 48, 59, 122, 179 see also spiders
jaguars 47, 65
kangaroos 178, 182
Keeling (Cocos) Islands, the 183, 186–87, 187, 188–92
kelp 81–82, 81
llamas 45, 60, 63
lizards 59 see also iguanas
locusts 122
Lyell, Charles 10, 132, 201: Principles of Geology (1830) 10
macaws 12–13
Magellan, Ferdinand 57, 57, 61, 70, 72, 154
Magellan, Strait of 66, 72, 74, 79, 80, 83, 107
maps, historic 14, 26, 40, 56, 70, 86, 100, 116, 132, 152, 170, 186, 199
marmosets 17
marsupials 178, 182
maté 93
Mauritius 184–85, 189, 192–94, 193
minerals/mining 94, 96, 97, 124–25, 124, 127, 128
Napoleon Bonaparte 18, 195, 195
natural selection see evolution, theory of
New Zealand 153, 157, 161–67, 176
Niño, el 46
O'Higgins, Bernardo 90, 96, 121, 125
Oceania 77, 150–67
ocelots 65
Owen, Richard 63, 201–02
Pacific Ocean 77, 83, 88, 91, 93, 100–13, 119, 134, 152–61
Panama Canal 88
Paraguay 48, 49, 53
Patagonia see Argentina
pelicans 168–69
penal colonies 79, 160, 172, 173, 173
penguins 28, 71, 79, 80, 80, 141, 141,
Peru 46, 90, 95, 108, 117, 121, 128–29, 134: Callao 128, 134; Lima 91, 128–29, 129; Machu Picchu 117
Peru Current, the 46, 141
petrels 108, 108
Pincheira, José Antonio 96
Pinochet, Gen. Augusto 88
Pirates 135, 136
Pizarro, Francisco 95, 129
platypuses, duck-billed 178, 178
Polar Current, the (South) 134
Polynesia 152–60, 164, 176
pumas 65, 65
rainforests 12–13, 15, 17, 19, 19, 23, 23, 47, 65, 82, 117, 197
ranching see cattle
Río de la Plata (Argentina/Uruguay) 40–41, 41,

42, 49, 58
rodents 32–33: see also capybaras; tucotucos
Rosas, Gen. Juan Manuel de 27, 35, 49, 53, 96
St. Helena 194–96
salt lakes 33–34
Samoa 152, 157
San Martín, José 90, 96, 121, 121
Scopes, John 205
scorpions 59
Scotland 9, 43, 180: Edinburgh 9, 9
sea lions 1, 132, 142,
sea otters 106, 107, 107
seals 28
seashells see shells
shells 36, 44, 59, 62–63, 76, 82, 90, 109–10, 119, 190
skunks 36, 36
slavery 20–22, 43, 164, 195, 198–99, 199
sloths 36, 36, 63
Social Darwinism 71, 77, 204–05
Solomon Islands, the 152
Solis, Juan Díaz de 42, 86
South Seas, the 77, 150–60
Spain, Spanish colonies 26, 33, 42, 44, 48, 53, 58, 72, 79, 81, 87, 90, 96, 111, 121, 125
spiders 58, 189
swans 106, 106
Tahiti 152–60, 193
tapirs 64, 64
Tasmania 180–82
Tasman, Abel 181, 181
tattoos 155, 156, 163, 163
Tierra del Fuego 11, 11, 60, 62, 68–83, 86, 88, 89, 91–92, 102, 104, 110
Tonga 152, 157
tortoises 132, 134, 135–36, 136, 137, 138, 138, 139, 143, 143, 144
toucans 15
toxodons 36, 44, 45, 63, 64
trees and forests 16, 18, 44, 75, 86, 91, 91, 92, 94, 102, 107, 110, 135, 148, 150–51, 154–57, 158–59, 166, 174, 177, 191, 191, 192–93, 197: petrified trees 123–24, 123 see also rainforests
tsunamis 112–13
Tuamoto Archipelago, the 154, 155
tucotucos 32, 32, 63
Uruguay 26, 35, 87: Maldonado 28–29, 33; Montevideo 28, 28, 49 see also Río de la Plata
Ussher, James 9
Valdivia, Pedro de 95
Van Diemen's Land (Tasmania) 180–82
volcanoes 88, 89, 89, 102, 109, 109, 112, 118, 123, 134, 138, 192, 197 see also Ascension Island; Ecuador: Galápagos Islands; Mauritius; Tahiti
Wallace, Alfred Russel 202–03, 202
water hogs (capybaras) 32, 37, 63
Wedgwood, Emma 202
Wedgwood, Josiah 8, 8, 21
whales 18
Wilberforce, Bishop Samuel 203